Reading Work

Literacies in the New Workplace

Reading Work
Literacies in the New Workplace

Mary Ellen Belfiore
Tracy A. Defoe
Sue Folinsbee
Judy Hunter
Nancy S. Jackson
In-Sites Research Group

LAWRENCE ERLBAUM ASSOCIATES, PUBLISHERS
2004   Mahwah, New Jersey   London

Lawrence Erlbaum Associates, Inc., Publishers
10 Industrial Avenue
Mahwah, New Jersey 07430

Cover photo by Vincenzo Pietropaolo
Cover design by Kathryn Houghtaling Lacey

Library of Congress Cataloging-in-Publication Data

Reading work : literacies in the new workplace / In-Sites
    Research Group ; Mary Ellen Belfiore ... [et al.].
    p. cm.
Includes bibliographical references and index.
ISBN 0-8058-4621-2 (cloth : alk. paper)
ISBN 0-8058-4622-0 (pbk. : alk. paper)
1. Workplace literacy. 2. Employees—Training of.
    I. Belfiore, Mary Ellen.   II. In-Sites Research Group.
LC149.7.R43   2003
658.3'124—dc22

2003049457
CIP

Printed in the United States of America
10 9 8 7 6 5 4 3 2 1

Dedicated to the sparkling memory of Ruth Farrell,
who took part in our research, read our drafts,
encouraged us to tell our stories
and left us too soon

Contents

Preface

This book is about understanding the meanings of literacies at work. Reading without a search for meanings is a contradiction in terms. So, too, is doing workplace literacy education without focusing on how people make sense of texts at work.

Yet often, that is exactly what workplace educators are asked to do. We are hired to teach the use of workplace documents and charts with a narrow focus on skills, rather than to educate for understanding and inclusion in the meanings of workplace life. In *Reading Work* we try to explore what might be missing from the familiar skills approach to literacy and workplace education. We think there is a better way. And we believe we are not alone.

For all these reasons, this book is also about bridging the divide between theory and practice in the field of workplace education. It attempts to strengthen the ties between recent social practice theories of literacy and the everyday events and dilemmas of education in the workplace. We argue that literacies at work can only be understood like threads in a tapestry. To see what they are, what they do and what they mean, we need to explore the patterns in the whole cloth, to discover the big picture. Ethnographic research is the tool that lets us do this, and stories are our principal means to share what we have learned.

We are a group of five workplace educators and academics who call ourselves the In-Sites Research Group. Our collaborative work process throughout the research and writing of this book is reflected in the listing of our names alphabetically as co-authors. We have worked together for nearly 5 years, learning many more, and sometimes different, things than we anticipated when we began. We have learned about the nuances of theory, about the complexity of workplaces, about the discipline and isolation of research, and about the stresses of collaborating across our own differences. We have stretched our own understandings, from the familiar terrain of "literacy" to the newer frontier of "literacies." We have transformed our own understandings of how literacies fit into everyday working life. Most challenging of all, we have tried to face the unsettling questions about what we do next, now that we see workplace education through a somewhat different lens.

Although the book is partly about theory, it is not written primarily for academics. Indeed, we do hope some academics will find it interesting and useful, particularly for teaching. But it is written mostly with workplace educators in mind, especially those who want to push the edges of their thinking and their praxis. For people with years of experience as educators, our workplace stories will likely recall familiar professional dilemmas. We hope they will also shed some new light, and encourage practitioners to reflect on their own toolkits of favorite solutions.

But even serious reflection involves risk, as we discovered in doing this research. It asks us to abandon our comfort zones; even aspects of our professional identities. So the book is about that, too. It is about how literacy workers can use some basic tools of research to investigate new questions and open new horizons in their own work. Doing research helps us learn how much we still have to learn; it makes us more reflective practitioners.

Reading Work has several distinct parts, offering different kinds of reading for a varied audience.

In the introduction, we offer the general reader a glimpse of the changing ideas about literacy/cies that have given rise to this book. We also review recent thinking about the emerging "new workplace" and its implications for workplace education. All these ideas have informed our research and also point to the significance of our findings for a wide range of workplaces, educators and learners.

Part I is made up of four chapters that primarily tell stories of working life from our research sites. The narratives are told directly by the researcher in each setting and aim to shed light on the texture of work processes and the nature of "literacies-in-use" in these settings. These workplaces include a food processing plant, a textile factory, an urban tourist hotel and a high-tech metal parts manufacturer. They are diverse in their products, their levels of technological innovation, their degrees of conformity to the "new workplace" and the cultural profiles of their workforce. Nevertheless, they show a great deal of similarity in the dynamics and dilemmas surrounding the changing practice of workplace literacies.

Part II consists of four chapters that reflect in different ways on what can be learned from this research. Chapter 5 explores key moments of teaching and learning in our research sites that illustrate barriers to both learning and using literacies in the classroom and on the job. Chapter 6 explores how a social practice view of literacies can pose new challenges, as well as offer new horizons, in the practice of workplace education. Chapter 7 offers a more in-depth discussion of social practice theories, illustrating how they shape our research stories. It also invites readers to think about ways that these theories relate to their own everyday practice as educators. Chapter 8 offers a brief conversation among the five of us on the joys and pitfalls of collaborative research.

Finally, the appendix offers a glimpse behind the scenes into how we did the research and a few suggested readings for those who want to know more about research methods.

Altogether, we have tried not just to build, but also to walk, a bridge from theory to practice and back. It has been a challenging trip, and only our readers can judge how successful we have been.

We hope a variety of readers will be interested in taking this journey: academics or practitioners who teach workplace educators; practicing workplace educators, trainers and instructors; administrators and planners of workplace programs; human resource managers, supervisors or quality coordinators who believe education can make a difference; unionists advocating for better education programs for their members; and policy-makers interested in satisfying all these other stakeholders and seeing maximum results from workplace learning.

ACKNOWLEDGMENTS

We have many people to thank for support and assistance in this project. First and foremost, we want to thank the National Literacy Secretariat, Human Resources Development Canada, for their generous support of the In-Sites research project. We appreciate their recognition of growing national and international interest in exploring workplace literacies from a social perspective, and their willingness to take a risk that this research would bear results. A special thanks to Brigid Hayes, Program Manager, for her vision and expert direction along the way.

We are grateful to Ryerson University for providing academic housing for the In-Sites project. We are especially thankful to the Ryerson Office of Research Services for their support through all stages of our work. Rose Jackson, Projects and Administration Coordinator, Robert Mochocki and Elizabeth Ing have generously and patiently prepared our financial statements and advised us on budgetary matters.

We wholeheartedly thank all the people in our research sites who not only accepted our proposals to be part of this project but also welcomed and assisted us for the months we were with them. Our thanks to company and union presidents, managers, supervisors, staff and especially to workers who allowed us to be part of their working lives.

Our gratitude goes as well to the many colleagues in workplace education who helped us examine how our research findings could be communicated to educators, and how we could build that bridge between theory and practice. We met you privately and publicly, in small conversations and in conference presentations and workshops. We thank Judith Bond, Karen Geraci and Lynette Plett, for meeting and challenging us when we were just developing our ideas on research and practice, and the late Ruth Farrell for her comments on early drafts. We acknowledge the assistance of ABC CANADA and Tara Goldstein in preparing early drafts of a proposal for this project. Thank you for starting us out on this learning journey.

We each want to acknowledge colleagues and friends whose inspiration and wisdom we have drawn on in this project: John Antonellis, Deborah Barndt, Geraldine Castleton, Richard Darville, Lesley Farrell, Chris Holland, Paul Jurmo, Tamara Levine, Andrea Nash, Virginia Sauve.

We want to express our great appreciation to Naomi Silverman at Lawrence Erlbaum Associates for her supportive guidance, reassuring conversations and humor when we most needed it. We thank the LEA reviewers Tara Goldstein, Chris Holland, Catherine Kell and Andrea Nash whose insightful comments helped us rethink and reshape our work. Thanks to Erica Kica, Editorial Assistant, for answers to our many questions and for keeping us connected and on track with LEA's publication schedule. For getting us through the production phase, our sincere thanks to Eileen Meehan, Book Production Supervisor, Art Lizza, Vice President of Production, and LEA staff for helping us transform ideas, images and words into the real thing.

We also want to thank Dianna Bodnar for her careful and thoughtful attention to our manuscript in the first editing stage. For preparation of the manuscript and design ideas, we thank Shelley MacDonald of To The Letter Word Processing, Inc. For indexing our book, thanks to Mary Newberry.

Finally we thank our families and friends who have been supportive of our preoccupation with this project over several years. Thank you for enduring absences and isolation at the computer, listening and quelling anxieties and celebrating completion.

—*In-Sites Research Group*
Toronto, Canada
2003

Introduction:
Reading Work

Nancy Jackson

Adult literacy is a powerful idea that ignites hope around the world. Over many decades it has mobilized the efforts of national governments, international organizations, humanitarian agencies, scores of educators and volunteers and, most recently, the business community. As business interest grows, so does the focus on workplaces as the site of both "the literacy problem" and its hoped-for solutions.

Today literacy advocates, educators, policymakers, researchers and theorists are all grappling with new and changing understandings of problems and priorities. First and most importantly, the word "literacy" itself has come to have many meanings, suggesting diverse —and sometimes conflicting—priorities for action. In common usage, the term "literacy" still most often refers to the basic, functional elements of reading and writing. But as the world changes, more and more voices are adopting the broader and more inclusive concept of "literacies" or even "multi-literacies." These expanded terms signal the growing range of media (print, film, video, computer) and domains of know-how that have become integral to participation in contemporary life. They also recognize the many educational challenges associated with the growing cultural and linguistic diversity of societies around the globe. Finally, they point to the many kinds of specialized knowledge (such as media literacy and environmental literacy)

1

that shape identity and membership in social groups, including workplaces.

Second, many people are arguing that, across all these forms and modes of literacies, what enables people to participate is more than "functional skills." Effective literacy in any domain happens only when skills are learned and used in a manner that is integrated with understanding and action. It follows that the most successful approaches to teaching or promoting literacies—for young or old, in school, work, family or community—might not be to treat them as isolated generic, functional and transferable skills. The alternative is to rethink the nature of literacy or literacies themselves, to see them not as discrete skills separate from or prerequisite to participation in social life, but as integral parts of everyday cultural knowledge and action. In this view, the meanings of literacy practices are not fixed or constant. They derive their meanings from the local situations and actions in which they occur.

Throughout this book, we try to emphasize this way of thinking by using phrases like "literacy-in-use" or "meanings-in-use." They remind us that being literate means not just performing tasks, but understanding and participating as a member of a social group. We have also found the metaphor of a tapestry very helpful. We see the workplace as a tapestry and literacies as multiple threads woven into the whole. The threads are many and densely interwoven to make a whole cloth. Without the threads, there is no cloth, no pattern, no tapestry. And conversely, when we take one strand out of the tapestry to examine it, it becomes "just" a thread. It loses the meaning and beauty it has as part of the weave.

Perhaps a similar thing happens with literacy in the workplace. To have a whole working environment, we need many threads, including literacy threads. But if we take individual literacy threads out of their place in the weave of everyday working life, extracting them from situations in which they are lived, we lose the meaning they derive from being part of the whole. This idea is both remarkably simple and yet complicated, especially when it comes to learning. When the lived meanings are stripped away from literacy practices, so are the many conditions needed for effective learning. We will illustrate this point many times in our stories in later chapters.

These ideas are not new. Indeed, they have been generating international discussion and debate in the fields of both school and adult literacies for as long as two decades (e.g., see Cook-Gumperz, 1986; Street, 1984). Similar debates are increasingly taking place about approaching second-language learning from more social and cultural perspectives, and we have seen much relevance of these ideas to our work on literacies and workplaces (see Goldstein, 1997; Mawer, 1999).

In the process of writing this book, we have read, listened, reflected, discussed, debated and experimented with many of these ideas, individually and as a group. Sometimes we agreed, sometimes we disagreed and sometimes we just felt overwhelmed. Throughout the chapters that follow, we share some of these deliberations and identify some of these ideas and their authors, for those who want to read more.

In deciding to put the word "literacies" in the title of this book, we have committed ourselves to the path of greater complexity. We have also sometimes written "language and literacies" as a couplet, without really exploring all the nuances of this pairing. We have not yet fully mastered all the implications of these shifts in language and ways of thinking, and we are inconsistent in our usage. But we are committed to getting started, to learning as we go and inviting others to learn along with us.

FROM LITERACY TO LITERACIES AT WORK

This book looks specifically at the nature of literacies in contemporary workplace settings. This focus on work adds its own complexities to our topic. For the past two decades, workplaces have been under enormous pressure for change to survive in conditions of increasing international competitiveness. As work changes, so do the nature and meanings of the literacies-in-use in all kinds of working environments. New electronic technologies and new management methods have brought an avalanche of new "texts" into workplace life. Examples include computerized manuals and records of Standard Operating Procedures; software programs providing a script for employees interacting with the public; and intensified use of visuals like charts, tables, graphs, symbols and photos, all in addition to greater use of traditional modes of communication like bulletin boards and chalk boards.

All these forms of literacy have an increasingly central role, not only in getting work done, but also in crafting distinctive workplace cultures in which people have a sense of identity and belonging. We have come to see that understanding the nature of workplace literacies also means learning something about these changing technologies, meanings and cultures of work. This has challenged us to become more "workplace literate" as well. We will try to share some of these discoveries, both in this introduction and in the chapters that follow.

The case studies in this book, Chapters 1 to 4, are based on ethnographic research in four quite different sites. The firm we call "Triple Z" (Chapter 1) is a food processing plant that grew up from a family farm to a supplier for the international fast food industry. "Texco" (Chapter 2) is a rapidly expanding textile factory that makes specialty products for international markets. "The Urban Hotel" (Chapter 3) is a state-of-the-art tourist hotel that is part of a multinational chain. And "Metalco" (Chapter 4) is a high-technology metals manufacturing company that already counts itself as world class.

Each researcher in our group spent from 6 to 8 months in one of these workplaces, got to know people and their work and listened to their stories. Our goal was to look systematically at what people actually do and what they understand when they participate in various literacies in these workplaces. We also wanted to know what is happening when people do not engage with these literacies, even though they are expected to do so. Through this kind of close-up exploration of front-line experience at work, we have tried to understand the nature of literacies at work and what they mean from the point of view of people actually doing them.

Significantly, we discovered that there is not one answer to these questions. There are diverse and sometimes conflicting answers, depending on where people are located in the culture and power relationships of the workplace. A picture of multiple and contrasting meanings of literacies-in-use has gradually emerged as the common thread guiding our research and our writing. But also and importantly, we have come to see it as the principal challenge we face as workplace educators trying to reflect on and revise our practice (see Chapter 6).

In the remainder of this Introduction, we provide just a glimpse of the main ideas that have shaped our thinking on this journey. This includes various strands of literacy theory and research associated with social practice, sociocultural or "the new literacy studies" approaches to defining literacies. It also includes recent research and debates about how workplaces are changing, and what those changes have to do with literacies and learners. Finally, we provide a brief synopsis of the chapters to follow, as an aid and invitation to the many readers who do not like to read books from front to back.

A "SOCIAL PRACTICE" VIEW

I believe that, in order to understand literacy at work, one must situate one's study of literacy not only within the immediate work environment, but also within the larger cultural, social, and historical milieu. It's not sufficient, I would argue, to simply go into a workplace and collect the documents people are required to read and build a curriculum around those. One needs, rather, to take into account how work is organized and how that organization affects who is required, allowed, expected to read and write what and why .... (Hull, 1995, p. 7)

We have been guided in this work by many teachers, researchers and theorists around the world who have been talking for nearly two decades about a paradigm shift in thinking about the nature of literacy itself. This shift means a turn away from thinking about literacy as simply the isolated skills of reading and writing. Attention is shifting to how children and adults alike understand and use many forms of text and images as part of their identities and their membership in schools, families and communities; as employees in workplaces; and as citizens in public life. This view treats literacies as plural and as complex, multifaceted social and cultural practices (see Barton, 1994a; Cope & Kalantzis, 1999; Gee, 1990; Hamilton, 2000).

These newer views involve shifting away from treating all forms of literacy as a discrete set of "skills" to be mastered by individuals. They even involve more than putting skills in "context" in the manner familiar to second-language teachers. They call for a change in how we define literacy itself, stretching its fundamental meaning to include the ways that reading and writing are intimately interwoven with knowledge, activities, intentions, social relationships and cultural meanings.

Various labels are associated with this broader way of thinking. "Sociocultural," "socially situated," "social relational" or even an "ecological" view of literacy are all terms reflecting subtle differences in emphasis and interpretation. But according to Mary Hamilton (2000),

> the essence of this approach is that literacy competence and need cannot be understood in terms of absolute levels of skill, but are relational concepts, defined by the social and communicative practices with which individuals engage in the various domains of their life world. (p. 1)

It involves looking "beyond texts themselves to what people do with literacy, with whom, where and how." For some, it includes focusing attention "… on the cultural practices within which the written word is embedded—the ways in which texts are socially regulated and used" (Hamilton, 2000, p. 1).

British theorist Brian Street (1993) and his colleagues have called this approach "the new literacy studies," and described it as "an understanding of literacy which places it in its wider context of institutional purposes and power relationships" (Prinsloo & Breier, 1996; Street, 1993). This broad social focus has opened up new perspectives on studies of literacies in many settings, schools, communities and families. Only recently has the subfield of workplace literacy begun to respond to this challenge. (See Chapter 7 for more detailed discussions of relevant theories of language and literacy.)

One of the earliest North American workplace researchers to take such a broad social approach in a workplace context was Sheryl Gowen, in her 1992 study of a literacy program for African American workers in a southern U.S. hospital. Gowen's ethnographic research reveals that what managers interpreted as poor literacy skills were sometimes acts of resistance. One story shows how workers, using their local knowledge of their working environment, purposely did not follow directions outlined in the official text. They did this to protect themselves from infected needles in an area of the hospital with AIDS patients. This need for defensive action arose because doctors and nurses also did not follow written procedures. The real problem in this situation could not be resolved through more or better teaching of "literacy skills."

In a similar study of workplace English as a Second Language (ESL) programs in Canada, Goldstein (1994) argues that, paradoxically, English classes in the workplace can create liabilities rather than benefits for some immigrant workers. In her study of female factory workers where Portuguese is their language at work, Goldstein shows us how ESL classes can contribute to breaking down existing social relations and communities of practice by encouraging workers to use English with one another. This problem could not be solved by more or better teaching of language skills.

Since the early 1990s, Glynda Hull at the University of California, Berkeley, has been leading the call in North America to "amend, qualify and fundamentally change the popular discourse on literacy and work" (Hull, 1993, p. 44). She argues that dominant approaches to understanding literacy do not make visible how "literacy is made" in the every day lives of workers. Instead, literacy is defined as a series of tasks that are limited in scope, underestimate the capacities of workers and serve to maintain managers' control over work processes. According to Hull, we need to rethink these traditional conceptions of literacy and the approaches to workplace training that follow right across the industrialized world.

In a similar vein, American workplace researcher Charles Darrah (1990, 1997) argues against relying too heavily on prevailing views of "skill requirements" as the starting point for understanding what it means to be literate in the workplace. According to Darrah (1997), starting with this notion "abstracts" people's actions from the situation in which they take place, making workers appear as "isolated actors" and skills appear as strictly individual traits. He and others direct us to broaden our attention to the study of work itself, and how it is organized as a social and cultural activity:

> the concept of skill requirements abstracts people from the specific concrete context in which they work by treating the workplace as a mere backdrop to their actions.... All this directs attention to whether a particular worker "possesses particular skills," rather than to how jobs are shaped and organized and how that shaping provides incentives and disincentives for individuals in learning and performing at work. (p. 252)

When we follow the lead of these researchers and shift our gaze, different things come into focus. For instance, most workplace observers report that individuals sometimes resist doing even the simplest forms of literacy work, such as recording figures, filling out checklists and signing their names. Managers and supervisors commonly attribute such failure to lack of skills and abilities, or lack of confidence among front-line workers, and often propose training solutions. At the same time, the literature is also full of observations that the very same workers who appear "unable" or "hesitant" to deal with even simple text in one setting may get along very well with the texts they encounter in another. This supports the idea that literacy/cies may not be best understood as a matter of abstract, transportable skills. It may be more useful to see literacies as forms of understanding that are embedded in particular relationships and occasions.

RETHINKING THE "LITERACY CRISIS"

Recognizing the broader meaning of literacies, and the socially constructed nature of competing meanings, has brought many familiar issues into a new focus in international debates. Even the popular notion of "literacy crisis" itself has come under scrutiny. Critics argue that it has been used as a political weapon at various times in history to make inflated claims that blame workers' alleged "skill deficits" for such broad and complex social problems as poverty, unemployment, workplace accidents and disease; even lagging productivity (Graff, 1979, 1997; Holland, Frank, & Cooke, 1998; Turk & Unda, 1991).

Castleton's (1999) analysis of policy texts in Australia illustrates this stance of implicit blame. Her research finds that institutional texts portray workers as having inadequate literacy skills, and that key stakeholders such as government, labor and workplace literacy practitioners, as well as business managers, support these views as "common sense." She calls this a "virtual and virtuous" reality that covers up important silences, stories that are not being told about the experience, skills and abilities and daily working conditions of workers. Hull (1997) also highlights examples from government texts and other articles that report on worker deficiencies and illiteracy as a threat to economic prosperity for all. Like other critics, she questions this position, saying, "I will argue that the popular discourse of workplace literacy tends to underestimate and devalue human potential and mischaracterize literacy as a curative for problems that literacy alone cannot solve" (p. 11; see also Turk & Unda, 1991).

The growing chorus of voices calling for fundamental change in public thinking and action about literacy and literacy learning is both compelling and somewhat daunting. If traditional ways of thinking are as "pervasive and unquestioned" (Hull, 1997, p. 7) as Hull suggests, change will not be easy. There is much invested in the current policy discourse, and the tools to implement its vision. How is it possible to row against this powerful current, and who stands to gain by efforts to do so?

We have often discussed this question in our research group. Some days we have felt isolated by our efforts to pull against the tide; on better days, we have regained our courage. Over time, we have come to believe that all parties stand to gain from a more complex and comprehensive view of how literacies are lived at work. This includes managers and human resource officers who are under enormous pressure to be more effective in making change happen in a brutally competitive environment. It includes educators and trainers for whom juggling competing interests and conflicting realities is a basic survival skill, although little acknowledged and explored. Surely the benefits of the approach extend to workers themselves, who tell us they feel "damned if you do and damned if you don't" participate in the forms of literacy learning and use that are currently being expected of them. It includes unionists who have long been calling for more worker-centered approaches to education and training. Finally, we believe there is much to be gained by policy-makers as well, faced with the perennial challenge of trying to show results that will please all these other masters.

BEING LITERATE IN THE NEW WORKPLACE

> To be literate in a workplace means being a master of a complex set of rules and strategies which govern who uses texts, and how, and for what purposes. [To be literate is to know] ... when to speak, when to be quiet, when to write, when to reveal what was written, and when and whether and how to respond to texts already written.... (Hull, 1995, p. 19)

Volumes have been written in the last two decades about workplace culture, the majority of it part of a sea change in the philosophy of management for workplaces of all kinds, both private- and public-sector. This management literature (see Boyett & Conn, 1992; Story, 1994) argues, in brief, that the "high-performance" workplace creates a culture of "empowerment" where workers take ownership of their work by participating in problem solving and decision making through teamwork.

A more skeptical body of literature written from a cultural studies perspective argues that this new work culture tries (not always successfully) to create "new kinds of people" who align their goals with those of the team, the company and the market. According to Gee et al. (1996), these "new capitalist" businesses seek quite overtly to create "core values" and "distinctive social identities," and to mold employees who share "ways of thinking, interacting, valuing, and so forth" (pp. 20–21). Regardless of their success in shaping individual identities, these aims are intimately tied up with the uses of literacies, including language and literacy instruction, in the workplace.

While cultural critics debate the power and significance of this new workplace "Discourse" (Gee, Hull, & Lankshear, 1996), managers face more pragmatic pressures. Many of these ideas have become a new orthodoxy, accepted as a measure of management competence and as the terms of survival in the new competitive marketplace. Among managers, terms like "high-performance" (or "lean," or, a few years ago, "flexible") refer to a workplace that aims to achieve more with less. It operates in a highly competitive market, changes quickly in response to its customers and "competes on quality" as well as cost (see Womack, Jones, &

Roos, 1990). Human resource managers in such an environment focus on building "shared vision," "high commitment" and some degree of decision-making in work teams. All this promises higher productivity as well as greater employee satisfaction in their work. It is also widely reported to increase and intensify literacy requirements for the workforce (for further discussion, see Castleton, 2000; Hull & Grubb, 1999; Lankshear, 1997).

Central to understanding high-performance management and the special emphasis it places on literacies are two highly intertwined concepts: Continuous Improvement and Quality Assurance. The basic principle of Continuous Improvement is the systematic use of an ongoing cycle of planning, executing, checking and refining operations to improve efficiencies and eliminate waste in all aspects of the production process. All this depends on intensive record-keeping, referred to in management jargon as "speaking with data." Data comes from many sources, including the most routine use of charts and checklists, sometimes computerized, as part of the daily work tasks of employees in all kinds of workplaces. Whether by hand or by computer, "speaking with data" depends on the literacy practices of front-line workers. This connection is at the center of the widespread concern about "rising skill requirements" at work (Jackson, 2000).

Quality Assurance and related safety initiatives also depend fundamentally on literacies, including a wide range of print, graphs, charts and symbols. They require an organization to specify, implement, monitor and record their compliance with Standard Operating Procedures in all areas of the work process. Compliance with all these steps is enforced through an on-site inspection called an "audit," leading to official certification by various national or international bodies, like ISO (International Organization for Standards) or HACCP (Hazard Analysis and Critical Control Point), a food safety certification program. Such certifications are increasingly essential to doing business in the international marketplace.

Some of the "meanings-in-use" of ISO documentation practices are illustrated in the workplace stories found in later chapters of this book, particularly Texco (Chapter 2) and Metalco (Chapter 4). For instance, among other requirements, ISO imposes methods for "product identification and traceability" during all stages of production or service delivery. This includes being able to identify specific personnel involved in each phase of the operation, often achieved through signatures on checklists and charts. Individual adherence to certified procedures is also monitored through the use of "Non-Conformance Reports," through which all employees are encouraged to file a written record of trouble spots that come to their attention. But actually doing so turns out to be a complex cultural act that even experienced and skilled workers can hesitate to participate in, as we show in the chapter about Texco.

Quality systems like ISO also require a highly formal system to control all documents relating to the requirements of the certification. All operational texts must be from a controlled source, and all other documents must be excluded from controlled areas to prevent their unintended use. "Nonconforming" use of paperwork of any kind becomes a violation of quality regulations. All this has considerable implications for the meanings-in-use of literacies, as our stories from Metalco illustrate.

There is much debate internationally about whether this picture of high-performance workplaces is more mythical than real (Cappelli et al., 1997; Legge, 1995; Pollert, 1991). In our research, we have not taken sides in that debate, but attempted to investigate the high-performance workplace as a work in progress—an incremental movement, in theory and in practice, toward a particular way of doing business. In theory, these ideas have clearly made their way into the management literature across the industrialized world and become a standard by which success is measured (see Hodgetts, 1998). As such, they are having a broad influence on thinking and talking in an increasingly international culture of management. In practice, we indeed found many of these ideas in use in all four sites of our research, although with great variation in the degree and style of implementation from site to site.

For instance, Metalco had a long track record of keeping abreast of high-performance manufacturing methods and a well-established reputation in the league of "world class manufacturing." By contrast, Triple Z was scrambling to get certified for the first time under the international food safety certification system HACCP, amid threats of plant closure. But wherever they were located along the high-performance grid or on the "Quality Journey" (as in The Urban Hotel), we found in these workplaces many common activities and dynamics that are recognizable as part of this change process. This included the growing reliance on multiple literacies, including print, graphics and other visuals, electronic texts and an emphasis on building a literate workplace culture. This universe of multiple texts, as well as multiple understandings of their meanings-in-use, became the focus of our attention.

CHANGING WORK, CHANGING MEANINGS

It is conventional to interpret many of these workplace developments as evidence of higher skill requirements across the workplace; much current literacy programming follows from this assumption (for a critique, see Holland et al., 1998; Hull, 1997). Our research, like those in whose footsteps we follow, is precisely about questioning and investigating more closely the exact nature of these changes and their implications for literacies and learning. We try to show how significant changes in the roles and functions of texts at work lead not simply to higher skill requirements, but to important changes in the meanings of these literate practices. Changing meanings, in turn, have powerful implications that complicate the picture of learning across the workplace. Not only does the rationale for learning change, but so does the experience of participating in the many kinds of formal and informal instruction that are on offer (see Chapter 1 on Triple Z and Chapter 5 on Workplace Learning).

Meanings of literacies also differ significantly according to one's location in the work process. Managers and others at the top of the workplace hierarchy know very well how to use print and visual text as the basis of their decision making and as a means of giving directions for others to follow. For them, literacies are an essential vehicle to get things done and exercise their power. That power involves getting other people to comply: to read and understand instructions, to follow procedures and to keep records of having done so. All this is part of working in a literate environment.

At The Urban Hotel (Chapter 3) posters and photos on the wall remind employees to smile, and computer scripts remind them to say not "Hi," but "Good Morning, Mrs. Jones." These reminders are part of multiple literacies-in-use. However, for the workers on the front line, in the hotel as elsewhere, participation in these literacies is not about exercising power, but about complying with the power of others. Meanings are different for them than for managers, and they have their own ways of negotiating these relationships of power. Sometimes it involves resisting the script.

Similarly, in the manufacturing sector, front-line work has traditionally involved relatively little paper or other forms of textual communication. Work has been done mostly through an oral culture, relying on a personal chain of command in which supervisors were key. In this context, paperwork has either had very little presence, or has been associated primarily with disciplinary procedures. In that case, its meaning for front-line workers has been negative, or even threatening, as reflected in the way workers talk about being "written up" by their supervisors. In these environments, some other paperwork may have been in use, but often in ways that were under the control of the workers themselves, like keeping private notebooks in their pockets or beside their workstation. In these situations, literacy has had very different meanings, like the sense of autonomy and pride associated with scribbling little notes "to help me remember" (see Chapter 1 on Triple Z and Chapter 2 on Texco).

Today, employees in the middle of these workplace hierarchies—the traditional place of supervisors or inspectors—are often caught in a transition between cultures. Individuals of the "old school" tend to focus directly on delivering a service or getting a product "out the door" as their understanding of keeping the customers happy. They often see paperwork as an "add-on" and a second priority. By contrast, middle-level employees trained in the new management methods will know that documenting work has become nearly tantamount to doing it in the new data-driven business environment. The workplace environment can be a maze of divergent and sometimes conflicting understandings about the value and the meanings of texts.

In the chapters that follow, we try to illustrate these divergent views and perspectives of employees from a variety of levels and locations within the four workplaces where we did research. We paint a highly textured picture of workplaces as complex social, cultural and communicative environments full of agreements and disagreements, satisfactions and dissatisfactions, participation and resistance, confidence and apprehension and risk and opportunity related to changing work requirements.

We certainly do not touch on all the issues that contribute to this web of workplace understandings. Though we worked in highly multicultural and multilingual environments, we did not try to make these differences pivotal to our analysis. We did try to make visible these aspects of individual identity and social interaction in our descriptions of workplace life. But we decided to stop there, because we were not working with a coherent theoretical framework to guide us in making an informed analysis based on language, ethnicity or race. These same workplaces would be rich sites for such an investigation, and we encourage others to pursue this path.

In this complex tapestry, the process of workplace change is never smooth and seamless. It is bumpy, full of knots and marked by differing experiences, views (even different realities) and understandings about the value and the benefits of change in general, and of literacies in particular. According to social practice views, it is precisely these multiple meanings that will govern the success or failure of teaching, learning and participating in literacies at work. This point is important not only for managers trying to implement workplace change. It is also central for educators who are trying to promote and support literacy development in the workplace. Acting on this view involves a shift that complicates the operational definition of literacies and literacy learning. And we have learned that making this shift turns out to be an "incremental journey" for educators, including ourselves, as surely as for managers.

So the road ahead is a challenge, but an exciting and hopeful one. We firmly believe in workplace education, and think it can only become more important—for businesses, for unions and for individuals—as time goes by. It is important for businesses because they want to survive in a competitive world, and for unions because they want to build workplaces where all workers are valued. But success for either of these depends on finding approaches to workplace education that actually work for individual learners. We dedicate our efforts in this book to them.

THE BOOK AT A GLANCE

The remainder of this book is in two parts, and speaks with several different voices. Part I presents stories of literacies-in-use in the four worksites where we did research. We tell these stories through the eyes and the voice of our own experience doing ethnographic fieldwork, and through our attempts to use social practice theories to understand what we saw.

In Chapter 1, Mary Ellen Belfiore introduces Triple Z, a food processing plant that is trying to stay in business by achieving certification in international standards for food safety. This will require a quantum leap for this aging plant, which has an older, immigrant workforce whose own hard work has built the good reputation of the company. Workers, staff, supervisors and managers interpret new demands for data and documentation in different ways. Most workers consider the paperwork peripheral to production, and to their own understanding of their jobs. Yet they clearly feel the pressure and potency of managers' drive for documentation. Mary Ellen shows how the demand for paperwork has created a climate often charged with stress and contradictory local meanings of literacies-in-use. She illustrates this in stories such as a meeting about a production error where problem solving turns into a disciplinary session. The research reveals how managers' aspirations for worker participation in this food safety system are inextricably woven into a tapestry of pride and fear.

In Chapter 2, Sue Folinsbee takes us to the production line at Texco, a small textile manufacturing plant competing in the global market. There we see how the documentary processes required by the quality systems of ISO (International Organization for Standards) cause dilemmas for both workers and managers. She uses the factory's two entrances as a metaphor for understanding the chasm between managers' vision for a literate workforce and the daily experience of workers. Sue's research shows how for managers, paperwork is the lifeblood of quality systems that will keep the company in business. But for individual workers, participation in literacy practices is about social relationships involving power, risk and blame. So workers get contradictory messages. Stories to illustrate this point are drawn from managers' and workers' different understandings of the Non-Conformance Report (NCR) and other documents common to ISO procedures in many workplaces.

In Chapter 3, Judy Hunter offers a glimpse of working life at The Urban Hotel. She shows that quality service is a central business strategy in the hotel, just like quality production in the manufacturing sites. Literacies figure centrally in its implementation. Hotel managers see the challenge as bringing workers into the hotel's Quality Journey through effective top-down communication about what is expected of them on the job. Many kinds of print, visual and computer texts are used to represent, teach and regulate a standard corporate image and identity of the ideal hotelier. But as Judy shows, employees do not always engage with these texts or their intended messages. Housekeeping staff tend to ignore texts that conflict with their own knowledge and experience of the work culture behind the scenes in the hotel. But they engage willingly in literacy practices that serve as practical memory aids for their everyday work tasks, thus enhancing their sense of power, autonomy and value as workers. As in the other sites, the research shows that it is not so much skill levels or even clear communications that make the difference to participation in hotel literacies, but the social meanings attached to them.

In Chapter 4, Tracy Defoe opens the doors to Metalco, a high-tech metal parts manufacturer. Here managers aim to achieve a culture of worker participation within a no-blame atmosphere of data-driven decision making. In this environment, the research shows the different meanings of production process documents for Machine Operators, Quality Assurance workers and managers. Working through these layers of understanding, Tracy discovers a skills paradox. In one part of the plant, workers with low literacy skills are keeping perfect process charts, whereas in another, workers with higher literacy skills are keeping incomplete ones. This challenges the logic of a strictly skills-based approach to workplace education. Another incident illustrates the potential inflexibility of participation in such a workplace when a homemade checklist is found in violation of the rules in an internal ISO audit. Metalco's stories show the continuum of contradictions on the Quality Journey and the influence of managers on participation in literacies.

In Part II of the book, we put back on our familiar hats as workplace educators and academics and try to share some reflections on what we have learned, and what we hope others may learn, from these workplaces.

In Chapter 5, Mary Ellen Belfiore and Sue Folinsbee look more closely at how literacies figure in formal job training. Drawing on the tapestry metaphor, they identify the "literacy thread" in two formal job training sessions in their research sites, and follow where it leads onto the plant floor. They examine the connection between how literacies are learned and used in the training room and how they are enacted on the job. By following this link, they highlight the importance of the meanings-in-use of literacy practices. These different and often contradictory meanings determine how and whether people will use their literacies and their learning. The two sessions observed here share common facilitation and teaching methods: reading aloud with a group of employees, and/or stand-up presentations with dense, jargon-filled text. Both of these techniques impede rather than enhance the kind of communication that would lead to better compliance with paperwork requirements. But the training sessions differ in how they deal with the issue of use. One trainer pushes literacy and documentation practices beyond the training room to get answers about barriers to compliance in the real practice on the floor. In the second training session, it is the researcher who uncovers the contradictions between the ideal promoted in the training and the actual use of documentation in work practices. Both scenarios offer insights for workplace educators.

In Chapter 6, the three workplace educators on the research team, Tracy Defoe, Sue Folinsbee and Mary Ellen Belfiore, come together to reflect on the implications of these research findings for the practice of workplace education. They explore challenging but practical questions about translating insights from a social practice perspective back into everyday life. They ask, what does or should "practice" mean for workplace educators? Should and can we expand the scope of our vision and action? How do we "read" a workplace? What can we do about multiple or contradictory meanings of workplace texts? What can we learn when we encounter resistance? What about our own risks as educators? They share their own struggles to integrate these complexities into their practice as workplace educators. Finally, they invite others who believe in the power of workplace education to meet real learning needs, and even to be transformative, to join them in getting these issues on the agenda for broader dialogue.

In Chapter 7, Judy Hunter takes a closer look at theory, this time with the aim of demystifying social practice theories of literacies. She debunks the popular belief that theory belongs only in the domain of experts, arguing that practical theories are a routine part of how we answer our own questions and make sense of things every day. This is in keeping with social practice theories that focus not on what words or texts mean, but on how people create meaning in the context of using them. Judy contrasts this approach with cognitive theories that have been the staple of language and literacy educators since the 1970s. She examines selected social theories of literacy and language to show how they can provide frameworks for deepening our practical understanding of literacies-in-use. Stories from other chapters in the book provide concrete illustrations. Finally, Judy urges practitioners to bring their own knowledge to the field, to take an active part in critical analysis and development of theories and inform themselves to enrich their practice.

In Chapter 8 we draw to a close with excerpts from our own conversations about the experience of doing collaborative research. This exchange actually took place on e-mail over a period of several months. We have chosen "snapshots" of this correspondence that we hope will be relevant to other researchers. We try here to share our excitement, discoveries and delights along the research journey. We also try to make visible some of the dilemmas involved in our encounters with theory, with workplace life, with the stresses of fieldwork and writing and with learning to work together across our differences throughout the life of the project.

Finally, the Appendix offers a narrative account of the various stages of the research process, how we handled common dilemmas of collecting data and some of what we learned about ethnography as an art rather than a science.

Photo by Vincenzo Pietropaolo

PART I

"Literacies in Use" in Workplace Settings

These first four chapters primarily tell stories of working life from each of our four research sites. The narratives are told directly by the individual researcher who worked in each setting for 6 to 8 months. They focus on the texture of work processes and the nature of literacies-in-use in these settings. These workplaces include a food processing plant (chap. 1), a textile factory (chap. 2), an urban tourist hotel (chap. 3), and a high-tech metal parts manufacturer (chap. 4). They are diverse in their products, their levels of technological innovation, their degrees of conformity to the "new workplace" and the social profiles of their workforce. Nevertheless, they show a great deal of similarity in the dynamics and dilemmas surrounding the changing practice of literacy/cies.

1

Literacies, Compliance and Certification

Mary Ellen Belfiore

ZOWEY, ZINGY, ZESTY: LIFE AT TRIPLE Z[1]

I take public transit to Triple Z, unlike most of the employees, who drive or carpool to this suburban factory. My last stop on the rapid transit line gives me a prairielike view to the north of classic suburban sprawl overtaking the once rich, fertile farmland of southern Ontario. When I exit the transit station, I'm in one of those large, anonymous and endlessly reproducible shopping malls with department stores, super stores and specialty boutiques. After walking across parking lots and six-lane mini-highways, I make my way up the small hill to the worksite and catch that distinctive zowey, zingy, zesty smell in the air. The company manufactures pickled condiments and relishes for an international market, but concentrates on large North American retailers and fast food chains. Right across the street is a cookie factory specializing in chocolate chip, crunch and fudge varieties. Depending on the direction of the wind, unexpected sweet or sour breezes invade the otherwise sterile-feeling environment.

---

[1]All names used in the text are pseudonyms. Zowey, zingy, zesty are words from a poster displayed in the cafeteria.

The worksite was a landmark in the area for decades before the shopping mall and town center took the limelight. Triple Z sits on the original farm where a Dutch immigrant family started the business in 1939. They grew the cucumbers, packed them in brine and sold them in bulk to institutions and restaurants. By 1950, they were packing in jars, and the whole operation was still done by hand. The family farm and business grew over the decades to 100,000 square feet of production facilities and office space. Now Triple Z is a subsidiary of a United States-based, multinational food producer that is publicly traded.

Triple Z has an older workforce in the plant. "Old building and old people," as one disgruntled worker put it, worried that his company would not be able to make the necessary changes to keep customers satisfied with products, costs and documented procedures. There are 113 plant workers on the seniority list, which dates from 1960. The average age of the workforce is mid 40s, with a strong Italian representation. About 40% of the workers are Italian or Italian Canadian. Over the last 15 years, immigrants from India, Southeast Asia, China, Eastern Europe and Russia have joined the ranks in all levels of the organization. Age, language, country of origin and education are the significant factors that create tensions among workers, as well as between workers and staff, supervisors and managers.

Despite these tensions, the plant operates successfully, although always susceptible to takeover, sale or closure in the volatile market of publicly traded companies. Talk of closure and fear of job loss punctuates many of my conversations with plant employees. A major reduction in the workforce in the last decade followed by many changes in management personnel, work organization and documented disciplinary procedures have left workers with an uncertainty about the future. Managers try to reassure them by citing higher profits, ongoing capital investments to make improvements in the old plant, and the announcement of new training plans to update the skills of mechanics and other plant employees. At the same time, the plant manager frankly states to employees that "if we aren't going to be here in the future, it won't be your fault or your decision. It's up to the Board of Directors sitting in the USA."[2]

Several years prior to this research, I had worked for a year as an education consultant with Triple Z, helping them set up an English as a Second Language (ESL) workplace program, hire instructors and evaluate the program. At that time, the company took advantage of an industrywide, government-sponsored opportunity to offer basic skills programs to their multicultural and aging workforce. Middle-aged and older workers attended the program, which addressed both workplace and personal oral communication and literacy. The union presi-

---

[2]Quotations in the text are from transcriptions of taped interviews and verbatim notes unless otherwise noted in the text as approximations or recall of dialogue.

dent, the first non-white and non-Italian to get elected, commented on its results:

> People can fill out their own forms now, which in the past they couldn't. There's more confidence in people. They're just like, OK. They can read the sheet now, so there's not problems. Which in the past, you give them a form or something, and it was like, they'd run away from it. But now you can actually see them looking at it and trying to read it. They might not understand everything, but they got the basics of what the form is trying to get to. So ... it helped a lot in communication, because now people can talk to each other. Right? So that will help in whatever training has to come further on down the road. In the past, no one could understand each other, right? There would be Italians and Indians. There was no "Hi" and "Bye" and this and that, but now they'll get in conversations and all that, and they're starting to understand each other.

The union president said people have the "basics" now, and from what managers as well as many workers told me, his view is widely held. More workers have more understanding (although not full comprehension) and more confidence with oral and written communication. Language and literacy skills have improved over the last few years, people said, with the help of the ESL course, with the change to English-speaking supervisors, and as workers have had to deal with more required documentation for safety and quality in production.

The company discontinued the ESL program after two sessions, since numbers dwindled and managers turned their attention and financial support to job-specific training. Managers supported the program when interest was high, but put their money into other training when fewer workers signed up, scheduling problems arose, vacations interfered, and not enough new recruits were encouraged to join. At the same time, the company embarked on major new initiatives requiring job training: a maintenance upgrade program and food safety certification. Managers decided that employees could continue learning English through these companywide training opportunities. Subsequently, they made an "English-only" policy for written information in the plant to break the dependency on translations and the use of first languages.

LITERACIES IN USE AT TRIPLE Z

The stories in this chapter reveal how literacies in use are woven into the social fabric of the workplace tapestry. What we commonly think of as skills is just one dimension in a multidimensional picture of literacy practice. Our research takes a social practice view of literacy to gain a complex, interwoven view of which literacies are practiced at Triple Z, how they are lived and why. This chapter shows how workers, staff, supervisors and managers experience the move from a traditional manufacturing operation based in oral communication into the first stages of a print-driven and certified quality/safety system. Literate practices are at the core of the certification system, which relies on employees' documentation and the analyses drawn from it. The certification system is far-reaching and ensures that literacy is tightly woven into the company's operation. The physical plant, the production process, employee training, job design, disciplinary procedures—all these and more are now supposed to be structured, monitored and controlled through the employees' own documentation. Thus, work is now textually mediated for everyone at Triple Z. These changes are central to any understanding of the multiple literacy demands at this workplace.

The majority of plant workers at Triple Z are immigrants; many came to Canada with less than secondary school education from their own countries. Many have difficulty reading and writing in their mother tongue as well as in English. Some native speakers of English (Canadian, Caribbean and Indian or South Asian) in the plant as well as in the supervisory group also have difficulties with print communication. The increased demand for documentation on the job has added new layers of responsibility and accountability, stress and risk to working life at all levels.

Triple Z has jumped into the document-driven work culture, especially through its efforts to gain international certification in food safety. The company had never used formal process control systems such as Statistical Process Control (SPC); its production monitoring was minimal and developed in-house. Now, with international standards for quality and safety demanded by its customers, statistical data collection has become part of everyone's job. Almost all plant workers have production forms or checklists to match their jobs. Documentation includes checking off items, writing "Yes" or "No," recording amounts of product or tasks completed, indicating errors and adding comments in short phrases or sentences. Frequency of documentation varies from job to job. Some machine operators have to fill in data hourly or half-hourly; others complete their checklists at the end of the shift; and still others document their work at the end of their rotation on the line. Increased paperwork for lead hands and supervisors also gives managers more data for monitoring and planning production output, monitoring the quality and safety systems, and, most recently, tracking employee performance and disciplinary infractions.

Managers in the plant see the documentation as an essential part of everyone's work, demonstrating the "criticalness" of each job as the production manager describes it. By contrast, I observed that workers and supervisors still see the documentation as an add-on to their production responsibilities; they see their first and most important responsibility as keeping the line moving. Furthermore, completing paperwork requirements increases accountability and can be risky, especially when workers are asked to document their own mistakes or those of their co-workers. Managers tell workers that their paperwork will protect them by making clear that correct procedures were followed and any deviations explained when the product's quality or safety is questioned by a customer. These measures are part of traceability in manufacturing. But workers often experience a different reality in their use of literacy, as the stories in this chapter show. Every day workers gauge the risk versus opportunity factors of literacy use and seem to act in what they see as their and their co-workers' own best interests. Thus, literacy use is a negotiated act, not a simple execution of skills.

Print communication has increased in other ways since I was last at Triple Z. An employee handbook is now available, which covers the expected workplace and manufacturing practices that employees must follow, as well as the procedures for disciplinary action. Workers sometimes get printed information at their monthly general meetings to update the handbook or refresh them on a certain issue. More information is posted on the bulletin boards throughout the plant area: the names of people on shift rotations for the next two weeks, job postings, notices about holiday and plant closure dates, letters to the company praising or criticizing the products, and the amounts of product processed and packed each day. The seniority list is posted in a locked glass case in the bulletin board area. During presentations, meetings and training sessions, managers and trainers often convey their important information on overheads. Posters outlining the procedures for safety and quality assurance mark different locations on the assembly line. Sanitation checklists are publicly on display in the cafeteria, change rooms and common hallways. So in all aspects of work life, employees see print taking a more predominant role; they are now working in and working for the culture of documentation.

THE PHYSICAL PLANT

Food Processing

The factory site has a tank farm, loading docks and one production/office building. The tank farm is an outdoor area with 600 large wooden vats that hold the cucumbers in brine. The vats are approximately 10 feet high and 20 feet in diameter; most are about 50 years old. Six newer vats made of turquoise plastic are preferred by maintenance staff because they don't leak and they don't need constant repair. The acidity of the brine eats away at the wood and rusts the iron runners that support the wooden vats. Workers in this area operate forklifts to transport large loads of cucumbers from storage areas to conveyers leading into the production area. Only two women in the plant have forklift licenses, so this is a male domain for much of the year; the women, younger workers with good communication skills, join the crew in the peak busy season in the summer.

The driveway entrance to the site leads right to the security booth and the loading docks. I walk up that driveway with delivery trucks on my heels. The factory is off to the left and the plant parking lot and tank farm off to the right. I enter at the employees' door, which is closest to the mini parking lot, and get a whiff of that zingy odor. The main door, with no street access, is reserved for salespeople and office deliveries. As in many industrial settings, the parking lot reveals the class system at the plant. Those 10 or 15 spaces located closest to the employees' entrance are reserved for managers, supervisors and office staff. The other 150 to 200 spaces are located on the other side of the security booth and the loading docks. By the unwritten rules that everyone is expected to follow, prime spaces, closer to the entrance, go by seniority. A female worker with 39 years of experience glows when she tells me that she has the best space since she's temporarily number 1 on the seniority list.

The factory building houses the older production section as well as the newer additions for the office staff, the cafeteria and workers' lockers. The factory floor itself is divided into several distinct areas: food processing, indoor vats for the washing and storage of cucumbers soon to be used and the warehouse. In the food processing area, relishes and sauces are made in four large vats in the kettle room and then moved through pipes to the production lines. The kettle room is filled with pickling vapors rising out of the kettles—looking like witches' brews. Male heavy laborers work the kettle room, where they shovel ingredients from containers to the vats before the start of each product run. All day long, forklift drivers drop off more supplies, from herbs, spices and salt, to liquids and chemicals.

The production lines are traditionally set up with conveyer belts moving the product through various stages. Operators monitor the machinery and the movement of the product, looking for defects in each stage. There are three separate lines for products being packed in glass jars and plastic containers. The process is mostly automated, with only occasional human contact with the food ingredients. First steps in the process are receiving and sorting the ingredients, mostly cucumbers either pickled or fresh. Then workers wash the glass jars, fill them with the product and cap the jars. The throbbing sounds of heavy machinery are mixed with the clanging of jars as they move along the line. All three lines feed into the final steps of the process: pasteurizing, labeling the jars, packing in boxes, labeling the boxes and finally stacking them on pallets (arranging and wrapping the boxes on layers of skids). In the winter months or the nongrowing season in southern Ontario, Triple Z only runs one of these lines with its permanent workforce of just over 100 people. In the summer, the fresh produce pours in and all three lines are running with the workforce tripling to about 350.

The Human Resources Director, a young White Canadian woman with 5 years in the company, describes operators' jobs as repetitive tasks. My field notes recall her description: "It's just the same every day. Some can remember and some can't. If they can't, they dump glass." (Dumping glass is a repetitive task where workers dump glass jars onto the conveyer belt to be washed and then filled with product—a job with little variation and almost no paperwork.) She feels workers who never move beyond dumping glass or never want to are the people who "just want to pack pickles and go home. They don't want to learn."

From the perspective of managers and supervisors, workers' disengagement from the company's goals to move ahead is disappointing and frustrating. But this director's comments about workers struck me as condescending and a simplification of motivational factors. In another conversation, describing the hiring of seasonal workers, I asked her if there were any assessments or tests in place for screening applicants. She responded that all they had to be was "warm and standing up" to do the job. Yet, in staff meetings I sometimes heard another side of the same woman, what struck me as her principled, administrative side. She would argue for workers' rights under the collective agreement and strongly disagree with any attempts to circumvent it. She presented plans for training that recognized the benefits of small groups, discussion and hands-on learning. She told me that getting out the employee handbook and developing orientation sessions for seasonal workers was satisfying, because employees had never gotten that information before. These different sides of the Human Resources (HR) Director reminded me that no employee can be characterized as a single type, and that contradictory positions, behaviors and attitudes are all part of the complexity of living and working together.

Following the request of the HR Director and the Plant Manager, I was on site from the late fall to early summer. I began the research at the start of the slow season, with only the permanent workforce. I ended just before the height of the busy season, with about double the number of workers on site. I spent a concentrated period of time in the label room for those final steps in the production process (pasteurizing through "palletizing"). Let me introduce you to one of the workers there.

Earl operates the palletizer, a 15-foot-high computerized machine that packs a set number of cartons per layer and a set number of layers for each pallet or skid. This machine is the last big piece of equipment in the production process. Earl, a 6'4" Black Caribbean man, is classified as a heavy laborer. He enthusiastically shows me his machinery and his knowledge of its idiosyncrasies, its delicate reflecting disks that read the steps and the errors in the packing process, and as he says, the "brains" of the machine—the electronic core that drives its inner workings through repeated patterns. At the end of his tour, I am struck by the intricacy of this huge piece of equipment and feel the pride of the worker who knows it well.

Like many other experienced operators, Earl is in sync with his machine. He knows the smooth sounds that make him smile and the rough ones that warn him to be watchful. To me it all sounds like a racket. As we talk about 15 feet away from the machine, the tilt of his head and the quick movements of his eyes reveal what the sounds mean to him. "I watch what that machine does all the time. When I'm watching, nothing goes wrong. But when I talk, something goes wrong. When I'm not watching, something goes wrong. It's like it's jealous or something. Yeah. It gets jealous."

Although he's got his pattern sheet and a binder with the codes and a graphic display of the finished pallets (he only uses them when he's training someone), Earl does his job by memory: "We have to remember everything. Different boxes, different products, we have to remember it all ... You have to know—no guesses."

Knowing is most important for Earl. For him, knowing is remembering, not looking in a book or checking the pattern sheet for a code. When I ask him how he remembers it all, he just laughs. For Earl, as for most operators, paperwork always takes second place to keeping the machinery running. Asked about his paperwork, he says: "I don't like it. It's a hassle. I hate it. When the machine is down, boxes coming off the skids, I can't deal with it. I have to fix my machine first."

Earl has several forms to fill out every shift: monitoring the operation of the palletizer and recording tracking numbers on skids he has wrapped and marked. His forms are often not up to date with the hourly checks, and the lab technicians have been trying to get him to keep his documentation in order. I observe that Earl often pushes away from paperwork and print by leaving it for another time. He hesitates and labors over his checks or his initials on the form, and emphasizes that it's remembering, not referring to print material, that counts in his job. Although to me he doesn't seem comfortable with print, many of the older Italian workers assume he is perfectly comfortable because he *speaks* English. What I see as discomfort may be caused by a variety of factors: production priorities, pressures, intimidation, reading and writing problems, risk, loss of face. At this early stage I have yet to uncover what factors are at play.

Off in a different processing area of the plant, the pouch line runs separately from the other lines, Here sliced pickles are packed in clear plastic pouches for fast food retailers like McDonalds, Burger King and Subway. This line has no slow season; it runs 24 hours a day, 3 shifts a day, 7 days a week. It also has the greatest number of machine breakdowns and downtime. For most workers, supervisors and staff, it is a source of frustration, tension and high pressure. Mechanics are in wait for the next problem, and they are rarely disappointed. On bad days there could be 40 stoppages on the line. The machinery seems highly sensitive for such a harsh environment. The acid in the product and in the air causes rust and corrosion, so the equipment needs regular attention. When the line is running well, the work is fast and repetitive. Small whole cucumbers move along a conveyor belt from the indoor vats and the sorting area. Operators sort the cucumbers by hand, removing damaged or bruised ones. Then equipment slices, shakes and separates them in preparation for the final steps, where computerized machinery puts them into sealed pouches and boxes them. When I was at the pouch line, I was always conscious of how any brief conversation I had with workers could easily distract them. Once distracted, the likelihood of mistakes increases and can lead to boxes of leaking pouches with product to be recycled or repackaged. These mistakes are costly, and the workers feel the pressure, tensions and risks associated with them.

Management and Nonproduction Areas

On the other side of the doors to the plant floor are the cafeteria, change rooms and the offices for salaried staff and managers. The offices are similar to many manufacturing sites: painted and carpeted in beige tones, with some enclosed offices and some spaces defined only by panels. Staff often eat lunch in a small meeting room and make their coffee and snacks in a mini kitchen in their area. Now that senior managers and the finance staff for the multinational have moved to the Canadian headquarters, some production managers (maintenance and quality assurance) have moved to this carpeted area. The production manager, her staff, the quality lab and the supervisors all occupy a much less attractive office area closer to the plant floor, but use all the service areas reserved for office staff and managers.

The change rooms, cafeteria and hallway joining them are nonproduction areas used by workers. In the hallway, workers punch in, exchange greetings during shift changes and check bulletin boards for shift assignments each week. The cafeteria is the meeting place for the two 15-minute meal breaks per day, and for informal get-togethers as well as formal general meetings and presentations. I spend hours in the cafeteria, where I find a steady stream of workers coming on and off the staggered shifts, eating meals or heading for the enclosed smoking room. The informal atmosphere in the cafeteria gives me a chance to talk to people off the line, share lunch, exchange recipes and family stories. I get to share some of my own Italian American history and culture with them. I also get opportunities to ask some of my many questions about work, although I feel somewhat intrusive when I pursue work issues because I know that people want a change of pace on their breaks. Workers can also find me there at odd hours scribbling in my notebook or drawing pictures of the scenes around me.

Halfway through my research, the bulletin board in the cafeteria gets a facelift. The new display, called "Sweet and Sour," is part of managers' efforts to keep people informed about the business and to share stories of success and failure. The sweet side of the bulletin board has a smile face with letters from customers praising the condiments made by the workers at Triple Z. Two customers wrote poems (one titled an ode) to the products and others wrote paragraphs of detail about their enjoyment, their family picnics and their reasons for choosing Triple Z pickles and relishes. Very few workers ever look at this part of the bulletin board, keeping mostly to the seniority list and the winning lottery numbers. I ask quite a few workers if they've seen the new display and they are always surprised when I point to the letters, talk about them or read them their praises. The sour side has a big frown and graphs charting reasons for customer complaints such as texture, taste, and foreign matter. I don't have extended conversations with workers about the bulletin board information, because they seem to lose interest fairly quickly after their initial surprise. It seems that workers still expect that any news is "sour" news. For instance, before one employee general meeting, a worker asked me, "What have we done wrong now?" From my vantage point, managers' efforts to share success stories have not yet had the desired effect they hoped for: bringing the big picture of Triple Z's business down to the floor. The managers see their efforts as part of the drive to create responsible workers who take ownership of their jobs because they know what their good work means for the company and ultimately for their jobs.

"I GO TO JAIL"

One particularly revealing conversation takes place in the cafeteria, when I ask six workers (five women and one man) to sign the consent form for our research at one of their 15-minute meal breaks. When I give everyone a consent form to look over, I notice there is a quick change of mood in the group. The friendly and chatty atmosphere turns quiet and tense. My field notes describe the moment: "skeptical, a bit fearful and nervous."

Of this group, I suspect that only Rocco, in his early 40s, can read English with adequate comprehension. As the former union president (a post he'd held for 20 years), he's often engaged me in conversations about workers' lack of language skills, their inability to fill out forms correctly and managers' refusals to provide ongoing educational support. He reads the consent form, signs it without any explanation, and walks away. The women range in age from late 40s to late 50s, and they've had little formal education in their own home countries, Italy and Poland. I begin to go through the short consent form, reading sections and paraphrasing others. I carefully read out and talk about my responsibilities: not to use their names or the name of the company, not to talk to others about what they tell me and not to show my notes to anyone.

They all look skeptical and concerned, but Adelina seems the most fearful as she keeps looking at the paper and tightening up her face. Her usually bright and inviting face becomes full of fear. From my reflections on my field notes: "This was quite a moment. I could really sense the hesitation, the intimidation, the fear of unfamiliar paperwork. Signing a name—what will it mean?"

Then Adelina blurts out, "I go to jail if I sign it." I reply, "No, I'll go to jail. You can send me to jail!" I say that half laughing, trying to diffuse her anxiety by saying something almost as outrageous as she did. She looks very surprised and wants to understand this confusing situation. Filomena and Neva both ask for more information about why they have to sign. I try to explain the university's rules on consent as simply as I can, and emphasize that by signing they protect themselves. I am the one who has to worry and stick to the rules; otherwise they can get me in trouble.

Keeping a copy of the paper seems to calm some of their fears. My field notes recall that "Adelina is less nervous, but clearly not certain of what signing a paper can mean for her." With a mixed sense of resignation and yet bravely taking the leap, Neva signs the form and the others follow, perhaps encouraged by her rather dramatic agreement. She notices one of my cards on the table and asks to have one. I pass one over to her and give out cards to everyone—a gesture to demonstrate my sincerity, even though I realize it is highly unlikely anyone will ever refer to them.

This experience with "going to jail" brought home to me the strength of the workers' fears about documentation and the intimidating nature of unfamiliar written statements. Even though I thought I was familiar and trusted, their reaction to this formal literacy exercise was immediate distrust and hesitation. Although they trusted me enough to tell me details of their work life, my asking them for signatures introduced a new element that signaled danger. Only later in my fieldwork did I learn what some elements of that danger were: different meanings of paperwork, honesty, and protection of self and others.

The lab technicians told workers that their paperwork would protect them, just as I tried to tell them about my consent forms. But most had never experienced this use or meaning of documentation. The idea of signing a consent form to protect themselves made no sense, because their lived literacy practice often told them otherwise. In their own experience, paperwork could easily get them into trouble, as the story of the meeting will later show. My own understanding was beginning to change.

After months of research, I could see that for many workers, every aspect of literacy practice could be risky. This sense of risk is a barrier to what workplace educators are expected to do. It is important to make visible these contradictory meanings so that learning will be successful and our efforts rewarded. Not only do we have to deal with the print that is part of everyone's job, we also have to create space for the different meanings of texts to be understood, challenged and discussed. We need those spaces in language and literacy classes, job training, production meetings and general employee meetings; that is, whenever text is part of talk and work. Just as the women had different understandings of my consent form, so too will workers, staff, supervisors and managers find different meanings in workplace texts. Those meanings help determine why and how people will engage with literacy or not.

THE WORKFORCE: "WE DON'T SING ANYMORE"

The veteran Italian workers, both male and female, with 30 to 40 years of experience still seem to be a significant force in the plant. Of the top 28 people on the seniority list who began working in the 1960s, 26 are Italian. I feel comfortable in the multiethnic environment at Triple Z because I am Italian American, a second generation of southern Italians born in eastern United States. My mother and father were born in the United States, educated in English and were anxious to be accepted as "American." In the United States, I am seen as Italian; in Canada, I am American; at Triple Z, I am that assimilated Italian who has lost touch with the language. Workers shake their heads in dismay when I say I can only speak a little Italian. Nevertheless, I gravitate to the Italian population because I find enough familiar customs that make my entrée into this community easier. They open up to me more readily once our distant ties are known, ancestries placed and arrival dates in North America established. Although this Italian community is very different from my own, we recognize a common heritage that spans generations on both sides of the ocean.

These workers have a collective memory of working together, living together, growing up in Canada here at this plant, speaking Italian and singing Italian songs while they worked. They began with a small community of 15 or 20 workers who worked side by side with the original Dutch owners, packing by hand, using one washroom, sharing food, stories, and songs of the old and new worlds, and later on bringing their children to work here in the summers. One worker, Rosa, with 39 years experience and maybe the last of the singers, reminisces about the early days:

> When we pack pickles by hand in the summer, we sing like crazy. You can hear us up to the 401 [highway]. We happy. We work like crazy. Those jars go through like the wind [she snaps her arms and whistles like a sudden wind coming up].... We scare to complain because maybe they send us home. We all Italian and no understand nothing.... Now all mix up. But Italian people, we build this place.

One day I accompany Rosa on her daily rounds to complete her checklist of light janitorial duties. She ushers me into the ladies' change room, where I sit down on one of the long, low benches with her and two other workers. I gaze around the walls and see the strong presence of the Italian Catholic women, who have taken one area and turned it into a shrine to the Madonna. The wall is covered with different portraits of the Virgin and a few female saints, all distinctly representing people's towns in Italy. There are large posters and oversized postcards of the Madonna on the wall and colorful plastic models of her on a shelf just under the picture display. Plastic flowers also decorate this chapel-like area. When I comment on the display, the women gladly tell me which representations they have contributed and the town they come from. I imagine that what started out as one large poster of the Madonna soon mushroomed into a whole show, not only of religion but of regional affiliation. Some locker doors are open and I can see more pictures of the Madonna covering the interior of the doors also, similar to the movie star photos we might find elsewhere.

Rosa, like many other workers, talks frequently about the future of Triple Z: "If this place close, I feel bad here. We grow here—like my house. We grow up here. Our kids work here. We work hard to make this place, so sometime I feel bad when I see things."

What things does she see? Certainly, a changing workforce that doesn't share that earlier collective experience. But from my observations, even more jarring for these veterans is the larger superstructure of work systems that has engulfed their once small, tightly knit work world: a management team aiming for ever-increasing efficiencies; face-to-face trust replaced by standardized and impersonal rules; paperwork that should protect them but in the end incriminates them; and the steady stream of new managers and supervisors who don't speak Italian, have never done the job and yet seem to act like they know it better than the workers do.

COMPANY INITIATIVES

During my stay at Triple Z, four company initiatives were of overriding importance in the economic health of the company: food safety certification, the "pay-for-knowledge" training program in the maintenance department, Continuous Improvement teams aiming to "drive the costs out of manufacturing" by eliminating waste, and the "fight for capital," as the accountant put it, to buy new equipment for a Canadian operation in a United States-based multinational company. Each of these initiatives influences the workers both positively and negatively. They ease workers' frustration of dealing with troublesome equipment. But they also increase their workload. They introduce more responsibilities such as documentation and committee work, resulting in greater accountability. And they make workers painfully aware of the cost of waste, be it time or product. The union president, a forklift driver in the tank farm, comments about the new awareness of workers and the ever-present fear of closure:

> We're competing with the Americans now, so you have to improve. Or else you're out of business. So we have to cut down on the waste. We've got to make sure the lines are running.... So everyone's trying their best. Be-

cause you know if the line's down for an hour or something, it's going to cost us in the long run. But in the past, there was no real competition from the Americans or anything, and people didn't really care. Oh, it was an hour down. We can relax. Now people are more worried.... OK, why is this line down for an hour? Let's get it going ... every second now you've got to make sure your product's good ... everyone understands now. Like in the past, 10, 15 years ago, if this placed closed, you'd find another job, no problems. Nowadays, you can't do that no more.

I am very conscious of the workers' awareness of downtime and the cost to production. Operators, lead hands, light and heavy laborers all express dismay and worry when the lines stop for any lengthy period of time. They talk about why the lines keep going down, often blaming the trainees in the maintenance upgrade program or the program itself. They frequently talk about the company closing if they can't keep lines running continuously. They question the managers' decision to train so many maintenance workers, resulting in slow repairs and hours lost. They laugh about the games they used to play when the lines stopped. Now, no one laughs; they look worried, shake their heads and wonder how all this change will end up.

At Triple Z, I see worlds and work cultures clashing: the push and shove of old against new; the veterans' experience of working by your wits and senses against the cold intricacies of today's computerized equipment and production statistics; the old value of a hard day's work against a frustrating shift dealing with machine breakdowns and anxiety about catching up on overdue deliveries; the old trust in what seemed like a safe food processing system against the current tightly monitored and documented system of audits and certifications. Back then, Rosa says, "Nobody walking around with paper. All Italian. No read and no write. And still the work go up here [productivity and profits increased]. Now what's the paper for?" Increasingly I come to see Rosa's question as central to the problems and tensions in this workplace.

For Triple Z's managers, the "paper" is for telling the government, "big box" customers and international fast food retailers that the relishes, condiments and pickles have been processed according to verified standards of safety. Much of the paper is demanded by government food inspection agencies, but a growing amount is to meet customer demands for quality and safety certification. This certification is now a requirement for securing and maintaining contracts with the company's most important U.S. retailers and fast food chains.

What stays constant? It seems only the smell and vapors of zowey, zingy, zesty. Just before I go out on the floor, I put on my white lab coat, hairnet (over the ears and all hair covered), steel-toed boots, safety glasses, and face mask. I push open the door to the production floor, and the atmosphere suddenly switches to pickle vapors, acid tingles and the varied roars of heavy machinery running at full tilt. I feel my nose and chest reacting to the acidic air while the rapid bass beat of the motors pounds my brain. The floor is wet and often slippery from pickling juices, water and pickle or relish debris. Workers hose down parts of the line at times to clean off ingredients or push them toward the drains. Nobody's kitchen ever looked like this. For me, it takes a lot of getting used to, and such a working life would never be easy.

HACCP AND HICCUPS

Hazard Analysis and Critical Control Point or HAACP is a food safety certification program based on paperwork. Employees develop and then use the documentation to identify, monitor, control and prevent hazards at critical points in the food production process. The Pillsbury Corporation first developed this control system with NASA to ensure safe food for space flights. It now has become the international standard for food production.

Wal-Mart demanded HACCP certification from its suppliers, and Triple Z began the certification process to satisfy them. Then Wendy's required it, and the company assumes a growing list of their prime customers in the United States will do so also. Triple Z produces 700,000 cases of product per year for Wal-Mart, a customer they can't afford to lose. For Len, the English-speaking, Canadian-born plant manager, "HACCP is a critical success factor. It absolutely needs to happen in order to protect our current and future business." He says that "Wal-Mart tends to be very demanding of their suppliers. And Wal-Mart for Triple Z is our number one customer. So when they say jump, we very quickly ask, 'How high?'"

How high a jump is HACCP for Triple Z? Len describes it as "definitely a quantum leap from where this plant has been in the past." The documentation demands, the precision and consistency needed in production, the increase in sanitation work, the wide range of training required for production workers and the high cost make this an all-consuming initiative for the company. This process demands everyone's participation to reach the customers' heights. The system is only as good and safe as the employees make it. Bozena, the quality assurance manager, says: "Whatever we have on paper, is it going to match what we are really doing in the plant?" For Triple Z, HACCP dominates many staff meetings and affects most every aspect of the physical plant as well as the work process. "Not surprisingly," says Len, "there have been some hiccups in that process."

Bozena, an Eastern European with English as her second language, began work at Triple Z as the Quality Assurance Manager. Now, she is also the HACCP Coordinator and responsible for implementing the certification program. Working with middle managers and staff, she has written the safety procedures, developed the monitoring systems based on documentation, designed and delivered training sessions, and carries most of the responsibility for preparing the company for the upcoming audits by external examiners. Preparation for HACCP certification begins by analyzing hazards to safety, which could be biological, chemical and physical, then identifying Critical Control Points (CCPs), where, as Bozena says, "loss of control may result in an unacceptable health risk." Critical limits are finally set at these points.

Triple Z did not have a certified quality system, so they used this opportunity to further develop and document quality procedures as well as good manufacturing practices (GMP). This safety certification is the first time standards of an international order have become the routine way of working for the company. Like most food processors, they had checks and measures for ensuring food safety, but usually for the finished product. Instead, through its paperwork, HACCP oversees every step of the entire process from receiving raw materials through production and onto storage, shipping, and customer information. A quantum leap indeed!

Returning to the company after a 4-year hiatus, I noticed some obvious differences in the physical plant, especially in sanitation and housekeeping. These differences, I discovered, were all part of the prerequisite program for HACCP. While I was on site, the company completed the initial audit of the documentation for the prerequisite program, trained people for the on-site inspection, passed that inspection, revised its documentation for the prerequisites, and was preparing the actual HACCP plan and inspection. This preparation included the documentation and audit of the detailed plans and procedures around CCPs, training workers and supervisors on CCPs, and training workers for the on-site inspection. By the time my data collection was finished, the company had already devoted almost 2 years to HACCP certification and was still several months away from the first official audit.

WORKERS AND HACCP

Unlike the workers' keen awareness of the costs of downtime, my observation was that they were only vaguely aware of the goals of HACCP, its broad implications and its importance in retaining the company's most lucrative accounts. When I spoke to them about procedures related to HACCP, they usually said that food safety was important for the consumer, for themselves and for the company, and that their reporting forms were important because "the government wants them." Indeed, HACCP certification is administered by a Canadian federal government agency, but few workers understood that the company's customers, not the government, insisted on it. With increasing frequency, managers, supervisors and staff inserted the word HACCP in their discussions with workers, but it seemed with little recognition.

Although the plant manager's strategy with the supervisors and staff was evident in the weekly staff meetings I attended as well as in their committee work, I could not discern a clear, consistent communication strategy on HACCP coming from the managers and supervisors to the workers. Thus, few workers could relate the explosion in paperwork, the standardized procedures and the disciplinary measures to HACCP audits. How many could talk about HACCP as a money-maker for the company—almost as important as making production quotas? Everyone from managers to workers had been driven solely by production for decades; now they had to give quality and safety just as much attention. Although external audits had been a constant in the plant for years, the HACCP audits carried the weight of international competition, a relatively new pressure for Triple Z. Managers felt they would live or die by this certification program. Len, the plant manager, commented on an information session on HACCP that he gave to the midnight shift in sanitation:

> People need to know that we have a number of Critical Control Points in the plant. They need to know what they are. The people that are working there need to be trained.... And I think the other aspect people need to know, absolutely, is the fact that HACCP is something that is driven by our customers, and not by Triple Z management. And that in fact—and this is another critical success factor, quite frankly ... if we miss somehow achieving HACCP certification, we will put not only our current business in jeopardy, but also future business.

Len may have been more successful in getting HACCP across to this shift because Franco, the lead hand, and Phil, the supervisor of the sanitation group, had spent the last year working with their employees to draw up the Standard Operating Procedures (SOPs) for HACCP. Phil, English-speaking and Canadian-born with limited literacy skills, leaned heavily on Franco, his Italian Canadian lead hand, for assistance with paperwork and job training. Their department was the only one I knew of that had involved workers in documenting their work procedures. They took a brief amount of time every night to gradually go through their operations, chemical safety information and changes. This group would be in the know, unlike most of the workers in other departments. The cooperative creation or at least the discussion of these procedures and their text was an important step. These daily discussions at least raised the possibility of acknowledging different meanings of text and barriers to action. Franco and Phil created the space for talk, questioning and change, even if the workers' decision-making powers were limited.

However, for most workers on the operating floor, HACCP meant following the rules: following standardized procedures for doing a job, especially at the Critical Control Points; obeying Good Manufacturing Practices (GMP) rules such as wearing hairnets correctly and not wearing jewelry of any type; and completing paperwork correctly and on time for each position. While I was there, two incidents related to GMP infractions (jewelry and hairnet) resulted in the company losing points on audits done by two of their fast food customers. Then the company tightened up on the GMP rules and stepped up the warnings to people who violated them. Managers and supervisors turned more frequently to "progressive discipline" to gain compliance (each repeated infraction results in a higher level of discipline, ending in dismissal). As Len said in a staff meeting: "There are two ways of getting things across: the cooperative approach and the discipline approach. They don't like the cooperative approach, then we'll do the discipline."

In fact, I saw discipline become the overriding message of many managers. Most often discipline was related to GMP infractions, such as jewelry, hairnet and smoking irregularities. But, as the next story shows, Liz the Production Manager was also preparing people for progressive discipline if their paperwork was consistently incomplete or incorrect. In another instance, Phil the Sanitation Supervisor said the workers had plenty of questions when they went over the standard procedures, like "Why not do it this way?" For example, some of his workers questioned wearing their rain suits while hosing down the machinery (the suits were hot and took time getting on and off). After explaining why, if they still insisted on "doing it their own way," the supervisor countered with: "If you continue doing that, I'll write you up." (The infraction is documented at each level of progressive discipline from verbal warnings to written warnings to dismissal.) Although workers might have a say, and a limited one at that, in determining sanitation procedures, ultimately those procedures had to receive the approval of external HACCP auditors. Bozena, the HACCP Coordinator, began a monthly GMP report keeping track of each worker's offenses— the documentation needed for progressive discipline—as the HR Director did with attendance. In an orientation session for seasonal employees, Bozena warned the temporary workers:

> We are strict about rules now because we are going for HACCP certification. They are not flexible at all. If you are caught chewing gum and you take it out immediately, you won't get a warning. But if you wait until break and don't take it out, then you will be written up. If you have three [warnings] in one month, then we'll take disciplinary action.

Veteran workers frequently complained about the changes in attitude of managers and supervisors over the last few years. What they described as originally listening, caring and respectful attitudes seemed now in their eyes to be one-way, rule-bound approaches to workplace life. The enforcement of GMP standards was a constant thorn dug in by lab technicians, supervisors, and managers. "Why?" remained a compelling question and a constant stumbling block.

THE CULTURE OF DOCUMENTATION: "I KNOW MY JOB. I KNOW WHAT I HAVE TO CLEAN. SO WHY DO THIS PAPER?"

HACCP operates through a documentation system that affects almost every employee in the company. While I was on site, new forms for procedures in the plant and for supervisory duties were introduced at almost every staff meeting I attended. Soon after, I would see the forms in operation and hear some of the reactions to them. Often, workers were unclear about why new forms were necessary or they saw no benefit for themselves in this additional work. Consider Rosa, who does light janitorial duties, and the checklists she now has to fill in to verify that she has cleaned or inspected all her work areas. Although the standard forms she uses satisfy HACCP concerns for sanitation, they fail to capture what the job means to her and why she gets satisfaction from her work. So for her, Rosa says, these forms have "no value, no value."

Rosa's Checklist

Rosa's work includes cleaning the cafeteria for each group of workers on staggered lunch hours, mopping the hallways and walls connected to the workers' entrance and cleaning the washrooms and lockers. She also has to give out gloves, aprons, hairnets, earplugs, masks and other safety equipment to workers daily. Rosa treats cleaning Triple Z like cleaning her own home. She cleans the pictures and the cases with displays because she says she loves to see them shine. Sometimes she brings in her own detergents, which give a "nice scent," even though HACCP demands use of a standard product. Variety rather than standardization seems to keep the job interesting for her. "I like my job. I like to clean. I was born this way."

Rosa takes a disciplined approach to work, monitoring herself on breaks, knowing what she wants to accomplish each day. She shows me special cleaning projects she has taken on because she sees a need, not because it's written down on a checklist. When I see her at the end of her shift, she's sitting at a cafeteria table with one of her checklists: "I have to do my homework," she says with a twinkle in her eye.

Two months after my arrival at the site, Phil, her supervisor, appeared with four new checklists and told her to fill them out every day: for the cafeteria, the women's and men's washrooms/change rooms, and the first aid room. Down the left side of the forms were the cleaning tasks for each area; across the top, numbers for each day of the month; at the bottom, lines for the month, year and her signature. After the first month or two, Phil also began to sign the form at the end of each month after reviewing Rosa's documentation. For Phil, these forms carry as much weight or more as inspecting the actual cleanliness of the areas. For Rosa, they are 20 minutes of "homework," separate from the real work done on the job. They are not indicative of what she sees as her high-quality work, her dedication or her value to the company.

Duties	1	2	3	4	5	6	7	8	9	10	11	12	13	14	...	28	29	30	31
CAFETERIA																			
Cleaned tables																			
Mopped floors																			
Washed windows																			
Cleaned appliances																			
Cleaned cupboards																			
Cleaned ventilation units																			
Disposed of garbage																			
Washed walls																			
Cleaned vertical blinds																			
LADIES WASHROOM																			
Mopped floor																			
Cleaned stalls																			
Cleaned sinks																			
Washed mirrors																			
Filled soap dispenser																			
Filled towel dispenser																			
Disposed of garbage																			

Date (day/month/year): _____   Initials: _____

FIG. 1.1. Light janitorial checklist. This figure is a composite from similar original documents adapted by the authors to preserve anonymity.

38

Rosa asks: "What's the paper for? For me, it mean nothing. For them and the government, it mean something."

Even though she questions the value of this paperwork, she accepts the fact that it has become part of her work; as a good worker, she'll do it. Filling out forms is not part of her habit yet and so "sometime I forget. Sometime they look for something with them." She may not know exactly what that something is and doesn't feel that her good work depends on knowing.

Rosa decided on her own way of marking the list. She uses a check (✓) to indicate cleaned and a slash (/) to indicate that she has only inspected it but not cleaned it. When HACCP auditors visited the plant, Rosa was one of the few people they questioned. Her checklists are hanging on the walls, visible to everyone, and the auditors asked her for an explanation of her marking. They left satisfied with her explanation and her distinctive marking system. Workers like Rosa find ways to own their jobs and to express their creativity even in situations that demand standardization, and even when such individual expressions may risk getting them into trouble.

In one of our rounds together, Rosa shows me an item on her checklist that she can't understand: "cleaned the stalls." "To tell you the true I no know what it mean," she says. Her knowledge and use of English on the job is adequate for getting her work done, but HACCP has introduced new words and new ways to talk about and write about the job. I associate "stalls" with showers and indeed there are shower stalls in this area which haven't been used for a long time. But Rosa thinks it refers to bathroom stalls, which she wants to bleach clean but hasn't got the help she needs to do it thoroughly. Still not certain what "stalls" means, she decides she will just keep putting her slash (/) to indicate that she has not cleaned the stalls but only inspected them.

Phil made up the checklists without speaking to her, unlike his cooperative approach with his night shift in sanitation. Some of the items like "cleaned stalls" are just not relevant in Rosa's view. She also refuses to carry out other checklist items, such as cleaning the ventilation outlets on the ceiling. She needs to use a ladder to clean them, and doesn't feel it is safe. "That's a man's job. He have men at night" is her response to that checklist item. She regularly marks a slash at this item. But she does take the ladder to clean some other areas that don't require her to stretch too far and be a potential safety hazard, like the tops of the cupboards and coat racks.

Although she doesn't know a few items on the forms, she reports what she has done that day to the best of her ability. When I did the rounds with her, she occasionally marked the lists inconsistently, putting a slash for a check or vice versa. Ultimately, Rosa wonders what the point of it is: "I know my job. I know what I have to clean. So why do this paper?"

She follows up with her own answer. The "government" wants it and "we have to follow the rules." Rosa does follow the rules mostly, changing her shoes, taking off her jewelry and using her safety glasses when she goes into the plant to collect paper garbage. She will probably eventually try to do what Phil asks her to, even if she doesn't agree, as long as it's safe. Lately, Rosa feels she's being pressured by Phil to do more cleaning work: "I fed up. Every morning Phil ask me something else, tell me something else. 'You clean behind those [vending] machines?' What he think? He move the machines out and of course I clean."

Indeed, Phil tells me that Rosa can do more and he would like her to be on the midnight shift so he can supervise her more closely. With HACCP he feels he needs to clean many more corners and document every one of them. His meaning of careful cleaning is different than hers. His checklist reflects HACCP sanitation concerns such as cleaned ventilation systems and sanitized washrooms. Rosa's special cleaning projects are not usually part of that list. Like a good house cleaner, Rosa wants a presentable as well as clean environment: a personal versus an institutional understanding of "clean." She sees what's dirty and attends to it whether or not it's part of the job as Phil has described it for her. "I clean the pictures yesterday so they shine. Where that on the list? See, I scrub my pail—half an hour I clean it. Where that on the list?" When she asks Phil for help, she says he hasn't been following through.

> What I check when they no care? I tell them the light broke, but they no fix it. What I check? Then I wash my hands [of it].... So I scream at Phil, "What I check if nobody care?"

Not only do the checklists ignore tasks that she considers important, but from Rosa's perspective, they are a cover-up for not caring. Real work in her eyes is her day-to-day labor along with the supervisor's cooperation and follow-through. What does cleaning mean? Surely not making checkmarks; rather, the mop, the pail of soapy detergent and the satisfaction in seeing a shining cafeteria for fellow workers.

I can see Phil and Rosa share many of the same concerns about cleanliness and responsibilities. At the moment, they don't share an understanding of HACCP requirements and of the paperwork. Their different meanings of the checklist reflect their job positions, their knowledge of HACCP and the company's goals, as well as their own perceptions of being a responsible worker ready to take on the demands of accountability. Phil, with the help of Franco, found more common ground with his midnight shift when they worked together on procedures and their checklists. With Rosa, his one-way approach to communication and required tasks is showing signs of breakdown. If Rosa and Phil sit down to review and revise her checklist together, new understandings might emerge for both of them.

More Views on HACCP Documentation: "Brand New and Learning for Everyone"

Documentation for HACCP is a prime focus for ongoing worker training and for repeated reminders and quasi-reprimands for supervisors who are falling behind. Len, the plant manager, often defends his supervisors when the HACCP Coordinator points out their shortcomings at staff meetings: "This is brand new—part of the brand-newness of HACCP, so it's learning for everyone." He also takes the long view when it comes to how quickly documentation could be "done right" on the floor:

> [HACCP] is effectively brand new, and you know, I'm one that has quite a bit of patience for this…. Since it is brand new, you've got to work with the employees, and I think that as long as you continue to do that, you'll finally get it done right. But I mean HACCP for this facility is definitely a quantum leap from where this plant has been in the past…. Given the various levels of literacy … I think we've done extremely well so far…. I would anticipate struggling a little bit even at that point because again this is all brand new stuff. So I think we'll definitely get there, but … we're going to have some bumps along the road.

Len is often willing to be patient with something new, unlike Liz the Production Manager, a Chinese Canadian with English as her second language. She sees the documentation and procedures at the Critical Control Points (CCPs) as *familiar* work that people have been doing. From her point of view,

> even though the employees have been already doing it for a number of years, they may not understand that they are looking after a Critical Control Point…. They might forget here and there about documenting on a timely basis. So when these individuals are trained, they will learn the criticalness of their own position that controls the CCPs….It's not really something new that we are interested in seeing. It's something they are familiar with already.

She is not going to be as patient, but rather will "take the route of progressive discipline" if necessary to get people to pay attention. What is new for her is workers understanding the "criticalness" of their own work. Training for her means giving new meaning and importance to familiar tasks. She feels that with this new understanding, workers will change their behaviors and attitudes. Otherwise, discipline will become the driving force.

Len at times also sees discipline as the only way through the resistance. He expresses his disappointment in a staff meeting:

> People are being told things aren't right, and yet they persist. I have to understand why. I'm not surprised, but I'm disappointed to the max. Same

as GMP with the hairnets. And people keep doing it. Do I have to say you're out of here for the day? I hope not. People on the line are held responsible for doing their job. Either you need to be trained up or you can play silly buggers. It's not acceptable.

Then his frustration: "I love you to the max but don't piss me off. We have to hold people accountable. We know people can do it when they want to."

In staff meetings, I see Len asking questions and searching for some clues to why people want to cooperate or not.

Erin, a young English-speaking, Canadian-born lab technician, "wants to." Newly hired, she listens attentively to what managers promote, and actively participates in the quality and standards drive. In addition to testing products, she, like the other technicians, has major responsibilities in the quality and HACCP programs. "There are standards for everything," Erin says. She feels this job is a good match for her interests, especially with the current documentation work on HACCP and quality: "I like forms. It's exciting. I make up forms. I like everything to be formal. It's a great time to be here. I can see the changes."

The changes that she has witnessed over her short 9 months are mostly with the operators. They had been writing in pencil, not signing their names or initials and not completing their checks as necessary. Now most of them are using pen when filling in the forms, signing their names and keeping up with their hourly checks. She attributes these changes to "us keeping on top of it, reinforcement and giving positive feedback." They also "see how much I write in point form and so they see it's part of the job." According to Erin, "it's good for them. They see we look at the sheets." She feels workers now understand that the lab takes the paperwork seriously because they see her reading over their sheets on the line, making her own comments and talking to them about their paperwork.

As a lab technician, she has her own meanings for literate practices: Documentation defines every job and should verify that the job has been done. Erin describes this essential aspect of her job: "If you don't write anything, it looks like you didn't do anything. All our actions are documented."

I observe that on the floor workers still see production numbers, jars rolling along the lines, as proof of work, not documentation. Most of them have not bought into the culture of documentation and adopted the literate work practices managers have been promoting. Keeping their eyes on jars speeding in front of them, pulling out defective products, dealing with the idiosyncrasies of older machinery—that's their work. For many, the paperwork is onerous, difficult and offers little satisfaction. On good days, they can pack 5,000 cases or more of product. How do you count the value of forms filled in?

Fernanda, an Italian operator with 20 years at the plant and a lead hand in the busy season, says: "When we start to do it [documentation for HACCP], nobody like it. Now, it's OK. We know how to do it but we no care.... Just a waste of time and that's it ... nobody care."

Other operators like Svetlana, an Eastern European with many years of experience, find increasing demands around print too stressful. They try to find ways to deal with the paperwork and still keep up their production. For instance, Svetlana thought she was doing a good thing by filling in all the hours ahead of time on her forms (8:00, 9:00, etc.) when there was a break. With that extra work done, all she would have to do was write "y" or "n" (for yes or no) under each hour. So, when she was told by the lab technician and the supervisor not to do it that way but rather to put in the *exact* time she documented (i.e., 8:25), she got upset. "Why she tell me that? ... I busy, no tell me. No bother me.... Working here for so many years and now more and more stress." From what I could observe and understand, Svetlana was never shown why the exact time was important for tracing safety and quality checks on recalled items. Unfortunately, she continued to be upset and confused as to why her hard work and good intentions were not appreciated.

More and more, the representatives of HACCP and quality look to paperwork to cover themselves and prove their productivity. Erin tells me: "If workers don't write down what they did, then it looks like nothing. I keep trying to get that message across.... We need people to write more. They need to make comments."

A MEETING ABOUT HACCP: "WHY ARE WE MAKING SO MANY MISTAKES?"[3]

Getting workers to "write down what they did" on their forms was one of the topics of HACCP-related training. Even after this training, employees were not filling out their HACCP documents correctly. After several incidents were recorded, a meeting was called in which literacy and language issues took center stage. The question for the meeting was, "Why are we making so many mistakes?" As became clear, there was not one simple answer, as workers tried to relate literacy to production demands, interpretations of the job, social relations and power dynamics.

This special meeting was called by Liz, the Production Manager, to find out how the company could make sure that the codes printed on the caps of the jars and on the boxes were correct. The previous day six people in the label room had all signed off "OK" for correct codes on the caps when in fact the "best before date" was incorrect. Workers, the lead hand, the lab technician, the mechanic and the supervisor had all

---

[3]An adapted version of this meeting story was published by TESL Ontario in Hunter, Belfiore, and Folinsbee (2001).

written "OK" on their forms. Production ran for 3 hours—almost 15,000 jars got through their documentation system—before the error was noticed.

The company had retrained people on how to complete these forms just a few weeks prior to this meeting. Repeated incidents of incorrect documentation cast in doubt the effectiveness of the lab's training and forced Liz to find a new approach: Get everyone involved in cap coding into one room and find out what was wrong.

Liz called 18 people into the meeting: "You all play an important role.... HACCP is an important part of our documentation for recall. Cap codes and case codes are very important.... All the key people are here. I need your help. I gathered you here to find out what can be done." The key people had the board room overflowing: line workers, mechanics, supervisors, laboratory head and technicians, the Maintenance Superintendent, and the Plant Manager. Liz frequently repeated throughout the meeting that everyone had a role to play in assuring quality and accuracy and that she was "not trying to find fault or point fingers."

She began with her answer to the problem of mis-documentation: more information on a check sheet and more signatures to ensure compliance and accuracy. As it happens, the coding machine broke down during the production run that day. The original code had been accurate but when the mechanic reprogrammed after fixing the machine, he put in the "best before" date incorrectly. According to reports at the meeting, everyone who signed OK had assumed that the date was the same as before and never checked it carefully again. "An honest mistake," said the lead hand afterward. "I looked at it, the mechanic, the supervisor, the lab. We all were there and none of us saw it."

To get the point across more directly, Liz went through four overheads showing forms with names of the operators and lab technicians who had filled them out for that production run. With rapid-fire instructions, she explained the date codes to everyone by pointing quickly to the small print on the screen. When in doubt about the codes, "Ask questions," urged a floor supervisor, "nobody will be angry if you ask questions." Liz drew attention to areas where the codes were incorrectly marked "OK" for the three hours the product ran. She repeated that she wasn't pointing fingers, but had to use the original forms to get some answers and some ideas about how to correct the problem. Neva, a label machine operator whose form was shown, said later, "I felt bad. Everyone made the mistake, but she showed my form."

Then, workers in the room began to give explanations, express their frustrations and offer suggestions. Vittorio, the mechanic: "It happened because no one paid attention.... Too much stress—that's the problem." Not following up on this opener, Liz kept looking for more answers: "What else can I do for you?" Rocco, the forklift driver, responded, "I have a suggestion that will solve all the problems. We need

Operator's Name: _____
Q.A. Analyst's Name: _____
Product Code: _____
Line #: _____
Cap Code: _____
Thermometer #: _____

Date: _____
Date Code: _____
Product: _____
Size & Type: _____
Best Before Date _____

		LABEL MACHINE OPERATOR													QA ANALYST		
TIME	(STD)																
Is the correct label being used?	Yes/No																
Is the label flagging or crooked?	#/48																
Label scuffed/torn?	#/48																
Exit temperature (center)	90-110 F																
Exit temperature (side)	Relish only																
Air blower on?	On/Off																
Cap codes correct/legible?	Yes/No																
Dud detector on?	On/Off																
Vacuum	5 mmHg (min)																
Headspace	3-5/16"																
Best before date OK?	Yes/No																

* Please indicate any problems, corrective action taken to fix problems, to whom the problem was report, and downtime (if any?) in the comments section below.

Operator's Comments:

Q.A.'s Comments:

Verified by: _____

FIG. I.2. Label machine area checklist. This figure is a composite from similar original documents adapted by the authors to preserve anonymity.

a lab tech every half hour to check. People don't know how to fill out the forms or why."

Liz replied that it was everyone's job to document the production process, including the operators: "Everyone is equally as important in these tasks. My reliance is on the staff on the floor." Then Svetlana, an operator, expressed frustration and blurted out, "People confuse. Need more checks. Sometimes not there the mechanics, the lab. I no like to argue [with] other people."

Liz didn't follow up on this comment. Svetlana later told me the confusion was because "the caps different, the codes in different places. We confuse. We have too much to do: fix boxes, look at caps, look at labels, too much." Her partner on the line, Filomena, reiterated the same message: "We work hard. We have lot to do. We need a person just walking around and checking. A person only in here [the label room area alone]."

None of these comments made it to the floor of the meeting. Instead, Liz continued showing people the forms that were incorrectly filled out and instructing them how to put in the exact time, and to write any problems in the comment section.

Liz: Is everybody comfortable with what I just explained?

Silence.

Len, the plant manager, interrupted the bad news of the meeting with praise for this group because they had noticed some serious errors in the past. "You've found foreign matter in the jars and you have helped us catch things others haven't noticed."

The last form to be shown on the overhead was the most incomplete. Earl, the palletizer or case packer operator, had twice not put in the hour he did his check, so it was impossible to use his form for tracing back on any recalled product.

Liz: Mis-documenting the time—it's very critical. The lab will only be auditing now, random audits [Not doing such regular checks as previously]. The key people are all of you present. This is how critical it is to us.

Hoping to wrap us this meeting, the Production Manager did one more check of her own:

Liz: You feel whatever is in place now is adequate to document and check adequately and correctly?

Silence.

Operator's Name: _____
Q.A. Analyst's Name: _____
Product Code: _____
Line #: _____
Size &Type: _____

Date: _____
Date Code: _____
Product: _____
Case Code: _____

		CASE PACKER OPERATOR																	QA ANALYST			
TIME	(STD)																					
Is the label scuffed or torn?	#/48 jars																					
Are there any broken jars?	Yes/No																					
UPC on cases scanning?	Yes/No # of 10																					
Is UPC sticker on case? (NOT APPLICABLE TO ALL PRODUCTS)	Yes/No																					
Is case product info correct?	Yes/No																					
Is the case code correct?	Yes/No																					
Is print quality good?	Yes/No																					
Finished product appearance?	Good/Poor																					
Finished product taste?	Good/Poor																					

* Please indicate any problems, corrective action taken to fix problems, to whom the problem was report, and downtime (if any?) in the comments section below.

Operator's Comments:

Q.A.'s Comments: Verified by: _____

FIG. I.3.   Case packer area checklist. This figure is a composite from similar original documents adapted by the authors to preserve anonymity.

47

> Liz: What else can I do?

A flurry of frustrated responses followed:

> Rocco: We need more lab techs.
> Floor Supervisor: No you don't. You guys can do it.
> Rocco: So why are we making so many mistakes?
> Liz: That's what we're asking you.

Neva, whose form had been shown on the overhead, was getting impatient and threw out the obvious: "Yesterday we made the changeover and we didn't look to check." After a pause, she answered the question before the managers asked her: "We're too busy to check."

Liz, probably feeling discomfort about showing Neva's form and sensing her upset, said once again:

> Liz: I'm not trying to point fingers and find fault. I want to find
>   the best way.

Rocco felt he had the best way—use the lab techs to do it.

> Rocco: Some specific people are getting paid to check the codes.
> Liz: It's the operator's job, too.

Contradictions in the Meeting

Even though Liz talked the words of employee importance and participation, her actions contradicted those words. She mentioned several times that she wasn't pointing fingers, yet workers like Neva and perhaps Earl felt singled out when everyone had made the same mistake. Rocco said that people were never carefully instructed on the how and why of their forms. Liz chose to ignore this part of Rocco's remark and concentrate on the contentious issue of whose job it was anyway.

Despite giving repeated invitations for input, Liz was not prepared to explore the issues workers brought up: stress, lack of time, more maintenance and lab support, and a full understanding of HACCP. Instead she used the meeting to advance managers' efforts toward worker responsibility and compliance on the job. For her, everyone who did the same task owned the job so she wanted to see everyone involved, both hourly and salaried employees. In her words, "In order to ... take the route of progressive discipline, you have to be fair to the entire group who is ... doing the same task."

In a follow-up interview, Liz explained that fairness involves highlighting the importance of coding for traceability in case of recall, identifying the "current paper flow" and reminding people of their responsibilities in the presence of everyone. Everyone gets the same information: "It's almost like an eye opener for everybody where everybody missed it." Rather than a fault-finding session, she saw the meeting as an opportunity for her to find out how to help and also to impress on all employees that "when they are assigned in that particular position, they should have ownership of that particular responsibility."

The comment in the meeting that the company should hire more lab techs to do checking was completely unacceptable to her. She is operating within the general framework of Lean Manufacturing with workers responsible for some decision-making and monitoring their own work. Liz said that "the floor employees are the ones that are steady. They're on that particular spot or area and they're equally responsible for what they should be doing correctly." Staff at all levels are carrying this same message to employees: a task is your responsibility and it's your responsibility to document that it went right or wrong and why.

Liz said what she heard at the meeting was that "this is something new, even though mechanically they are filling out the information. But mentally, they're not really paying attention to the information that they have documented." Workers and staff admitted at the meeting that their attention had lapsed. Their comments about being too busy and work too stressful never surfaced at the meeting or in subsequent discussions with Liz and the staff. Finally, she said what the meeting accomplished for her was raising awareness and addressing the issue of responsibility:

> like it opens their awareness a little bit more. And also, I guess ... address the level of responsibility, you know. Which in their mind they thought ... it should be someone else's job ... and meanwhile it is their own ... and not somebody else should be looking over their shoulder to catch their mistake. Should be done correctly the first time.

Liz's comments about people mechanically filling out the forms is important for workplace educators. She needs to raise awareness about her meaning of the forms so that the workers might think through their documentation in the future and see it as part of their job. Likewise, workers need real opportunities to be heard about their understandings, their "meanings-in-use" of the literate practices they engage in. (See the Triple Z story in chap. 5, Literacies and Learning at Work.) A skills approach to literacy addresses the mechanical aspects, while a social practice approach focuses on those meanings, contradictory as they may be, that are central to Liz, the workers and us.

With the pace of change at Triple Z, the assumption is that more work will be demanded and that everyone (workers, staff, supervisors and mangers) will continue to shoulder it. Employees at all levels of the organization complain about the reduction of the workforce and the stress as they take on more and more responsibilities. Rocco made this point in the meeting: With the paperwork, workers are doing the job of the lab technicians for less pay and at a lower status. But no manager will accept this any longer—it's all part of the job. Everyone at Triple Z talks about how much more work it takes now to get the product out. Much of this added work is a result of the culture of documentation that demands data, analysis, written verifications and a seemingly limitless explosion of paperwork. This paperwork is positioned as crucial in an organization where the lines of authority and discipline are being drawn tighter every day.

For Bozena, the HACCP Coordinator, documentation is her only source of information and verification when dealing with quality assurance and HACCP. She admits that most workers don't realize how she pores over their paperwork looking for clues on products that fall short of expected quality and have been returned or recalled. Like Liz, she also says the meeting raised attention to the importance of documentation and to "make sure they really understand what they are looking for." But even after the meeting, the lead hand in the label room, a mixed-race Caribbean man, also says that people don't understand why they are filling out forms.

> It's important, because if you don't know what you're doing, you don't care. We don't understand what's going on and that's what makes it difficult for everyone to change. If you explain, this is the reason why we are doing this, then people will do it.

Most workers don't know what the paper is for, who reads it, what people do with it. But they do know it can get them in trouble. Bozena also says she wants employees to understand "the necessity of completing the documents on a timely basis and telling the truth without fear." Yet, later that week, there was another coding problem in the label room and Bozena admitted that the situation wasn't resolved yet, but "maybe everyone got scared" at the meeting and this would motivate them.

Getting people scared and gaining compliance through discipline became more common in the talk of managers and supervisors during my time at Triple Z. Although Bozena says she wants people to document and work "without fear," it seems that "getting people scared" is an approach she will try when necessary. Likewise, Len, the Plant Manager, says he prefers the cooperative approach, but will settle for discipline when workers won't comply with managers' directives. While I was on site, managers, supervisors and staff began tracking workers who broke GMP rules as part of progressive discipline procedures. With recommendations from the last audit, these procedures now fold into HACCP documentation. Paperwork seems to be the next frontier for discipline. Liz says the meeting she called was to ensure that everyone heard the same message, a kind of "fairness" that she sees as necessary for progressive discipline. There already is a charged environment around paperwork: Workers resist doing paperwork that incriminates them or their co-workers and they can get into trouble even when they think they are doing what is expected. Consequently, fear, a time-honored motivator in workplaces, is also tightly interwoven with literacies at Triple Z.

Sara, a young English-speaking, Canadian-born lab technician with 5 years at the company, explains her view of the company's culture and paperwork. She has the trust of most line workers and recently trained them on completing their forms. She says they "lie because they want to keep themselves from getting into trouble."

> It's very hard for them to understand that if you made a mistake, I'm not going to get angry that you made that mistake. I will get angry if I find out you made a mistake and you're hiding it from me.... I think that they still are afraid.
>
> ... Even though we say it's okay to make a mistake, really, it's [the mistake] not always little. It's not okay, but the point is it's more okay to make a mistake and be honest than it is to make a mistake and lie. Because then you get in trouble not only for making a mistake, but for lying. I think that's where, for them they feel I'm damned if I do and damned if I don't.
>
> ... I feel bad for them sometimes. 'Cause you try and try, you tell them one thing: "no you're not in trouble if you tell us the truth." [Then we say] "But how can you have done that?" [laughs] [Workers say] "But you just said I wouldn't be in trouble." But I think it's getting slowly but surely better. They're starting to be a lot more honest than they were ... at least they're making an effort. Maybe they're not being totally honest on what the problem is, but they're at least getting, you know, the problem. Whereas before when I started, they would pretend they didn't know a thing. But then because of the old foremen who used to scream at you at the slightest mistake you make, of course you're going to try to hide it. Like who wants to be yelled at, you know.

Sara frames her comments about workers' behaviors in terms of honesty as a moral stance, but at the same time admits that often the real cause of mis-documentation is fear about getting into trouble. My sense is that workers might frame it as protecting themselves and their co-workers—their own moral stance—which is worth much more to them than a form filled out correctly. Neva, for instance, says that ladies up the line don't report a problem with a jar, but try to fix the cases themselves by repacking. If they do report the problem, it could be that three people haven't noticed it and then "we all get into trouble." Sara certainly realizes the contradictions in her own message and behaviors even though she doesn't indicate any intention of addressing them. Instead, she focuses on how the workers are getting "more honest" and hoping that slowly they will push through the contradictions and achieve the results she expects.

Sara gauges the change in attitudes toward paperwork by looking back 5 years ago, when the "old-style" foremen set a different standard and tolerance for production quotas and mistakes. In the beginning of the research, the union president described it to me this way:

> The old-style management is gone. The new-style management is in ... the old-style management was like in the '50s, they told you what to do. And now, it's more, more communication. That's the main thing.

When I ask him how people have responded to this change, he says:

> I think it's, what they say, they're out of jail now. More freedom. They can make an opinion. They can voice their opinion. Someone's going to listen. Might not be correct, but they're going to look into it, see what's best. In the past, no one would even open their mouth, 'cause they knew they wouldn't get nowhere.

I recalled that when I worked with the company as a consultant 4 years ago, many workers complained about the supervisors' behavior in the organizational needs assessment. During my research this time, I never observed workers getting yelled at, but I can see that they get into a different sort of trouble now. Mis-documentation, as Liz has said, is going to be met with progressive discipline. Warnings, suspensions and ultimately loss of one's job has become part of this new freedom. As other researchers have found (Darrah, 1997; du Gay, 1996; Gee et al., 1997; Graham, 1995), the authority, empowerment or freedom given to workers is limited and narrowly defined, often within a regulatory system set up or at least implemented by those who are in charge of the workplace. Consequently, the meanings workers attach to their paperwork are complex despite deceptively simple-looking forms. The meanings are often not positive, because this paperwork is part of the picture of stress, power struggles, work reorganization, more accountability and possibly disciplinary action. Their compliance in filling out the forms will depend not simply on learning how to read and write the form, but on addressing those issues that have created the different meanings that workers and managers hold about documentation.

This message about meanings is what workplace educators have to bring to the table when we meet employers and unions, when we negotiate educational activities, when we teach and evaluate the results. The tapestry metaphor we have been using might offer a way into these ideas. When we look closely at the tapestry, we see how literate practices are tightly woven in with all the systems of a workplace: work procedures, communication practices, social relations and power dynamics. Literacy is not a single thread to be pulled out and examined separately. Literacies are part of the tapestry and get their meanings from how they are woven into it. Our work as educators then is to look closely to find the patterns, make them visible and show how literacies are inseparable from all the other threads. If we bring this view of literacies to the workplace, to the funders and to other educators, we may have a greater impact by reaching more people and more systems in each workplace.

The Aftermath: 5 Weeks Later

Five weeks after the meeting there are increasing signs that workers have heeded the message from Liz and are trying to integrate the paperwork into their daily routines. In the label room, Neva shows me her paperwork when I stop to spend some time at her position. Ever since my time as an education consultant with the company, many workers associate me with the ESL class, call me "Teacher" and take the role of student when they want some help with English. Because I thoroughly enjoy workplace teaching, I sometimes find myself, as in the brief excerpt that follows, taking up the role of teacher and offering whatever help I can. I too have to gauge how my help affects their negotiation of the personal risk and benefits from producing more accurate documentation.

In this situation, Neva has written a short phrase, "cap code not good," in the comment section. I express pleasant surprise when I see it and interpret her smile back as her modest pride. "I really want to say 'cap code not work,'" she says. I take that as an invitation and offer to help. She asks how to spell "work" and succeeds in writing the sentence she wants to. I praise her work and also note that she has spelled "code" correctly. She says she copied it from the top of the page where the product code is indicated—a sign of some manipulation and use of print for her own ends. Her smile and her public display of her work show me she is pleased with her efforts and she says she knows it's just a start. As an educator, I also see it as just a place to start, meeting her at this point and making our way into the complex world of literacies at Triple Z.

Earl seems to be in a similar frame of mind at the palletizer. When I see him, he gestures to me to look at his forms, where he has been carefully keeping track of the half-hour checks. "I'm not going over the times now. I'm not going ahead." His paperwork is right up to date, although he is still writing in the standard half hour rather than the exact time. In response to my praise, he says, "I do it every day and I get confident. I build myself up.... Even the lab people are proud of me."

At the moment the paperwork seems an opportunity for Neva and Earl, albeit a risky opportunity, because they know there is still the potential for blame. The issues of more accountability for increased responsibilities on the job, added stress, and finding fault are still part of the environment. Although mentioned by staff and managers, these issues have not been examined as far as I can tell. As most workers see it, there really isn't a choice: Do it and show you are trying, or face disciplinary action. As work life becomes increasingly rule-bound and pressured by quality, safety and production demands, literacy becomes more precariously balanced between a potential risk and an opportunity for gain.

GETTING THE SYSTEM TO WORK FOR YOU

There are workers who find ways to use the system and its documentation to their advantage. They are generally people with adequate literacy skills who have jobs that give them some autonomy and independence. They have limited power to make decisions usually because they have job skills that few other workers have.

For instance, Sergio, a young Hispanic with English as his second language and the operator of the pasteurizer, can make the system work for him. He has the expert knowledge of how his machinery fits into the system, how his data can make him a prized worker, and how his documentation can benefit him. Fear and intimidation are not part of his picture. Whenever I see Sergio between the steaming tunnels, he has his notebook and papers in hand: charting temperatures, comparing notes from past runs of the same product and making new notes if he notices any different circumstances. Wherever he is, his papers and his notebook are not far away.

Sergio knows how to use the data to his advantage. Once when a product was returned, the production manager questioned him about the accuracy of the pasteurization process. He checked the date on the product code and went back to the circular graphs (which automatically graph time and temperatures) for that day to see when the product was in the pasteurizer. He found he wasn't on that shift, arriving just after the process was complete for that product. Consequently, he didn't personally have to account for a bad quality of product. In another one of my informal conversations with him, he showed me how he had written on the circular graph the length of time the machines were down in the label room to verify that the pasteurization process was being interrupted. If the product was recalled, then he could cover himself by showing that jars were held up in the pasteurizer because of other problems further down the line and not because of his work. In this case, the paperwork would protect him just as he had been told.

Franco, the lead hand in sanitation who is also the trainer for new employees, thinks HACCP has had an overall beneficial effect:

> At first I thought it was the government making sure we weren't lazy. Now I think it's important and good.... It's all about organizing, planning and problem-solving.... It keeps everyone in line and people realize how important their job is. It keeps people alert, too. In the past we waited four to five months to get repairs. Now [maintenance] fixes the problems quickly.... With HACCP, people communicate more, solve problems together, keep trying to do things together and try different things.

Franco has read about HACCP and learned the details over months of preparing documentation and training. He can point to the inconsistencies in their own documentation, see the holes in their efforts, explain the ramifications of passing or failing the certification and talk about the economics of this plant. His idea for HACCP training is a much more hands-on approach, in which supervisors point out HACCP-related procedures during work. For instance, he says when glass breaks and workers are cleaning up, that's the time to remind them "this is what HACCP means." As an educator, I see that his training would be interactive, in real time, at a real place, focused on explanation, and answering the "Why?" question people often ask.

On the whole, he feels that sanitation comes out ahead in this program. "The plant is a lot cleaner. We got a higher rating from AIB" (American Industrial Business, one of the plant's important auditors). His goals have become aligned with the company's goals, and benefits flow to him, to his department and to the company. He says he thoroughly enjoys learning and makes the best of whatever comes his way. He has taken communication and training courses with the financial assistance of the company. In the chemical training sessions that we both attended, he always came prepared, with questions to clarify workers' concerns and also his own inquisitiveness. As I interpreted it, with HACCP, sanitation is now being taken more seriously, given attention with time, training, money and power. The "dirty work" has now gained some respect. Through HACCP, this lead hand has become a trainer and will have continued work, job enhancement and learning ahead of him. He is another example of a production worker who has made the system work in his favor.

These two workers are representative of a somewhat younger group in the plant who come with a different comfort level around paperwork, and a different set of expectations about work, their role and the possibilities for participation and gain even in this atmosphere where risks of blame are real.

MORE GAIN THAN RISK: SERGIO'S WORK

Sergio, introduced in the earlier story, has been operating the pasteurizer for 7 years. From conversations and observations, I find him to be an avid investigator and learner in his passion for recording the details that define his job. The pasteurization process is intensive, requiring constant attention to numerical details and dealing with the many unexpected stoppages in production that affect the process and the quality of the product. This process is also a data generator and Sergio has to be on top of it all: circular charts automatically graphing time and temperatures; regular checks on temperature in the jars themselves; forms that show the calculation of speed, time and temperature; forms tracking broken jars; and, for his own information, a form tracking machine breakdowns in the label room that require Sergio to adjust the pasteurization process.

The pasteurizer occupies an area about 80 feet long and 30 feet wide, half of one wing of the plant. The pasteurizer and the label room share this section of the plant, and are the final steps in food processing at Triple Z. In the pasteurization area, there are three long heat tunnels, connected to the three production lines, for products to pass through. Each tunnel is divided into sections. Tunnel number 3, for instance, has 18 sections and 4 windows that the operator or lab technician opens to test the product at its different stages. The belt moving the product through the tunnel is set at a certain speed. Each product has a heat temperature and a time/speed formula for pasteurization. As the product moves through the tunnel, the heat increases to its desired level and then cools down. The belt speed determines how long the product will remain at that section and at a certain temperature. Near the end of the tunnels is a large bright-blue chiller machine, floor to ceiling height, which cools down products quickly if necessary. If the product is overheated or remains at a high heat for too long, the quality is questionable. Texture and taste may be compromised.

After pasteurization, the next step in the production process is labeling and packing the jars. When the label machine or the packer is down, the product backs up in the pasteurizer and can easily overcook. That's when Sergio has to be creative—"I have to run like mad; Oh my God"— open the steam valves, open one of the four windows of the tunnel, and add water with a hose to the chiller machine to cool off the product stuck in the pasteurizer.

Prior to Sergio's taking over this process, the operator would just "open that steam and let it blast" according to a recalled conversation I had with the maintenance supervisor, Hans. That's how Sergio had learned to handle the operation, until Hans brought him back materials on pasteurization that he had used in one of his maintenance courses in the United States. Sergio took the materials home to read and as Hans recalls, "that really changed him. He turned right around." He learned he could control the process, be more efficient in energy consumption and save the company money. Hans speaks glowingly of Sergio's ability to learn and apply that new learning. "Now we saved $300,000 in energy and it's mostly him. I told him, 'Here my boy, see these efficiencies. And it's mostly your work there.'"

In the summer when the plant is running at full tilt and the number of workers triple, all three of the lines and heat tunnels are operating. "In the summer, I get all the lines smoking," says Sergio. "If the first line running will be at 7:00 a.m., I know what the steam has to be. Then I go to the second line." I was fascinated by the intensity of the job, the fine tuning and the accompanying frenzy. Here are my field notes from one of my conversations with Sergio:

> He talked about the summer again and how he has to remember what's happening on each line and in each tunnel. He might write down a time

that he checked a temperature, for instance, 9:03. If he "opens up the steam," he has to check back again in 3 or 4 minutes. But maybe another line needs attention. If a packer machine is down, for instance, ... he has to run and take care of that [then there would be a backup in that tunnel in the pasteurizer]. "Oh my God, it's 10 minutes! I have to check that steam." So back he runs to the first line he was checking. It seems to me that it would almost be impossible to keep it all rolling. But I can tell he loves the hectic pace. I said, "Your eyes light up when you talk about it." "I love my job," he says.

I often noted how he seemed to enjoy the buzz, the constant demand for attention from his complicated machinery. He knows how each tunnel operates, dealing with the idiosyncrasies of the older tunnel number 1 and the higher-tech tunnels 2 and 3, which give him more possibilities for fine tuning. He knows how to read the tunnels, how to coax them, push them and handle them with care. On a day with "no steam," as Sergio says, he's bored. Some products, like the relish in plastic squeeze bottles, are only cooled down in the pasteurizer because the plastic would melt if heated. On slow days, I found Sergio in the label room helping out during his free time. But most days I found him enveloped in the clouds of steam coming out of the heat tunnels.

In the summer, Sergio's area is beyond the heat tolerance level for many workers, one of the reasons why it's very difficult for Triple Z to get workers to train on the pasteurizer. The HR Director says the company has trained a number of people over the years, but most refuse to continue working there due to the physical demands of the job in the warm weather and the responsibility entailed. Here is Sergio's view:

> People think my job is easy when they see me standing and looking at the windows [of the pasteurizer]. "Hey, your job is easy and I break my back with my job," they say. I tell them sometimes I use my back and sometimes I use this [he points to his head].
>
> I have lots of men and women try to do this job. After three days or a week they say no, not for me. If something goes wrong, it's their responsibility. If a customer [is] not happy, the boss comes to see them. They don't want the responsibility. They say they don't want this job.

SERGIO'S NOTEBOOK: "THE DETAILS ARE MY TEACHER"

Whenever I see Sergio in between the tunnels, he's got his notebook and papers in hand. His papers are numerous, because the pasteurization process is a data generator. For controlling the pasteurization process for each product, Sergio does not depend on his memory, but rather on his own custom-made book to guide him. "No guesses," he says. He uses his own notebook to check data, compare data from past runs and make new notes for any variation in his process. Wherever he is, his papers and his notebook are not far away. In my field notes, I commented on his literacy practices: "He's into paperwork—always writing himself notes. He uses paperwork to account for his actions. He could easily be called to explain himself when there are recalls."

Triple Z has an official binder for the pasteurizer, a simple two and half pages with only the most basic information: product name, pasteurization temperature, speed of the belt and label of the product. Sergio refers to it by saying, "The book is my boss." The fact is, no other manager knows this book or the process. But as Sergio says, "My boss can't help me if something goes wrong. I have to find the problem."

But this company book is only the beginning for him. Sergio described his early days on the job. He'd start with the company book, but then notice that different products required variations on the timing, that seasons affected the process (e.g., water is warmer in the summer so he would need less heating and more cooling time). He found that he could reduce the heat of the pasteurizer with different techniques, that he could finesse the chiller machine and much more. He realized every product had its nuances and that he couldn't remember them all. "The next time I ran the product I say, 'what was the pressure last time? What was the steam?' Oh my God, I don't remember. How cool the water? I don't remember. I need a book. I went to buy myself a little book."

He uses his "small book" to make notes and help him remember what he did with each product to ensure quality. The spiral notebook is about 4" × 7" with one or two pages devoted to each product. Near the top of the pages are the product name and size, printed carefully. Then come his details on the temperatures at different stages, the pounds of pressure/steam, the seconds per foot, the use of the chiller machine and seasonal differences. Because the tunnels operate differently, they also figure in his notes. His notes are legible, mostly printed, with Spanish liberally sprinkled throughout. "Bien" or "muy bien" notes the differences in how good a temperature or speed setting might be for this product in a certain tunnel. He uses Spanish to note corrections, the better settings, what to do and not to do with a product. Sometimes colored ink also distinguishes new information he wants to highlight about a particular product or run. "The details are my teacher," he says. "I look in my book and see what I did before. I look at the numbers on the machine now. They are the same or close. Beautiful. Oh thank you, God."

Here is an entry from my field notes where Sergio showed me one way he uses his book to check his own work:

He showed me how his entry on [this] product was right on. First stop temperature should be X and it was. Where the temperature was off a bit [at a later chart], he explained the pasteurizer needed repair and it was leaking, so he kept the heat higher than what he had noted in his book. His small book is also filled with added comments, changes. He needs a bigger book now—no room to add more info on some pages.

Indeed, his notebook is getting too small, as he finds himself writing in the margins or in between lines. "Now I need a bigger book because I have no more room to write," he says with surprise and a wide smile. With all his notes capturing his experience and know-how, he told me he doesn't have any problems with getting enough steam. "I'm serious. I get the lines smoking. Oh yes." If he didn't, he said, the supervisor would ask him why he wasn't doing his job.

I asked Sergio for a copy of one page from his notebook as an example of his literacy practices on the job. This page was first begun in November 1998 for a new product at that time. At the top, he wrote in the date, the page number in his book, the belt speed, name and size of the product and the word "new" slightly off to the right of the page. Then he wrote temperature readings for each of the five charts he checks—actual, control and "bien." He had comments on the pounds of pressure with changes in what might be needed, the temperature in the hot water window and in upper case letters: "Cool down product. Use chiller machine at all time." Some instructions to himself were circled or arrows pointed to comments made on certain runs when he discovered a better setting or technique. These comments looked almost boldfaced because he had written over them a number of times. Other notes were written horizontally on the vertical page next to the spiral margin. The last third of the page had newer information: "This is after January—year—2000," he wrote. Half Spanish and half English indicated what he considered now to be the normal speed of the belt, different from the standard speed he took from the company book, and the best pressure setting "to cook this product."

He gave me this copied page in a secretive fashion. I was standing near a line in the label room and he gestured that he had something for me. As I recall, he folded the paper over slightly so no writing was visible, making it clear to me that he didn't want anyone on the line to see it. "I have to use their book [the company's]. This is only to help me get better," he said, as he handed it over to me across the line. I assured him that it was only for me to look at but I could see he was worried that it might get into the wrong hands. Although he showed me his writing willingly and demonstrated what I thought to be ownership of his job, he seemed to have felt at risk if anyone in management or his co-workers saw that he was refining the calculations in the company's book.

In standardized certification systems, the use of nonstandard documents like Sergio's notebook is not official and could get workers into trouble in audits (see chap. 4, Literacies at Work in a Culture of Documentation). I never heard any discussions in staff meetings about nonstandard documents, so I assumed that they were not yet an issue at Triple Z. The company was still just writing up Standard Operating Procedures and job descriptions at the time of the research. After HACCP certification, the use of this kind of custom-made document would likely become more of an issue. For now, I knew Sergio felt uncertain about what might happen if his rich work literacy was discovered. There was risk in his enterprise, but the gains for himself and the company seemed much greater.

Sergio's notebook was totally his own creation, conceived and written by him and used only by him. I was not aware of any other hourly worker who kept such a detailed written account of their work practices, although no other operator's job required so much knowledge and precision for each different product. For Sergio, this literacy practice served several purposes. It confirmed his knowledge of the process; it helped him learn more and continually revise his process when new circumstances presented themselves; and it captured on paper his growth in knowledge and skills. It housed data for future comparisons; it was his research piece. The book was more than a reminder, it was making sense of his job in a valuable way, on paper. His practice captured not only his steps in the process but, more importantly, his thinking, his considered conclusions about what was "bien" or "muy bien" in different circumstances. Being the learner that he was, nothing seemed to be a final statement. I felt his research kept his interest and enthusiasm in his job alive.

CONCLUSION

Triple Z, like every workplace committed to success in contemporary manufacturing, is rife with contradictions. In this chapter, I have tried to uncover the disparate and often contradictory local meanings of literacy for workers, staff and managers. These diverse meanings are formed within the social fabric of work and arise from the different daily experiences of working life: managers carrying the message and the pressures from corporate headquarters, supervisors squeezed between managers and workers, and workers dealing within this tangle of meanings on the plant floor. In contrast to a one-dimensional view of literacy as skills, this view of print communication at Triple Z is multi-dimensional and complicates the picture of how people understand print and why they use it or not. What might appear to managers or educators as simply language or literacy difficulties, or even workers not doing their jobs, is likely to be a flag for much more. To be successful with literacy solutions, we need to go deeper and discover the fine details and intricate relations that create layers of meaning for literate practices.

The new demands for documentation at Triple Z affect everyone, albeit in different ways. Managers have a new reality to address in this document-driven culture where documentation takes on a kind of hyper-reality. Supervisors and staff, swamped with paperwork, struggle not only to keep up with but also to understand this new way of proving themselves through data. Most workers consider the paperwork peripheral to production, yet experience the pressures, urgency and potency of it. This paperwork, developed by others to validate their work for international corporate safety systems, has created new opportunities charged with risk.

Literate practices are powerfully shaped by these often contradictory conditions. Although some workers can find a place to create personal documentation in their own meaningful ways to enhance their work, most workers are not in jobs that afford them the opportunity, time or benefit to do so. Still, literacies continue to expand at Triple Z and meanings for literate practices change as workers, staff and managers experience the new workplace individually and collectively— changing practices in changing communities.

2

Paperwork as the Lifeblood of Quality

Sue Folinsbee

It's three p.m. My feet are killing me and my whole body aches. I am absolutely exhausted from being on my feet for eight hours in my new, stiff, unbearable steel-toed shoes. My hands feel dry and chapped. It's the end of my first full day as a participant observer at Texco,[1] a small, privately owned, nonunionized textile factory that makes specialized fabrics for a niche market around the world. The factory employs about 60 people. They're a mix of men and women; long-term employees and those just out of school; people born in Canada along with immigrants from Portugal, Greece, India and South America. The work force is mostly White, with few people of color. On the plant floor, men hold the majority of the higher paying jobs.

This chapter describes my experience as a researcher at Texco. My aim was to study literacy practices over 6 months, focusing on the nature of the work rather than on individual workers (see Darrah, 1997; Jackson, 2000). I am a workplace educator and consultant, but had

---

[1]The name of the factory and all names of people in this chapter are pseudonyms. Certain details and job titles have been changed to protect people's identities. Figure 2.1 is a generic version of a standard Non-Conformance Report.

not done any direct work with this company previously. My findings provide an alternative to some popular views about literacy and skills that identify workers' so-called "lack of skill" as the problem. These views suggest that if only the skill level of workers was increased, their participation in workplace literacy practices would improve. I will try to show why solutions might not be so straightforward.

Through the stories I tell in this chapter, I want to first show how literacy practices or "paperwork" are inextricably interwoven into all aspects of workplace life, especially how literacies are the lifeblood of ISO 9001, the quality system used by Texco. ISO stands for the International Organization for Standardization. It is a certified international quality system to ensure customer satisfaction, involving conformance to quality requirements, including reduction of variation and waste. Customers demand that their suppliers have ISO certification. Companies these days need to be certified to play in the global marketplace.

Second, I want to make explicit how the literacy or documentation requirements of systems like ISO pose contradictions and dilemmas for both workers and managers that are about "meanings in use" rather than just worker skills. I illustrate how the different meanings that workers and managers give to literacy practices reflect the power, social relations, work practices and values that are part of the larger company culture. In short, I want to stretch the reader's imagination about definitions of literacy and the implications that this might have for practice.

But first, some background on the workplace culture of Texco and the different understandings of this culture. These are critical to also comprehending the local meanings of workplace literacy practices found on the factory floor.

TWO ENTRANCES, TWO PERSPECTIVES

That first day at Texco is a cold dark morning in December, and it takes me just a little over an hour to drive to the plant from my home. I turn onto a small side road that I come to think of as "industrial row." The main building, like dozens of others in the area, looks like a squared-off hockey arena. There are two parking lots. One is close to the production workers' entrance that goes directly into the plant. The other one is on the left side of the building near the door where visitors, managers[2] and office staff enter. During my time at the site, I park in both lots and enter the building through both doors at different times. I first enter as a visitor but as I start to work and learn alongside the production workers, I use their door. When the time comes at the end of my research to make a presentation to managers and formally say my

---

[2]I use the word "managers" in the plural to refer to all employees who have a managerial or supervisory role.

"thank you's" to employees, I end as I began: I enter and leave through the visitor's door.

There is a definite contrast between what I see and experience as I enter the factory through these different doors. When I enter as a visitor, I walk into a small, quiet foyer with a wooden coat stand, comfortable loveseats and a small table with some current business magazines on it. The plaques and certificates displayed on the wall create an impression of good corporate citizenship. Thanks for donations and community participation paper one entire wall. A door leads inside to the main office area. Visitors must phone the person they want to see and wait for their contact person to come and meet them. The main office is quiet and orderly, with the light tapping of several office staff working on computers. When I enter by the production workers' door, I am enveloped by the muffled symphony of the weave room: the "chunk, chunk, chunk" of the looms and the harnesses going up and down at different speeds. The green chipped paint, the line of coat hooks and the stark wooden bench are a sharp contrast to the quiet elegance of the office foyer. The bulletin board with its notices, safety minutes, employee announcements and thank-you cards creates an impression of an everyday work life that differs greatly from the formality of the framed plaques in the office foyer.

As I pass through the door of the production foyer, the full force of the sound of looms doing their work assaults me. A bright room the size of a small gym is filled with five rows of different types of looms, four to five looms in a row. Each one is about the size of an upright piano. On this particular day, nine looms are in operation, weaving a variety of materials. I have a sense of ordered chaos as I scan the room. Boxes of yarn that will be used as fill in the weaving process litter the aisles between the rows of looms. Garbage bins overflow with waste from the sides of the woven materials. Bits of fuzz quietly float off the looms and scatter over the concrete floor. Several blinking lights on the looms indicate empty bobbins that need to be changed, yarn breakage or other problems that need to be taken care of.

Throughout the data collection and the year of writing after, I keep coming back to the visual impressions, the noises and the impact of the two entrances. They become a metaphor for understanding the chasm between the managers' vision for a literate workplace and the realities of worker participation in literacy practices.

Texco is ISO 9001 certified. This requires a whole battery of standard procedures and documents, bringing lots of new literacy expectations. But the process is full of dilemmas and contradictions, The quiet, ordered, comfortable visitor's entrance leading into the office reflects the ideal notion of how documentation and paperwork required by ISO should work, as outlined in the manuals, the ISO orientation and some conversations with managers. By contrast, the production entrance leading into the weave room reflects the messiness, the complexities and the lived experience of paperwork and documentation from the workers' point of view: fraught with risk and blame, and sometimes opportunity. The entrances also reflect the ideal values of company culture and the actual everyday workplace practices.

On the Plant Floor

A month into the research project I go out on the plant floor. I first observe and work as a "trainee" in areas throughout the plant, then zero in on its two largest areas: the Warp Room (where the yarn is prepared for weaving) and the Weave Room.

That first day as a participant observer provides a taste of what it is like to work on the factory floor and a glimpse of the lived experience of workers in "the new workplace." It's like an isolated piece of a large puzzle. Despite my many years of experience as a workplace consultant, it takes the entire length of my time at Texco to understand how all the pieces fit together in order to present a complete portrait of literacies and work. It is a picture full of contradictions and surprises.

Because I have largely worked with joint worker/manager committees to facilitate workplace education programs, being on the floor as a participant observer is a new experience for me. It is strange to be just observing and not working on a strategy that will eventually have concrete results. Although I have offered my consulting services to Texco as part of this project, this gets taken up in minimal ways during the 6 months, which leaves the workplace educator part of me strangely unsatisfied. I give some feedback to senior managers on a revised mission statement and company values, and on the company handbook. I also develop a list of adult education principles for one of the managers. A few times, I help people with their spelling and report writing at their request. However, these efforts seem piecemeal and I never do see any results of my feedback. This is also true of the final presentation that I give to managers at the end of the research period.

I am also conscious of trying to leave behind my preconceived notions of what I know about literacies and workplaces to really understand literacy practices in new ways. I wonder how both the workers and managers perceive me and my role as a researcher. At least trying out the work—tying knots, loading creels to prepare the yarn for warping, changing bobbins and helping with measurements—makes me feel more useful than just standing around, observing and asking questions.

TEXCO: AN EXAMPLE OF "THE NEW WORKPLACE"

In terms of stated vision and values, Texco has many of the characteristics described in the literature of "the new workplace." Jackson (2000) describes such a workplace as having management approaches that combine both the technical side, focusing on conformance to standards and statistical process controls, and the "soft" or human re-sources side, focusing on customer orientation and employee empowerment. With its emphasis on both standardization and docu-mentation through its ISO 9001 quality system, and on employee em-powerment, participation and learning, Texco can easily be recognized as an example of a "new workplace."

It can also be characterized as a company on the road to high perfor-mance. The ideal of the high-performance workplace described in the literature (see Jackson, 2000) emphasizes Continuous Improvement and achieving more with less, with every employee as part of a team to achieve workplace goals. Management methods focus on building align-ment to a shared vision and strong commitment from all employees. There is an emphasis on employee satisfaction. A high-performance workplace "operates in a highly competitive market, changes quickly in response to its 'customers,' and 'competes on quality' as well as cost" (Jackson, 2000, p. 3). Texco's focus on building employee commitment to achieve company goals, quick and flexible turnaround for customers, quality and product innovation are all marks of the high-performance workplace. Its attempts at employee empowerment and appreciation, including a profit-sharing plan, are also characteristic.

Texco's owner is young and described by many employees, both in the office and in the plant, as a charismatic leader. Many changes have occurred since his arrival. I hear many comments from both workers and managers about how much better things are at Texco since this new ownership. Sales doubled in the first 5 of the 6 years since the changeover. Six years ago, most of Texco's business was based in Can-ada. Today most is export to the United States, Asia, the Middle East, South America and Europe. One of the company's greatest challenges is to constantly innovate through its research and development depart-ment to beat out the competition and come out with the next new prod-uct to meet customers' future needs and demands. "You have to be seeding continuously, out chasing things down because they usually take six months to a year to come to fruition," says the VP of Sales and Marketing.

Texco prides itself on producing high quality products with a flexi-ble, quick turn around for its customers. I am told that the company is growing at a rate of about 8% a year and the plan is for the company to double in size over the next three years. I get a sense of optimism and goodwill among senior management.

TEXCO CULTURE: STATED VALUES AND PRACTICE

During my 6 months at Texco, I observe many contradictions between stated values and what happens on the factory floor. What I observe with respect to stated policy about how ISO documentation is sup-posed to work and what happens on the shop floor reflects these contraditions. The "rough spots" with respect to ISO paperwork are at the heart of these dilemmas. This section sets the stage for stories about the different understandings that managers and workers have about ISO documentation told later on in the chapter. During my research, I get a clear and consistent message from managers that making sure employees are happy and showing appreciation for them are of primary importance. If people are happy and feel appreciated, the theory goes, they will be focused on their work and more productive. Providing information for people, forums in which they can ask questions and express their views, profit-sharing and extra financial rewards, social events and personalized birthday cards are all examples of ways managers say that people are appreciated at Texco. "Kill people with kindness," says the CEO. "People are visible as individual people," the president tells me. Another consistent message is that it is important to make sure people's work is meaningful, to give them some control over this work, and to give them a chance to grow.

At the same time, managers say that the degree to which people are happy at work is inversely related to the amount of time they have been with the company. I hear that those people who have been around the longest have the greatest number of complaints, ranging from distrust and objections to supervisors' working styles to feeling they have no autonomy in their work. "This may be because we don't listen enough, or it could be because there are people who will always complain," says one manager. Another acknowledges, "We can always be better at listening."

Later, as I spend more time on the plant floor, I begin to think that the factors that managers say are important for people's happiness only work if their other basic needs around how work is organized and done are met. I also see that managers' appreciation is geared to the individual, and that although this is laudable, perhaps the systemic issues that keep people unhappy are invisible. For example, I observe that those workers who are valued, respected and empowered in their work, and have their basic concerns listened to, are more likely to be the ones that value the kinds of appreciations offered by managers. This is true of both office staff and workers on the production floor.

I am curious about how people can exercise control over their work and how empowered they are. One manager muses, "How far can we go? What would happen if there were no managers in the building for a week?" I also hear that managers would like workers to "push the boundaries"; that managers' concerns are not so much about how to operate machinery, but more about results. When I am on the floor, I find out that although certain workers see themselves as empowered and having control over their work, there are others who feel just the opposite. One issue I hear about centers around control and initiative. Workers are told that they should take the initiative, but when some do, they are told by their supervisor, "This is not your business." One worker tells me, "You're damned if you do and you're damned if you don't." This is an expression I hear a lot during my time at the site from several people working in different parts of the plant. The meanings behind this expression provide a good understanding of the dilemmas and stresses that workers may experience in the course of their work, especially concerning the documentation required by ISO.

I hear stories about people being chastised or reprimanded for either helping others or doing a piece of work that they weren't told to do. I also hear that although workers know there will be a problem with how they have been told to run a product, they will not say anything to their supervisors. Then when the problem happens, they say, "I knew it wouldn't work this way." I consistently hear that after numerous encounters where workers raise issues and nothing changes, they just don't bother any more. I ask one of the operators whether people write anything under the heading on the blackboard in the plant that says, "New Comments and New Ideas." She says, "Nobody writes nothing. Do you think they are going to listen to anything we have to say?" Many workers tell me that they are told that there is an "open door" communication policy. But some issues never get resolved and they fear that if they speak honestly about an opinion different from their managers', the managers will "keep an eye on them."

Many of the comments I hear from the shop floor are in direct contrast to the stated values I have heard about empowerment and initiative in the managers' offices. Whether workers participate in the documentation requirements has everything to do with these overall contradictions. The threads of paperwork are tightly interwoven into this messiness of everyday workplace life. As an educator, I am also aware that these contradictions become the conditions of teaching and learning in the workplace and sit right at the heart of the success or failure of educational initiatives trying to get people to participate.

THE ISO QUALITY SYSTEM:
UNDERSTANDING THE LITERACY THREAD

Because the requirements of ISO 9001 make documentation critical, the company has been transitioning from an oral culture to a written one. At Texco, literacies in the form of documentation and paperwork are central to the success of the ISO system, and this system is central to the success of the company.

I first learn about the role of documentation in the quality system at Texco from Brendon, the VP of Manufacturing, who tells me that quality is the "lifeblood of the organization" and that it is important that people are always looking at the quality of a product. Quality procedures like equipment set-ups, Standard Operating Procedures (SOPS) and quality checks are in place so that the customer gets a consistent, high-quality product. I also learn from managers about the place of paperwork in that system. I find out that it "lends order to processes." The president tells me that "[Paperwork] is something which is in effect a map that allows everybody to cross the same terrain, and know where the pitfalls are and know what things have to be done to cross that terrain properly and get safely to the other side of the processes, as it were."

If quality is the lifeblood of the organization, then paperwork and documentation are the lifeblood of quality. Paperwork at Texco controls every aspect of the work process from the time a customer order is received until a product goes out the door. There is an intricate system of tickets attached to every product. These tickets get entered in the computer during each stage of the work process so that at any one time a person should be able to find out exactly what stage a product is at in the factory. There are work orders for each part of the process, SOPs and instructions for set-ups, product specifications and checklists that workers must follow. Following written specifications and completing paperwork is all part of quality-control procedures.

A new aspect of documentation that is added to the operators' job while I am there is Statistical Process Control (SPC), requiring operators to record production data. In the Weave room it is the width of the product being woven and the number of picks per inch. In the Warp room it is the tension of the warped yarn across the width of the material. These figures are recorded for every product, then graphed by a senior project manager who works directly with the VP of Manufacturing. The graphs show whether a product is performing within the normal range of specifications. The idea is to make products as consistent as possible, by pinpointing when a product is deviating from the normal range of specifications before it becomes a problem. Everyone in the plant gets 4 hours of SPC training. It is a standard feature of high-performance management and a commonly required component of ISO certification.

I hear from managers that although the paperwork for ISO is generally working well, they would still like to see improvement in two areas. They want better completion of the forms that employees have to fill out when something goes wrong, and they want more responses in the "Comments" section of the form on how a product runs through each stage of its process for the purposes of new products being developed.

But I observe that there is still a gap between policy and actual practice in how paperwork is done. This gap is partially created by Texco's efforts to satisfy the dual goals of serving the requirements of the customer in a global and competitive marketplace, and following the ISO system that allows them to play in this global marketplace. In real life, the goals of meeting customer requirements for a quick turnaround and the time-consuming burden of following and completing the paperwork under ISO sometimes collide. The result: a short-changing of the procedures, which sometimes leads to costly mistakes, and a working culture that supports a mixed message about the importance of this paperwork. Some workers and supervisors still believe and tacitly promote production as the "real" work and paperwork as secondary. During this time of transition from an oral culture to a high concentration of paperwork, this mixed message may only serve to reinforce views that production is more important than paperwork. One of the workers tells me that "In the office they just have to do paperwork. We have to do our work and paperwork." Paperwork is not integrated with production in this person's mind. He sees it as something quite separate from the job he is doing. This view is widely shared by other workers.

More importantly, the mixed message about the value of paperwork causes a dilemma for workers. On one hand there is a constant formal message from managers about the importance of paperwork and documentation. On the other hand, they are asked directly or indirectly to engage in practices that short-circuit the paperwork or are given messages that tell them that production is more important.

A VIEW FROM MANAGERS

To find the source of these mixed messages, it is useful to explore some of the business challenges expressed by Texco's senior managers as they work to stay competitive in a global marketplace. Documentation required by ISO is an integral part of the larger business challenges.

Brendon, the VP of Manufacturing, says that Texco's competition is in the United States, Canada and "other places [we] do not even know about." He goes on to say, "In general we've survived because we're a bit more flexible with a quick turnaround. And our quality is very, very good. We're very customer-focused and our customers always say, you know, they get a good response, you can get good product from us."

My conversations with senior managers paint a picture of markets that are rapidly changing and the challenge to be always developing and working on new and innovative products. As Garth, the company president, explains, "The biggest challenge we have is to continue to innovate." He tells me that they operate in a market that is changing and very competitive. He explains they have to learn to adapt, listen to their customers and have the capability to respond to what they need. He gives me one example of why things change quickly. He explains that they have to be very careful about doing a lot of research and development work in cases where they get only small orders that only last a year before the competition can copy it:

> We have to stay ahead of everyone else and make the newest or the most technical [product] and make sure our quality is better. We have to make it as hard as possible for the competition to copy. But they will eventually; it's a fact of life these days unfortunately. So while you are servicing today's business, you have to be looking a year or two years out, because if you look at that [big contract] and say it's great and we're great, by the time the contract is finished you go, "Okay, what's in the pipeline?"

Assessing how Texco is handling these demands, Garth says, "We've got good systems I think internally. We have to have more discipline in using the things we've already got in place. We waste time when we don't do things properly the first time, simply because in our zeal to get moving sometimes, the new system we put in, like ISO, seems to slow things down." His comments about ISO help clarify the senior managers' points of view on documentation and quality.

THE IMPORTANCE OF PAPERWORK ACCORDING TO MANAGERS

Conversations with senior managers give me a good understanding of the pressures and tensions that they face to ensure that the proper documentation has been completed and customer needs have been served at the same time. I get a sense of the critical importance of ISO documentation to the company's goals and profits.

I ask Brendon which is more important, paperwork or production. "They're equally important, and in some respects the paperwork is more important than running the product," he explains. He tells me that because the yarns they are dealing with are so expensive, a warp made to the wrong specifications can cost up to $50,000 U.S., more than an operator's yearly salary. Warping prepares the yarn for weaving by ensuring that the required number of ends for the product being made are of the same length and the same tension. Every product at Texco has to be warped. Brendon explains that "You have to look at the paperwork and understand what you are trying to do. Some people guess and say, 'I make this stuff all the time' and they haven't noticed the change. Then they go ahead and run it [but it's wrong]." It's a costly mistake. In another example that shows the importance of paperwork, he says that they have struggled to get employees to understand that when you finish a warp, you must do the paperwork associated with the warp rather than waiting until the end of the day to do it:

> People think that if they can get another warp in, they are saving time and being efficient, But they forget that someone in the office is looking in the computer to see if the warp is complete, and if they don't see it entered, they will start making calls all because somebody hasn't entered their paperwork into the computer or done their recording on time. Six to ten conversations can happen to find out what happened with the warp. People tend to forget they are part of a team and that their action or lack of action costs money.

I ask why people don't always do the paperwork in the way it's supposed to be done. Brendon believes there are several reasons. Workers may not understand the ramifications of not doing the paperwork, because they didn't have to do much of it in the past. They may have worked at Texco for 10 years and only recently have been asked to do paperwork. They may not understand the value of it or may see it as an inconvenience to their core job. He recalls a past employee who once said, "I'm a loom fixer and that's all I do. Don't ask me to do paperwork. It's not in my job description." Brendon goes on to say that paperwork is harder than what most workers do and not something they may typically be good at. He says people don't want to do something they see as an inconvenience as opposed to the satisfaction they get out of managing their own work or making a warp or getting a loom to run. Brendon laments that his biggest frustration is when people make mistakes because they are not doing the paperwork and following checklists that are in place, even though there are systems in place to prevent this from happening. This costs the company money and he is the one who has to explain the mistakes to the owner, and to the employees when their profit-sharing is down. "It's very, very frustrating," he states.

Garth, the president, gives me his perspective on the challenges of paperwork:

> A classic example is for instance in new product development. We have an element in ISO called "contractor view," which covers how we deal with the customer order all the way through the systems, and makes sure everything is correct. We often have the same sorts of elements apply to developmental things. Often the customers are saying, "I want this in a rush," [and] we don't get proper paperwork done, so things will get out onto the floor but we do it incorrectly. We do it incorrectly because all the information that's necessary wasn't done the first time and we started something without having all the paper. So it's the road to hell being paved with people's good intentions, the good intention being that we move fast, but in fact what we do is slow us all down.

He explains that customers impose their requirements, but that Texco shouldn't be initiating anything unless all the paperwork or internal communications are done properly. In a past case, Texco didn't understand the customer's needs "as well as we should have." After they made up the material in the way they thought was good, they found out that the material was supposed to have a uniform tension for a laminating process that would follow. "So instead of having something we thought was terrific, we ended up having a $100,000 claim." One of the things Garth would like to see is more information and detail on the product [being documented] at the point of presales. He echoes Brendon when he suggests that people need "more whys" about doing the documentation that is part of the ISO system in place at Texco.

MY VIEW FROM THE FLOOR

I am a participant observer on the plant floor for 5 of the 6 months I am at the Texco site. I have many reasons for wanting to be out on the floor. First, I want to understand firsthand the work processes and how people engage in literacy practices. But I also want to experience some of the work that people do on the plant floor so I have the physical and emotional perspective on what it is like to do the work and be in this particular workplace. I want to understand people's own interpretation of their work and work lives. I also hope that being on the floor will give me a better understanding of where people are at, and build trust between myself and the operators.

I believe that understanding all these things firsthand will not only improve my own practice as a workplace educator but will also improve my ability to work with others who also do this work. I think I will be better positioned to work with managers, workers, and in-house trainers after this experience. This research opportunity is an ultimate professional development experience that I hope that I can share in an accessible and effective way with others who do not have the luxury to do what I am doing.

I ask people to think of me as a trainee, someone who knows nothing about their work. I begin by watching and asking questions. Slowly, I am given tasks to do, starting with easy things and progressing to more difficult tasks. During my time on the floor, I am impressed by the number of inventions and ideas that have been developed and implemented by workers that have improved both the quality and efficiency of the work processes. The workers I am with take the initiative to show and tell me about these inventions.

As I try to understand working life from the workers' point of view, I soon learn to ask questions outside the preconceived framework I had originally constructed as research questions. I am amazed at the information that people entrust to me in such a short time about what it is like to work there. I feel a deep sense of responsibility to their stories. This is quite different from how I usually do research (such as an Organizational Needs Assessment) as a workplace educator. I don't usually have time to just hang out with people. When I map the culture of the workplace and the literacy needs within that culture, I have to be focused and directive to get pertinent information that will determine what educational programs I should recommend and what the barriers and supports are to offering these programs within a short period of time.

The stories that workers paint for me about their lives at work are quite different from those I have heard from the managers. I spend time with both long-term and shorter term employees on different shifts and see similar patterns in their stories. The most consistent story I hear is about contradictions between what they are told and what actually happens during their workday.

HOW WORKERS SEE THE VALUE OF PAPERWORK

Workers at Texco are told that everything they have to do in their jobs is important, including paperwork, so in theory, a great deal of emphasis is put on paperwork. However, comments from both managers and workers show that this is not always the practice, for many different reasons.

The stories that workers tell me indicate that there are subtle and not-so-subtle messages that getting the product done and out the door is more important than paperwork. These stories show how workers and managers short-circuit the paperwork to quickly get the product to customers. In other situations workers are questioned about the amount of time they take to do paperwork. One worker told me that he was chastised by his supervisor for spending too much time doing paperwork when he should have been "running the product." Another worker explains to me that people do not fill in the paperwork because it is not valued. He tells me that he puts in a report for the same problem over and over again, but nothing is done about it.

Such stories are commonplace to workplace environments of all kinds. But as educators, we need to pay special attention because the conditions they describe often underpin the success or failure of teaching and learning at the workplace.

WORKERS' STORIES ABOUT DOCUMENTATION

The four groups of stories that follow focus on the different aspects of documentation required by ISO. They show that the dilemmas that both managers and workers face concerning ISO documentation are systemic issues rather than the problem of any individual. These dilemmas are found in both the ISO system itself and the different "meanings-in-use" that workers give to the paperwork required by ISO.

The first two groups of stories are about Non-Conformance Reports (NCRs) and the paperwork required for Research and Development products. Both reflect the dilemma caused by quality systems like ISO where the very documentation that workers are engaged in can be used against them. Jackson (2000) notes that through these kinds of literacy practices workers "participate in policing their own work, by providing the evidence which may be used against them by their superiors" (p. 8). The third group of stories describes the process for implementing a new checklist in the Warp Room, and the last is about workers' own writings that help them do their work. All four types of stories show that workers have different interpretations or "local meanings" for these four aspects of paperwork other than the official meaning. In all of the stories, why the documentation does or doesn't get completed requires a complex understanding of power relations and social relationships, the value placed on production work, and how work is organized according to the ISO requirements. Although the stories travel along different roads, there are clearly places where local meanings come together.

NCRS: WRITING PEOPLE UP OR WRITING INFORMATION DOWN?

When I ask one of the employees from the quality department what he would tell somebody like me who doesn't know much about ISO 9001,

1.	**Non-conformance source:** Was the source internal or external?	Source:_____	
2.	**Non-conformance type:**	product_____	process_____
3.	**Non-conformance details**		

Employee_____   **Date:**_____

4. **Immediate corrective action**

Supervisor:_____   **Date:**_____

5. **Follow up**
    ☐ Reclassify   ☐ Return   ☐ Scrap

Quality:_____   **Date:**_____

6. **Sign off**

Comments:

Quality:_____ **Signature:**_____   **Date:** _____

FIG. 2.1. Non-conformance report. This figure is a composite from similar original documents adapted by the authors to preserve anonymity.

he says, "Be prepared for a lot of paperwork." When I ask if he can tell me about that paperwork, he says:

> It's basically just documentation of every process … basically every little thing that you do within the plant starting from the time the product comes in the door to testing it in the lab, to processing it in twisting. Right down to the end, to the shipping out the door. And which also includes checklists, Non-Conformances, Standard Operating Procedures. It goes on and on, and on.

I am soon introduced to the Non-Conformance Report (NCR), a requirement of the ISO Standards. The concept of non-conformance means that something is wrong and that it needs to be fixed. Examples of non-conforming situations might include the wrong yarn being sent by a supplier, fabric that is not completed to specifications, or paperwork that has been entered into the computer incorrectly. The NCR is used by everyone in the company, from operators on the plant floor through to customer service representatives, front office staff and managers to document these non-conforming situations as part of the company's quality procedures.

The NCR report is one page long. The person completing the form must fill in the non-conforming source, identifying characteristics like the part number, the process where the non-conformance happened, the quantity of product affected, a description of the non-conformance, immediate correction action, and whether the problem can be repaired, reclassified or the product scrapped. The supervisor, the quality coordinator, and the person initiating the non-conformance must sign this form. In cases where the non-conformance means the product must be scrapped, the quality coordinator calculates the cost and records it on the form. She presents all the non-conformances at the daily production and senior managers' meetings.

I learn over my 6 months at the site that whether one completes an NCR is a bigger and more complicated picture than just knowing the mechanics of reading and writing. Completing NCRs also includes comfort level with the degree of risk or blame, and the time required in completing the report. This is tied up in how one deals with contradictory messages about paperwork from managers.

I learn that completing an NCR requires a complex and astute understanding of the power and social relationships at the workplace. I discover that although there are overlaps in managers' and workers' understanding of the purpose and the problems with NCRs, there are some quite clear distinctions between them.

MANAGERS' POINTS OF VIEW

Managers view the NCR as a useful tool to help people monitor their jobs by documenting things that are wrong and need to be fixed as part of a Continuous Improvement process. One of their concerns is that these reports do not always get completed or get completed in as much detail as required; people do not take the time to write down what is wrong. When I ask one of the production managers why that is, I am given a host of reasons. I am told that people are shy about putting their opinions on paper and that they will talk about problems but they rarely want to write it down and make it formal. They could be nervous about writing the wrong thing or it could be "a confidence thing." I am also told that some people do not have English as their first language. Managers also say that some people might be scared about their handwriting or spelling. Later on I learn about a potential communications course that will be offered to all employees. Part of the course will include a module on how to complete NCRs properly. Although managers interpret the NCR problem as something needing to be addressed by training, stories from the workers' point of view show quite different interpretations of why they are not completing NCRs the way managers want.

WORKERS' POINTS OF VIEW

Workers give some of the same reasons as managers for reports not being completed or detailed. However, observation and careful attention to conversations with workers shows they give other meanings to NCRs.

The language that plant floor workers use to describe the process of completing NCRs reveals they believe the forms have a different purpose than managers say they do. Terms like "writing me up," "writing them up" and "against me" abound in discussions about NCRs. This language reflects the terminology that is normally used to describe written disciplinary procedures or warnings that go into people's administrative files. This language reflects the self-policing implications of the documentation requirements of systems like ISO (Jackson, 2000).

Stories and conversations with people indicate that you could get "written up" by a superior but that you could potentially write up a co-worker or they you using an NCR. Some production workers (those who have a sense of power and security) "write people up" to get problems resolved even with a person from the office. But people also write NCRs to protect themselves.

The stories that follow reveal these conflicting meanings of NCRs within the workplace. They clearly show that whether people write NCRs is not just about skill level.

Using NCRs to Get Things Done

I hear the first story about NCRs early in my data collection from Janet, one of the quality coordinators who works in the lab. One Friday Ted, one of the shipper/receivers, calls the lab and says, "The yarn is in, it needs to be tested." But it doesn't get tested then, and Ted calls the lab again on Monday morning. Cameron, an employee in the quality department who normally does the testing, is busy with something else. So Ted writes an NCR saying the yarn has been sitting for more than 24 hours.

Janet tells me this is not really a non-conformance in that "nowhere in our procedures does it say that yarn has to be tested within 24 hours." This is Ted's way of trying to get something done. Rather than communicating to someone in the lab that he doesn't have a lot of room back there or that he needs the boxes moved out of the holding area so he can put some other stuff there, he writes up an NCR. As Janet explains, "Cameron gets on the defensive and says, 'Oh well, I'll find something to write him up on.' When the yarn is tested, Ted isn't printing tickets up on time. And so it works both ways." Janet thinks this was just Ted's way of getting things done, but that he should have used other channels because writing the NCR wasn't effective. When I ask why it wasn't effective, Janet tells me that "people's feathers were ruffled and people [i.e., Cameron] took it the wrong way even though it wasn't done out of badness."

Subsequent conversations with Ted indicate he writes NCRs on people because communicating through normal channels about problems doesn't get things done. "Writing NCRs is the only way to get things done and the only way people will learn." Ted is a long-term employee and a recognized informal leader among the workers. Although he says he has no fear of writing people up, he acknowledges that other people don't want to write NCRs because they don't want to get people into trouble.

Ted makes two very important points. His legitimate frustration about not having enough room in the holding area and his status in the plant allow him to use the NCR the way he does without fear of major repercussions. In some ways, one might applaud it as a creative strategy to get work done. However, in situations such as the next story, workers are clearly concerned about not completing an NCR to maintain good working relations with their co-workers on whom they depend—or conversely, completing a form that will ensure that they do not get blamed for a mistake.

Protecting a Co-Worker

This brief story takes place in the Yarn Preparation Department with Karen. Her story exemplifies Ted's point that people don't write NCRs because they don't want to get their co-workers into trouble. Karen tells me that one time she noticed her reed was dirty, a situation that requires an NCR because someone should have cleaned it. She did not write an NCR because she didn't want to get anyone in the Weave Room into trouble. But she says the funny thing is that one of the "fixers" (mechanics) in the Weave Room noticed the dirty reed and he wrote her up, even though he was the one who should have cleaned the equipment in the first place!

Protecting Oneself

When I spend time with Barb, a worker in Finishing and Inspection who examines fabrics, she tells me that they have a new log for writing details about NCRs. It is a whole page for writing comments. She says it is true that people do not want to write NCRs, especially in the Weave Room. But she tells me, "I want to write them because the customer will come back on me." She also tells me that she writes NCRs on problems from the Weave Room where an NCR should have been written. She says, "In the NCR, I say that an NCR wasn't done. The supervisor should talk to her people because it keeps happening. Maybe she thinks that NCRs from her department will look bad on her." In her job in Inspection, Barb clearly sees writing NCRs as a way of protecting herself from blame, even if it means pinpointing a problem from another department. Although she writes them in exactly the way intended by managers, she does it to protect her own interests. This story also shows that even supervisors might want to protect themselves from blame. It shows their relative lack of power and how they can also be vulnerable. According to Barb, "It is not good to be seen as having too many NCRs from your department."

Getting Back at Co-Workers

This fourth NCR story centers around a different worker, Mary, from Inspection and Finishing, who feels that Wendy, a Lab worker, has unfairly singled her out for mistakes. In the hierarchy of the workplace, it is clear that a worker from the Lab has more status than a production worker on the floor. Mary also tells me that "the Lab is a clique and that their attitude is not pleasant. You feel that they are talking about you when you go in and will again when you leave."

Several days later after this conversation, I go to a team meeting with Mary's group. One of Mary's supervisors, Ross, facilitates the meeting. In the meeting Ross brings up a mistake brought to him by Wendy. He doesn't mention names, but it is clear to Mary that Wendy is accusing her when she interjects: "She brought it up again? I did it again?" Ross sidesteps her question and reminds everyone to be diligent in doing things correctly. Mary interrupts Ross by saying, "Yeah, because I have a couple of things that maybe I should just write her up and start sending e-mails now. Was that me?"

Several weeks later, I follow up with Ross about the conversation in the team meeting. He tells me that people think that Wendy is at fault, but Ross thinks there is human error on both sides. He tells me that when Mary and her co-workers make mistakes, Wendy berates them, but when Wendy makes a mistake nothing happens, which is why Mary was saying she wants to write up an NCR on Wendy. He adds, "The idea of the NCR is to solve quality problems, not petty problems." When I ask Ross why people talk about writing people up, Ross says, "It's a written document. People think it's a black mark against them and think that senior management scours them [the NCRs] to find out who did mistakes. It's written and it's permanent." Ross understands the power of documentation and the potential blame that can be associated with it.

NCRs for the Month of March

I spend an hour one day going over a month's worth of NCRs with Jack, a Quality Coordinator, to better understand what people write about and to shed more light on the question of why people complete NCRs and why they don't. I am not able to do this until close to the end of my time at Texco. I find that this conversation is consistent with the contradictions and different local meanings that I have discovered through workers' stories. I also notice that although there are errors in grammar, spelling, and sentence structure in some of the reports, they don't seem to interfere with the message the writer of the NCR is trying to get across.

I find out that there are already 67 NCRs for the end of March. I learn through my time at the site that there is a tension around the numbers of NCRs being completed. On one hand, it is a good thing that people are completing NCRs because the problems are being documented, and on the other hand I learn that there are rewards, like theater tickets, for having no NCRs for a whole month. This seems to me to be contradictory.

Jack tells me that a lot of the NCRs stem from the Weave Room. When I ask why, he tells me that there are more opportunities for problems in the Weave Room because there are many products running on many looms. I have also learned through my time at the site that although a problem may require an NCR in the weaving process, the actual source of the problem may have originated from another process. Jack tells me that when Texco first got ISO certified, people did not write an NCR for smashes. A smash happens when more than 10 ends of the fabric break at the back of the loom. They would say, "Oh this is all in a day's work." But now people are writing down smashes so that Texco can track the root cause of the problem. Jack tells me that sometimes it can take a weaver hours to untangle the ends and retie them. Eleven smashes have been recorded so far in March. As we flip through the NCRs for the month of March, I am struck by the fact that there are lots of NCRs from the Weave Room, that others originate with the yarn supplier, and still others reside with outside finishers. Still others from different areas clearly show that the problem recorded on the NCR originated with the work of the person who completed the NCR.

What I observe with the NCRs I look at is that in many cases the degree of risk or blame for the writer is minimal. For example, smashes are "all in a day's work" for this kind of operation, even though there is a push to find the root cause and minimize them. In addition, there are lots of reasons why smashes occur, many of which have little to do with the weaver. It is also safe to write about outside suppliers and finishers. In one case it appeared that an NCR had occurred because the writer had forgotten to do something. I knew that in this case the person was well respected by managers and the only person who could do the particular job—a job that no-one wanted to do and that was often difficult. Therefore, I saw the risk of blame to this person as minimal.

I ask Jack about the kind of language that I have heard on the floor, such as "writing people up." Jack says, "That's funny because they don't write a particular person up, but they write it in such a way that you know who it is. They write it in terms of 'this process wasn't done because this ticket wasn't written or printed properly.' Then you can narrow it down to who it is." Jack makes explicit the hidden implication for blame in completing an NCR that shows up in the workers' stories about NCRs.

Summing up the NCR Stories

All the people in the NCR stories clearly understand the risks and benefits of the "writing me up game" with NCRs. Although none of the workers in the stories is using NCRs exactly according to managers' intentions, each worker's literate practice is different.

Ted writes up issues that are not "true" non-conformances to deal with his frustration in not getting things done through other channels.

Karen doesn't write one to preserve her relationship with a co-worker, who then writes one against her to protect himself. Wendy writes up Mary, and Mary would like to write up Wendy to get back at her for past injustices, but doesn't. In the hierarchy at this workplace, Wendy in the Lab—part of the front office—has more status and power than Mary. Barb always writes NCRs to protect herself from blame with customers and hence with managers, even if it means pointing the finger at another department.

These findings about the meanings-in-use of NCRs allow me to reflect on my role as a workplace educator. My experience as a researcher confirms my previous experience as an educator about the complexities of identifying a cause for why people do not engage in required literacy practices at work, and the fallacy of not exploring the social context (through the input of all interest groups) for all angles on the situation. However, it is the first time I have actually seen the complexities unfold layer by layer, right before my eyes. It is powerful to see something as simple as filling in a one-page form embedded in the complex dynamics of power and social relationships at the workplace. These experiences as a researcher encourage and sharpen my understanding as an educator to continue to expand my facilitative role in the workplace beyond just educational programs. New insights from the research give me ways to assist workplaces by coming up with strategies to address issues and rocky places around literacy practices. True, some people could benefit from improved writing skills and the procedures for completing forms. However, taking only this approach would fail to consider other underlying reasons for why people choose not to engage in this literacy practice.

R&D: "DOING EXACTLY WHAT THE PAPERWORK SAYS"

The following story examines why workers do or do not participate in completing the documentation required for Research and Development (R&D).

During my 6 months at Texco, I discover that there is a lot of paperwork that goes with new R&D products. In one instance, I count 14 pieces of paperwork in a red folder that signifies an R&D product. Various managers tell me that there are three major purposes of such paperwork. It is a requirement for ISO, but it also "makes sure that the operators doing the work really understand what they are trying to do from beginning to end." The third purpose is for operators to provide very specific details on what is working and what isn't. One manager tells me that "in most cases we are going to ask them to do something different from what they do every day." "The process is very open," I hear from another. Although there is a framework for running any new product, the expectation is that operators will use their expertise to determine whether something will work, and provide written feedback.

The operators' completed documentation also provides a guide for set-ups when the product is transferred over to manufacturing. The process for handing over R&D projects to manufacturing is well defined. One of the engineers, Harold, looks over all the comments and feedback and transfers the different set-ups for running the product to a manufacturing form. When the fabric is run in manufacturing, it is initially inspected and in many cases receives ongoing visual inspection to make sure it is running properly.

One of the recurring themes that I hear from managers throughout my time at Texco is the fact that people do not complete the paperwork in enough detail when there is a test run of a new fabric. The Plant Manager explains that when they make a brand-new product they don't know how it's is going to perform. They have an idea about how it will run through the equipment, but they always ask for feedback. He notes, "So there's paperwork for each department with an area for what has to be done and then [an area] for comments." The Plant Manager tells me, "It is rare that we get good comments from the operators that are doing the job ... it's always something is 'OK.' 'OK' doesn't tell you a great deal except it was okay. But if you did it again the next person's 'OK' might be 'well, it wasn't so good.'" He describes why he thinks people might not do the paperwork:

> I think it's a bit of nervousness. They don't want to say everything was great in case later on it's found that it isn't so great. And I say, "Well, why did you write that?" So it's a confidence thing; some of it's English as a second language and some of it's people are scared that their writing is kind of scribbley or, you know, unreadable or their spelling is bad, that's part of it.

These are familiar explanations, but I am curious to get a fuller picture on why people do not provide more details on R&D paperwork. It is not until the end of the data collection period that I spiral deeper and deeper to gain a more complete understanding of the issues, the complexities and contradictions around R&D paperwork.

The General Meeting on R&D

The third general employee meeting I attend while I am at the site is run by one of the senior managers, Raymond. This particular meeting focuses on the importance of R&D to the business, and the importance of paperwork to R&D.

The general meeting is held in the lunchroom. It is crowded, and people are standing as well as sitting, contributing to the hum of voices and the feeling of anticipation. An overhead project and a screen are set up at the front of the room. The meeting begins with the president introducing Raymond and the purpose of the meeting, which is to focus on the importance of R&D to the company. Throughout his presentation, Raymond uses overheads to make his points. Closer to the end of the presentation he shows actual products made by the company.

He begins: "Only 16 out of the first 100 businesses that were in business a hundred years ago are still in business today. Why is that?" He then responds to his own question, "They weren't making products … the products were obsolete."

A discussion follows about companies and products that became obsolete and why companies like Dictaphone went out of business. Raymond emphasizes that R&D's business is to make these new products, to ensure that Texco is changing and up-to-date. "Change is hard, but it is part of life. Change is essential for business."

Then he goes through the different products and materials that are made at Texco. As he talks about the products, he shows people the items. He also talks about the process of R&D and how long it takes to get the right product. You have to make many attempts, and it's not always easy. "But one should not give up," he says. "Look at the results."

At the end of the presentation, Raymond asks people to write their comments on the R&D paperwork, even though he acknowledges it is tedious. He talks about the importance of their comments for running the orders later. "If all the proper set-ups are not written down, people will forget because of the length of time between the R&D and the customer orders." Brendon, the VP of Manufacturing, also emphasizes the need for paperwork at the meeting. Everything that has come before in this presentation has set the stage for convincing people to be more diligent in completing the R&D paperwork. This is confirmed later in my conversation with Brendon after the meeting.

Throughout this meeting, I ponder how its message plays out in everyday life. How does everyday work practice encourage or discourage operators to fill out the paperwork when they are working with R&D samples? Is just telling people more about the big picture of R&D and about the finished products enough to encourage operators to engage in the paperwork?

Later, I talk to Brendon about the purpose of this meeting. I ask him his sense of what people got out the meeting. He tells me that people like to hear about what's interesting. If you can give them something interesting at the same time you *ask* for something, you might get what you ask for. He thinks that people like to get information about where Texco's products go and what's involved. What managers wanted to get out of this meeting was to get people to "write stuff down" about running the product: "their thoughts, comments and helpful hints," because different people may be running the product 9 months away. He adds that Raymond's presentation was supposed to spur people on to do more work, think more and ask more questions about the end product. The idea was, according to Brendon, that if people have more information about why things are being done, like the end product, they will be able to add their value. If they don't know why, they can't help. His feeling is that people don't have enough information about where a product is going and tend to focus on the immediate task at hand. Then they do exactly what the paperwork says rather than write "this would be a good idea" or "try that."

I like this emphasis on understanding. But I find myself thinking that it only partly reflects what is going on. Differences in power, privileges and pay also contribute to why workers do not get as involved in the process of making products as managers hope. The idea of getting people's opinions during the R&D process might directly contradict the standardized procedures they are supposed to follow when they are making regular products. "Doing exactly what the paperwork says" is what they are supposed to do. On one hand, the company wants the operators' creativity, but on the other hand it wants them to religiously follow written SOPS and set-ups required by ISO for regular manufacturing products. This makes the problem of not writing information down more complicated than Brendon thinks. As illustrated in the following stories, the reasons people do not write their ideas down are multiple and complex, just as they were in the case of NCRs. The very nature of the ISO quality program stifles the creativity, input, and imagination that managers want workers to use in the R&D process. It is one of several major contradictions that we learn more about next.

Managers' Perspectives on R&D Paperwork

I hear a consistent message from managers that operators need to improve the level of detail in their written feedback when R&D products are run. They have lots of views about why this doesn't happen. Some managers say that operators often don't get enough of the big picture: what the product is supposed to be used for or what it is supposed to do. They say operators are focused on the technical set-up for the product: the width, the ends, the number of pics, and so on. They are not thinking that the product is going to be a snowboard or skis. According to managers, they think: "I'm going to do exactly what the paperwork says rather than write 'This would be a good idea' or 'Try this.'" I also hear that often people don't take time to read all the information.

According to one manager:

> They feel they're too busy, that they have other things to do. So they don't want to be perceived as stopping and just reading, except that's what you want them to do when they are doing R&D.... They think they know production because they've done it before and it's a lot more routine and easier to do. When it comes to [R&D] paperwork, it's stop and [change] modes. You know, go from this "have to be efficient" mode to this "have to be thinking, reading and writing" mode.

This manager clearly understands the opposing expectations the company demands of people through the ISO systems. However, he doesn't acknowledge this as a major problem for workers, in terms of expecting them to be creative and thoughtful when they do R & D paperwork, but to pay attention to standardized procedures and paperwork for regular manufacturing products.

Ironically, one of the other managers has this to tell me about the R&D paperwork:

> ... like I said in the beginning, the paperwork is absolutely essential because the fabric is still in the design stage. But it's pretty time-consuming and in some ways cumbersome in that we have to really cover everything in the paperwork. We cannot assume that people will use their imagination or their intelligence. It's [the paperwork] almost like "stupidity-proof," and that is sometimes frustrating because we thought that people should be able to anticipate what they've been doing [because they have been] weaving for a long time in most cases. So there is a lot of details we have to cover and it's really time-consuming.

I find these comments contradictory for a number of reasons. First, this manager acknowledges the time it takes to do the paperwork. Second, although he says he wants feedback on how things are running from operators, his use of a phrase like "stupidity-proof" suggests he holds a low opinion of their capabilities and holds them responsible for the fact that there has to be so much paperwork.

Reasons such as fear of being blamed for a mistake, not understanding the "big picture," and conflicting expectations seem to contribute to why people don't complete the R&D paperwork in more detail. But I sense there are still deeper contradictions around managers' expectations.

Managers are aware on some level of the policing aspect of the R&D paperwork, as revealed through workers' comments about how a sample run could get them into trouble later. But I saw no indication that they are aware of the deep ramifications that this self-policing process could have on operators' consistent lack of detail in R&D paperwork.

They are also aware that operators work with R&D samples under a different set of expectations than those required to run regular products. However, both managers I talk to fail to consider how this contradiction in expectations contributes to the problem of resistance to paperwork. Sometimes workers are meant to be efficient, productive, and not spend too much time reading; other times they are supposed to switch to being creative, thinking and literate. These opposing expectations clash with full force.

A View From the Quality Department: Albert's Perspective on R&D Paperwork

Albert is an employee who works in the Quality Department. He has his own theories about why people do not complete R&D paperwork. He tells me that before the new ownership, documentation took place on an ad hoc basis:

> There was no formal way of doing it. Quite often what would happen is that we would run a sample and some records were taken, but there was little about machinery set-up and things like that. A lot was not recorded, and you never knew who was recording what. Now it's more formally documented. There's still work to be done, but it's improving all the time.

He tells me that communication between R&D and the shop floor needs to be improved. Albert says that improperly completed paperwork has to do with language problems, cultural differences, and documents that are too technical for people to understand, which makes it too hard for them to know what to record. He thinks that when two or three operators are working on a project, they may leave it to the others to take responsibility. He also says that it could be an issue of forgetting or lack of discipline. Albert puts the reasons for the problem of poorly completed R&D paperwork primarily on the shoulders of the operator. But he also suggests that some problems may exist with how R&D designs the paperwork, an idea I have not heard before. This makes me even more curious about the larger complexities and contradictions.

Sandy's Story on Circumventing R&D Documentation

I get a different picture through conversations and stories from some of the production workers. Sandy works in Finishing and Inspection. When I am with her on the floor, she tells me, "They say paperwork is more important than production, but when it comes to the crunch, no." She tells me that the supervisors will get on the bandwagon about paperwork until someone needs something right away. Then the supervisors or someone from R&D want to cut 500 meters without a Finishing Order—that is, without the proper paperwork required under ISO.

She explains that she can get a call from a supervisor to do a "rush" for R&D. "Larry will ask you to cut it without the paperwork and then he will come back on you and say 'Why did you do it?'" She says, "Supervisors are covered, but we are damned if we do and damned if we don't!" They want to do it without paperwork because they want to get a sample out to the customer fast. She tells me that in team meetings they are told not to touch anything that doesn't have paperwork. "For a month we are told not we can't do anything for R&D without paperwork. Then Larry says 'just do this and I will cover you.' Sally calls down and says just do this and this. But then they will get back on the bandwagon again because perhaps Brendon gets after people." When I ask Sandy why this happens she tells me that "R&D has hot new items they want to get out to the customers in a hurry." She adds, "But it only takes a couple of seconds to do a work order."

This is one of several stories I hear about R&D circumventing paperwork or documentation required by ISO. Although there is a great desire for operators to complete R&D paperwork, some staff from R&D do not appear to respect the need to do so themselves—another reason why operators may be reluctant to do it.

Tom's Frustrations: Experience Silenced

I spend an evening in Yarn Preparation working with Tom, an operator. He tells me he works for Texco because he likes the people. Before Texco, he worked at a place where he made more money, but where managers did not "talk nice." He tells me that he "talks straight," and that he has gotten into trouble for saying what is on his mind. Sometimes he has ideas for how things might be run in a different way, and says he always talks about it before he runs something. He also tells me that "people with a lot of experience will be told to run something in a certain way, when they will know that it would run better in a different way. But they won't say anything until the first way fails." I ask Tom why. He tells me, "Giving input is not something that is valued or welcomed."

He goes on to say that people do not sign off on the R&D work and do not want to fill in the paperwork: "People are frustrated and fed up that their paperwork is not valued. So not signing it or not doing it is a quiet sign of resistance." He tells me that people make suggestions for changes on the R&D work, but then the product comes back the next time with none of the changes made. He also says that "when new things are run, experienced people are never consulted."

Tom tells me that people are "pissed off" that their experience and knowledge are not utilized. When I ask him why this is, he tells me that he believes some managers and supervisors need to think they are more important than their subordinates. He comments, "If you make your subordinates bigger and smarter than you, they will take care of your work and you can just sit on the chair." Tom seems to be saying that if managers and supervisors would trust and use the expertise of their employees, the work, including the paperwork, would get done without as many problems.

R&D Paperwork: Conclusions

There are many reasons why the R&D paperwork is not being completed with the detail required by managers. However, I do not believe that the main reasons are because workers do not understand the "big picture" or that they are have poor writing skills. And I emphatically do not believe it is because they lack initiative, leadership skills or ability.

Poorly completed paperwork has more to do with contradictions that work in at least three major ways. One is between the different expectations set out by the ISO standards for Manufacturing and R&D work. A second contradiction is that their written feedback on R&D products can be used against them, a fact that some managers acknowledge. The final contradiction is between managers' requests for creativity and feedback, and their failure to pay attention to the feedback they do get or to believe that workers are capable of it. Some managers do not seem to truly value workers' feedback or their experience as operators. This shows up in stories from all levels of the workplace. The stakes are clearly high. Operators' very words can be held against them at a later date. And because they have the least amount of power in the workplace hierarchy, they can be blamed when they break these rules at the request of those with more status and power. Yet at the same time they are expected to faithfully do the paperwork for the same department that demanded that they break the rules.

CHECKLISTS: THE NEW FORM FOR WARPER SET-UP

This next group of stories focuses on a revised checklist for setting up a product on the warper. Remember that warping is a separate process that prepares the yarn for weaving by ensuring that the required number of ends for the product being made are of the same length and the same tension. Every product at Texco has to be warped. Generally, there are two operators working on the warping process at a time.

A new checklist has been designed by the Quality Department to address mistakes that have been made in the warping process. It serves different interests and gives rise to different meanings for those who designed it and those who have to use it. I have been fortunate to observe the implementation of the new warp set-up checklist over a number of weeks. One of the quality coordinators says it is easier for the operators than the old one and that its purpose is to prevent mistakes. The workers I talk to do not like it at all because they say it takes more time before actual production, and more time away from production.

From the Workers' Point of View

I observe that although workers could fill in the old checklist while the Warper was rotating, they must use the new checklist before starting the machine, while they do the product set-up on the computer. Each time operators check a function on the computer (like customer order number, product number, width, number of sections, width of each section, number of ends, and so on), they must check it off on the new checklist. However, not only does this take more time to do (because they have to do it "up front,") but it is also confusing because the list of items on the computer set-up are not in the same order as those on the check list. (In the original version of this revised checklist, not only did operators have to complete the list before they started, but then they also had to find someone else to go through the checklist with them to check it a second time. The idea is that a second person was needed to prevent mistakes. Apparently, this was abandoned.)

The new checklist has been developed without operators' input, by people who do not do the job. The operators view it as a clear assessment of their own incompetence. One of the operators tells me that if she "doesn't know her job after all this time, then something is wrong." When I ask if they had input into the design of the new checklist, I am given a withering look. "Get real. Where would you get such an idea?" one worker says. "Yes … we tell them what we don't like, but they still make us do it."

I find it curious that the Quality Coordinators who have designed the new checklist think it is easier and it saves time, when watching the operators shows it actually takes more. And it is precious time in an environment where the work on the floor often seems to be valued over paperwork. Operators are expected to do the paperwork, but they are not supposed to take any extra time to do it. The environment they are working does not empower them or use their input. Their expertise is not valued (they are not asked to solve the problem) and their competence is questioned (initially they not only had to complete a checklist designed by someone else, they also had to have someone else check their work).

Some have found solutions by doing the paperwork efficiently while the warper is running. This way they do double duty without losing time, even though technically they are supposed to complete the form as they complete each part of the process.

At the same time, it's clear that the old form was not really useful. Copying information from one piece of paper to fill in the blanks on another form is not helpful. I see the logic of the story from the Quality Department's point of view. However, the issue that is central to this story has more to do with actual literacy practices in use and how they are connected to issues of empowerment, control over one's work, and initiative. It is about who gets their suggestions taken up. I see a clear difference between the managers' stated values and vision about empowerment and initiative and what sometimes happens on the factory floor as illustrated through this story. It reflects the ongoing risks and disappointments workers can experience in taking initiative with paperwork or literacy practices. It is a story about who gets to exercise power in these practices, and it is a story about workers feeling "kept in their place."

Two things tend to happen when the operators use the new checklist. The operator either checks everything off when the warp is finished, or gets confused and checks off the wrong items because they are not in the same order as the set-up on the computer screen. Kerri, one of the operators, says that the new checklist doesn't work anyway because there are only a few things that she changes each time. She says she could see doing the checklist for a new product, but not ones they run all the time. She always "scans the specs [on the computer] twice with special attention to the things she changes."

I can see why the operators might want to check the list off later. They don't see a good reason for doing it while they do the set-up, and they have no ownership of it. All they know is that it is not going to benefit them to take more time to do their production work in this environment.

Another requirement of both old and new checklists is that operators have to put down the time it takes to do the different parts of warping, like loading the creel, tying knots, pulling knots and putting the yarn through the reed, doing the warp and beaming it off. I observed and later was told by an operator that this can be difficult because more than one person will do a task, people go back and forth between tasks, or some of the tasks are done by a previous shift. This makes it very difficult to accurately note the amount of time taken to do the tasks. Managers say they need this information for scheduling purposes, to determine how long it will take to do a warp for a particular product.

A Quality Coordinator's Perspective

I talk to one of the Quality Coordinators and several other employees in the Quality Department about the checklist. Peter tells me that the old checklist was revised to "make it easier for the operators." He explains that the previous procedures for checking the set-up were not working. He tells me that "everyone makes mistakes, can forget and that it is important to have someone else confirm what they have done is correct." The implication is that the revised checklists ask operators to both go through the list individually, then to get it checked by another operator to help them avoid making a mistake. Peter tells me that he and other internal auditors will be inspecting operators at random, picking some items on the checklist to see if they have been set up properly.

Janet, one of the Quality Coordinators, tells me that the old checklist had a lot of blank spaces, that it wasn't being used effectively, and that it was more time-consuming. She says that operators were just transferring information to them that was written elsewhere. She says that basically the same information is on the new checklist, but just in a different way. "They don't really have to write it down. The check list is for them to double check their work." She says that operators don't need to write the information down again, that they just need to see if they have punched things in correctly and check it off on the list. That's why it is supposed to be easier for them.

I ask Janet how people have reacted to the new form. She explains that initially there was a lot of resistance because operators didn't understand that the purpose of the new form was to save time and be easier to complete. Janet says that because they are now able to use a checklist with boxes, they can note things like the cut mark for products where there had been a recurring number of small mistakes, in addition to other important things to check that were never included before. She rejects the view that the new checklist is more difficult for the operators and takes more time than the old one.

I bring up the question of how difficult operators say it is to calculate the time it takes to do various tasks required on the checklist. Janet says that she knows it is difficult, and I ask her about the suggestion in the team meeting from one of the operators about taking an average. She explains that this will be a time-consuming task and that she has spoken to the Plant Manager and Supervisor about it. There is a conflict between the Supervisor and the Manager about whether it is necessary to write the time down each time. The Supervisor thinks it is; the Manager doesn't really know if they need it. Janet emphasizes to me that it is not her job to decide. She says, "But I should follow up with him [the Plant Manager] because if it's unnecessary and if it's not going to help us in terms of scheduling, then I need to know that, and that will calm the area down." She adds that she thinks it's hard, but people have to take responsibility for calculating their own times. I say that I notice that operators are going around looking for the Warper to report the time they took to do a particular task. She agrees this is happening, but thinks that it is not up to the Warper to go and get everyone's time, and that it is not necessary.

Janet gets to what I think is the crux of the matter when she says, "I think they [operators] are worried that we are doing it [implementing the new checklist] to assess how well they do their jobs, but that's not how we are using it." She reiterates the need to have times for scheduling and meeting customer needs. She reemphasizes the fact that people think they are being tested for how much time it takes. We end the conversation with Janet acknowledging that she would like to just average the time so there would be an end to all this conflict.

Out of curiosity, I ask Kerri what would make a good checklist. She tells me that a good checklist would be much shorter and only include those variables that change with each new work order for warping. In a team meeting that I attend, she also suggests that if the time it takes to do things is needed for scheduling, why don't managers take an average of the time it takes people to do the work? As an aside she tells me, "If they are taking averages with SPC for everything else, why not for this, too?" Managers seemed to respond positively to this suggestion, but 2 weeks later, it hasn't been taken up. During my time at the site, it was never resolved.

From the operators' point of view, the requirement of putting down the time it takes to do tasks seems like a form of control, and an assessment of how long it takes an individual operator to do things. But this is full of contradictions. First, because of the nature of how people work on things—sometimes working together, sometimes not, other times working on several tasks at once—it is difficult if not impossible to be accurate about the precise amount of time it takes to do a warp from beginning to end. Second, it takes time for the person who is completing the paperwork to go and ask these other people what their time was to do some portion of the task.

About a month and a half later, I talk to Peter again. The checklists still aren't being filled out in the way they're supposed to be. He tells me that quite often "somebody will go through an entire job, they'll get it done and then they'll go to the checklist and check the list off." He says that people think it's too trivial to do it up front, even though it is really essential to the running of the machine. He says, "They go through it and say 'Well, did I do that, yes I did that, did I do this, yes I did.'" He tells me that waiting until the end to check off the list is a problem of discipline. When I ask what he means, he says, "Just self-discipline. Some people are better at it than others. I'm bad that way myself, but you know, I don't have to. I am not involved with the actual paperwork any more. But I'm not a good one for writing and e-mails and stuff like that. I tend to even leave myself messages to remind myself to do things and I think a lot of people are the same way." We talk about whether this problem of not making the writing a priority is a lack of confidence or a lack of discipline. Peter says, "In my own case I don't have a lack of confidence in it, I just have a lack of discipline." He tells me about a manager who would much rather go to a person and discuss something with them than write something, and that he tends to be the same way.

I am curious about the contradiction here. It seems to be okay for staff people and managers to prefer an oral mode of working, but it is not okay for operators. If people in a leadership position don't make writing or paperwork a priority, how can operators be expected to? I also note that Peter equates everybody else's reasons for not doing the paperwork in the way it is intended with his own personal reasons. He doesn't seem to see any underlying systemic issues in this situation.

We then move on to talk about the internal audit. I ask Peter to explain what he would do. He tell me that he might randomly check jobs to make sure that there are SOPS at the work stations and that he might ask someone what the SOP is for a particular job to make sure they are following what the paperwork says. I ask him whether he would check how people are doing set-ups in the Warp or Weave Room as part of the internal audit process. He confirms that checking sets-ups is something they are going to start doing. He explains that set-ups and checklists are part of SOPs. SOPs in the Warp Room include entering data into the computer, checking to see that you have the proper number of ends on a creel, and that you have selected the proper reed. He tells me:

> I can't wait because I'm going to be auditing, and that's the exact audit I'm going to do this month. And that's the one where we introduced a new checklist. And I've seen instances where it has not been done. We implemented it for a reason and the main reason was because there were quite a few mistakes. And the whole purpose of implementing it in the form we

did was to try to eliminate these mistakes. So would you fly on an air-
plane knowing that the pilot hadn't done his checklist?

It sounds to me like Peter is hoping the audit will catch the operators
in the Warp Room completing their set-up checklist after the fact. His
analogy between using the checklist to ensure that a plane and its pas-
sengers are safe, and following one to set up the warper to run fabric,
shows that he understands the quality discourse primarily from the
perspective of managers.

Summing Up the Checklist Story

These different perspectives on and stories about the new checklist for
set-up in Warping present me with a tangle of different interests, different local meanings and people working at cross-purposes. My status
as a participant observer is invaluable to getting a holistic picture of
what's happening and the contradictions here. I have worked with both
the old and new checklists; I have worked with the operators to account for the time tasks have taken; I have been in team meetings
where issues about the checklist have been raised.

As a workplace educator, it seems to me that encouraging workers to
engage in a literacy practice such as completing the checklist requires a
different sort of strategy. I envision a meeting where the key players, especially the operators, are at the table with managers and Quality Department staff who value and respect their expertise. Everyone
discusses the small mistakes that are occurring. Managers ask operators for their input about how to address this problem. If a new checklist
is the answer, I would expect that the operators would be asked what the
checklist should look like in order for it to work for them. They might
even design a first draft with input from Quality Department staff. Then I
see a period where they would test out the checklist, followed by another
meeting to discuss how it is working. All parties discuss whether the
mistakes have been reduced. Adjustments are made to improve the
checklist further still. And operators do not resist the checklist because
they helped design it themselves, and feel pride and ownership in it. The
mistakes that have been occurring have diminished.

WORKERS' NOTEBOOKS[3]

This final group of stories is the flip side of the previous three. It is about
workers taking the initiative to engage in literacy practices beyond the
official requirements for documentation by developing their own notebooks to aid them in their daily work tasks. But these workers are not
rewarded for taking this initiative. In fact, they hide the notebooks from
view, tucking them away in a drawer or a pocket somewhere. At Texco,

---

[3]Portions of this story have already been published by TESL Ontario in Hunter,
Belfiore, and Folinsbee, 2001.

many of the long-term warpers and fixers (mechanics) have created their own literacies for their own purposes: to have more control over their work, and to be able to work more safely, more efficiently and more accurately. They pool their knowledge and experience and share this among themselves, both verbally and in writing. Understanding how these literacies are created is important to make visible how workers gain and share knowledge as a community, and how they maintain some control over their work in the face of increasing standardization. Ironically, it is often the long-term employees who most often keep these notebooks who are frequently accused of being unable to adjust to change and most in need of better literacy skills. Ironically, too, under the ISO system these worker notebooks exist as uncontrolled, non-standard documents, and their use could be considered a non-conformance, especially when the external auditor comes around.

Workers on Their Notebooks

Early on in the research I discover that several workers have their own spiral notebooks with diagrams, calculations and instructions on how to perform different work procedures. Although I am very interested in these notebooks, they seem to me to be private and off limits. It takes me a long time to ask to look at them at work stations, and then to borrow them in order to read them, make notes and finally interview the workers who created them. One worker, Jerri, has had her notebook for 15 years, using it when she runs into problems. Co-workers Sam and Miranda use their notebooks regularly. Other workers also use these notebooks or have access to the information in them. In one case, more experienced workers look at the notes and give feedback to the notebook writer. Jerri tells me that she has designed her notebook specifically so her co-workers can use it. Her book is neatly laid out in careful handwriting, divided into sections with the problem or task to be done outlined in blue and the solution written in red. Miranda's book, too, is clearly laid out with headings that describe the task to be done, followed by the steps to complete the task. The development of these literacies can, in some cases, strengthen the bonds and relationships among workers or even departments as a community. These worker literacies are embedded in an informal mentoring process that exists among them quite separate from, yet still connected to, the ISO procedures that govern their work.

I am curious about why people go to the trouble to write their own notes when they could use the manuals. My suspicions are confirmed. Both Jerri and Sam tell me that it is quicker and easier to refer to their own notes as opposed to looking something up in the manual.

As an educator, I find this revealing in view of the fact that many workplace literacy programs would attempt to "teach" participants document literacy skills so they can read the manual. Although this may be a realistic goal in some cases, I see other factors to consider.

First, much of the learning that occurs happens in cooperation and mentoring among a group of people. Literacy is embedded in this group process. Second, even when people use literacy to do their work, as with the worker notebooks, they may see the official form of literacy (the manual) as inadequate or inefficient.

Jerri says:

> When we got the machine in ... we each got a manual. And it's like about an inch thick. It has a lot of information, and it's really you know, you have to sit down and think about what they're writing ... because sometimes it doesn't make sense when you're first reading it. So basically what I did is that I just put together a book so that I wouldn't have to go in that big manual every time I needed some information and pull my hair out trying to find it.

Sam explains it this way:

> Yes, it [the information] is in a manual [but] I do it for my own because I can read my own writing, and there's less jargon in my book than there is in a manual. Like for instance, left-hand side, four to five millimeters; that's all I need to know. I don't need to know anything else—right-hand side three millimeters. That's all I need to know. I don't need to know it's the distance from here to here because I know where the distance is. That part of it I know; the three to four to five I don't know sometimes.

Where Workers Get Information for Their Notebooks

Information that goes into workers' notebooks sometimes comes from people, not directly from manuals, spec sheets or other formal documentation. It is gleaned from more experienced workers and technicians, from supervisors and from workers' own experience. In fact, supervisors, process engineers with supervisory responsibilities, and more experienced employees will provide information or changes to go into people's private notebooks. Jerri gets most of her information from the outside technician for the new warper and from lessons gained from her own experience with the warper.

> Before the technician left, I took it upon myself ... and, well, I figured if it's for myself, it's for the other girls, too, at the same time. I questioned Michelle on a lot of things. How to do this, what do you do when this happens. Like what I could think of, I questioned her on it, and she gave me some answers. And another thing, it's from experience, what happened to us [during] the first few weeks of working machines, like things that we learned.

Sam gets his information from more experienced fixers and the process engineer. As he puts it, it's just from people.

> It's from Garrett, it's from Tom, from Tim, from Alistair. Alistair, he's so smart I can't believe it.... He comes in here ... he knows the Dornier

[type of loom], I grab him anytime I've got a problem, so I bustle around and grab him and say, "Here I can't get this, it's not working out right," or "Did I do this right?" ... [I] always want somebody to check my work. Because I don't want to make a mistake that can cause someone else an injury, you know.

What Managers Think of Worker Notebooks

Sam tells me that managers don't know he has a notebook—it just has never come up as a topic of conversation. He does volunteer, however, that the more experienced fixers look at his notebook and give him positive feedback. Sam explains:

> Garrett [experienced fixer] says it's a good idea. But Garrett he can re-member. He has a memory like an elephant, he never forgets. I've had Garrett, I've had Tom [experienced fixer] come up and read my notes. But hey, I've got no problem with that, if you see something there that you know you don't think it's right, or you think I should change, by all means tell me. Because if you don't, I'm going to make that mistake forever and ever and ever.

He goes to explain that Garrett has given him positive feedback on the contents of his notebook. He told Sam, "Oh yeah, that's good, you know if it works for you, it works for you. Like all the information is there." Sam's comments indicate he experiences a high level of trust with these more experienced fixers. As mentors, they contribute positively to the literacy he is creating to help him learn a new job.

Miranda and Jerri both indicate that supervisors know about their notebooks. Jerri says that they seem to like them, and that they are always telling Miranda to put things in her book.

Miranda's Bilingual Notebook

Miranda's story is connected not only to the stories of other workers across our sites, but also to the much larger story of the contradictions of the new data-driven workplace.

Miranda is one of the first workers I meet and work with at my site. She works in one of the most high-tech parts of the plant, on a new computerized warper, where she must enter all the elements of product set-up into the computer. She also enters tickets into an AS400 computer system as part of traceability under ISO. An experienced worker, she has been at this plant for 15 years and in the textile industry for 28. She confides to me that she did not have the opportunity to go too far in school in Greece and that she finds entering data in the AS400 computer system difficult. She is one of a small group of women in the warp room who befriend me while I am at Texco. I spend many hours working with Miranda as a participant observer over the period of several weeks that I am in the Warp Room. While Miranda teaches me the details of warping, we share stories about families, learning, school and good food.

Miranda explains to me with enthusiasm that most of the notes in her notebook are related to how to enter things into the AS400 computer:

> You want to know the truth? This is for myself. See, I am not used to com-
> puter and stuff and anything I have to use to put though any work orders
> and stuff, I need to know which buttons to push through. So I have to
> have it, and some of it I don't know by heart, you know. But sometimes I
> get stuck, which is very often and I have to have a book.

I notice that Miranda's book is an interesting mix of Greek and English. Miranda explains to me that a lot of what she gets for her book is from one of the supervisors who sometimes speaks too fast. "So I have written down a little bit of Greek and a little bit of English. So afterwards I'll put in English and make it clearer." The pages of her book are filled with instructions for using the AS400. The pages are printed in English with chunks of Greek interspersed. Miranda emphasizes that she uses her book every day to help enter and transfer tickets and work orders into the system.

Jerri tells me that under the ISO system, these worker notebooks count as uncontrolled, non-standard documents. Their use could be considered a non-conformance, especially when the external auditor comes around. She explains it this way:

> Well because we're ISO, like so anything that we have in information and
> stuff has to be documented and everything. And this isn't really a docu-
> ment, it's just to help us along when we have problems or something. It's
> not really a document, so that's why we're not supposed to advertise our
> notebooks.

When I ask her why, she says that it is not a standard way of proceeding. She goes on to tell me that if an auditor saw the book, it would result in a non-conformance.

> Because basically these are kind of like specs, like they're not specs but
> they're specs. You understand what I'm trying to say. It's how to do things
> like a procedure, so they should be under a procedure, an SOP or under
> a spec. They should have a revision number ... it should be [an official]
> document.

If it is true that using these notes is a violation of ISO standards, it brings up a remarkable contradiction. Workers are using the program in their own way. They have developed literacies to help make their own work easier and less frustrating. In making their own work easier, they are also meeting managers' objectives for quality and efficiency. Maybe this is why I hear that managers turn a blind eye to the notebooks, even though they might know it is a violation of the ISO standards. The operators are told by managers to put their books away when the auditor comes. Herein lies the contradiction. Although workers are pushed to take initiative and continuously improve in "the new workplace," they might actually be penalized for this under a system like ISO by getting a non-conformance written up about them.

Although Miranda would score low on writing skills according to how we assess literacy these days, by following some threads of her literacies, she is highly literate in many respects. She is able to make literacy do what she wants, to have control over her work and do her work well.

Concluding Thoughts on Workers' Notebooks

In all of the worksites we researched for this project, there are workers who use print creatively. That is, they create their own forms, their own manuals or notebooks to help them with their work. In some instances, the workers' documents capture the collective experience of people in a certain department. They use their own manuals and forms rather than the standard ones for a variety of reasons. Many point to the inadequacy of the standard documents to get across information clearly, effectively or in a way that gives workers a feeling of control over their own jobs. People construct their own ways of using literacy in their jobs that make sense to them, but don't necessarily correspond to the standard. As a result, they create their own records outside the standard documents. These are the products of workers on the floor, the same workers who are often characterized in the dominant discussion about literacies and work as the ones with deficits. These are the stories we often don't hear.

A starting place for investigation into literacies in the workplace should assume a rich community of practice that workers like Miranda engage in to be successful and competent in the new workplace, rather than assume a lack of literacy skills in isolated individuals. As an educator, when I work with companies, I always suggest that they pay attention to the principles of clear language and design as part of everyday good writing practice. If I had been a workplace educator at Texco, I might have recommended that they rewrite certain documents in clear language for areas where people were using their own notebooks. But as a researcher, I found out the reason people create their own texts is far more complex than not being able to read and understand manuals. It has more to do with ownership, control and finding a place to "empower" themselves, regardless of their literacy skills, in workplace settings where this is becoming increasing difficult to do.

CONCLUSION—BACK TO THE TWO DOORS

In the beginning of the chapter I used the two different entrances for production workers and for office staff and managers as a metaphor to talk about the contradictions and dilemmas between of the ideals of ISO documentation and its lived reality on the plant floor. All of the stories from my time at Texco as a researcher revolve around the different perspectives and interests that the doors represent.

Now I want to use the metaphor of the different entrances to reflect on what they mean for those for us who are involved in workplace education and training. It took me the entire length of my time at Texco to understand the meanings that the two doors held for thinking about literacies at work. I learned about both the policies governing the ISO quality system, the reality of lived experience on the plant floor and the difference between policy and practice. How does all of this affect my own practice?

I have always been a strong proponent of careful program planning through a joint planning process. Based on the different interests that showed up in my research, I now believe even more strongly in this joint planning process. However, because I understand a lot more about the power of systems like ISO and the contradictions and different local meanings on the floor, I would ask very different questions in my front-end consultations with worker-manager committees, while conducting needs analyses and making recommendations. My questions now would probe the ideals and the realities of how systems play out. Whether the project was examining ISO, a Quality Journey, or any other system in which literacy plays a central role, I would spend more time looking for meanings below the surface.

In the past, I would have focused more on issues like people's educational needs and desires as woven threads within the work culture, but with less attention to systems. I would now look for contradictions in those systems. I would be more systematic in my own framework and thinking. I think that workplaces in the past were reluctant to address communications or larger systemic issues because as educators we did not tie them into something that management cared about enough. That may still be true, even with a better framework and understanding. However, in the New Workplace, managers are required to care about communication systems because they too are accountable for making them work.

I can also see that my new knowledge is dangerous. I will always have to be careful not to ask unwelcome questions that, because of my inside knowledge, could expose workers and make things worse for them, or might embarrass or anger managers.

My increased knowledge and understanding about the cycle of risk, opportunity and blame that workers are exposed to through workplace literacy practices is a double-edged sword. Increased knowledge provides greater opportunities to address the trouble spots with these practices. But on the other hand, it also increases the degree of risk and blame for everyone involved—including the workplace educator.

3
Working Life and Literacies at The Urban Hotel

Judy Hunter

When I told them I was planning to do my research in a hotel, the project team warned me that I'd have to change my appearance. I'd have to start with some new clothes. So when I had my first interview with the Human Resources Manager at The Urban Hotel, I wore a matching home-sewn linen skirt and loose jacket, with a pair of reasonably comfortable dress shoes. As I walked through the lobby with the eyes of a prospective researcher rather than a harried traveler, I realized I was hardly prepared. The Urban employees, besides running an impressively large hotel, had stepped out of magazine illustrations. Even with their ethnic diversity, there was a homogeneity in their look, the kind promoted through the mass media. Their grooming and makeup were impeccable, their clothes didn't wrinkle, and their smiles never faltered. They were youthful, vital, attractive people. When the Human Resources Manager accepted my proposal, I was delighted. Straight away I headed to a seconds shop on the west side and bought several outfits, added new makeup and nail polish, and practiced smiling when I talked. Although I did not yet understand the deeper identity or the cultural implications of my new look, I could at least blend in while I was learning what it meant to work in a large, big-city hotel.

My first steps in the project were to introduce myself to the top managers and get an overview of the hotel history and official corporate image. I started by interviewing them and then focused on three departments that they suggested for observing print communication. Since the hotel was so large, with 800–900 employees, I would not have been able to spend time in every department. As it happened, I spent most of my time at the front desk and in housekeeping. I also visited banquet and conference sales and the café for shorter periods. Altogether I was in the hotel on average 2 days a week from September 1999 to June 2000. Although I felt constant anxiety about my presence and my ability to fit in inconspicuously, to see inside people's working lives and to see how literate activity was interwoven with their jobs, most people were quite accepting of me. They were used to being shadowed by new employees, and talked to me easily about their work and what they were doing. Several invited me on their breaks, and when I got a very short haircut gathered around to touch it. After a few weeks I caught myself reflecting the hotel's body language. My posture and gestures had a new dimension. I began to say "Excellent!" I was on my way to learning about the complex interweaving of literacies, people and hotel working life.

THE ORGANIZATION OF CORPORATE SERVICE: HIERARCHY AND IDENTITIES

Besides the importance of excellence, The Urban Hotel shared many features of the globalized corporation. The hotel was owned and managed by multinational corporations, with a recent history of merger, acquisition and expansion. In 1998 the chain was bought by another multinational chain, a new president came on board, and the hotel had to respond to new policies, new demands for improved quality, and a new image consistent with the new corporate ownership. Unlike other companies in similar situations, the hotel was not being restructured. At the time I visited, the changes mostly involved cosmetic modifications to the logo and the building, and an increased pressure to compete successfully. Since the mid-'90s, as the managers told me, various changes had emanated from head office, ranging from a Continuous Quality Improvement program to redesigned logos. Quality improvement, customer service, and worker empowerment marked the hotel as a member of "the new workplace."

The hotel also saw itself as a responsible corporate community member. It sponsored charities. It bought an artist-decorated moose statue[1]; it regularly involved employees in charity bicycling and other

---

[1]The mayor of Toronto commissioned a number of artist-decorated fiberglass moose statues that businesses bid on to adorn the outside fronts of their buildings and attract tourists.

events. Likewise, it saw itself as an employee supporter. At Christmas it sponsored an employee party and a Santa Claus party for employees' children. It offered guaranteed in-house training of 12 hours a year for each employee.

Another feature of the new workplace was the flattened hierarchy.[2] But the hotel was noticeably hierarchical in work responsibilities, privileges and workers' appearances. The hierarchy could be set in roughly three categories: Directors, managers and assistant managers made decisions, formally evaluated and supervised others and "owned" various responsibilities for the work done in their departments. They generally decided what was written versus what was spoken, and composed and designed text that would be received and acted on by others, even though many of the text-based communications in the hotel had been in place over a number of years. Front-line workers, the focus of my observations, were unionized and nonunionized. Nonunionized employees worked in jobs that demanded regular face-to-face guest interaction, coordination of services, and tracking of guests' needs and status. They included guest service agents (who did check-ins), floor managers, and conference and catering agents. Literacy activities were closely tied to keeping track of the workload. These employees spent much of their time monitoring and recording tasks, and inputting and retrieving data, as well as dealing with guests and other employees. Unionized workers tended to be service deliverers, cleaners, fixers, laundry workers, food servers and Room Attendants. They spent much less time with print material than nonunionized workers. For them, the bulk of work was service delivery; responsibilities like ticking off checklists were their main literacy activities.

Despite the hierarchical structure, The Urban Hotel embraced a uniform image, an ideal hotel culture, which it attempted to project to all guests. To use Gee's (1990, 1996) term, it was a "Discourse"[3] created by carefully selected objects, arrangements of space, personal appearance, language, ways of interacting, values, attitudes and behavior, through which people display different kinds of identities. Gee (1990) further distinguishes primary discourses, those people are born with and socialized into through the family, from secondary discourses, or those "which crucially involve social institutions beyond the family" (p. 151). All employees were pressed to conform to the ideal Urban Hotel image

---

[2]Researchers like du Gay (1996) and Garrick and Usher (1999) see it as a key attribute of the restructured workplace. However, others like Graham (1995) and Darrah (1997), for example, in manufacturing sector research, have found claims about flattened hierarchies to be superficial and unsubstantiated.

[3]Gee differentiates "Discourse" (capital D) from "discourse" (small d), which was often used by linguists to refer to stretches of language in use. However, postmodernists like Foucault and those influenced by his work use the term "discourse" similarly to Gee's "Discourse." This chapter follows Gee's convention to avoid confusion. Other researchers and theorists also use terms like "culture" (du Gay, 1996) and "community of practice" (Lave, 1996) with similar meanings.

or discourse, a secondary discourse for all. Print materials were one of the key vehicles for entrenching this. Alongside the ideal Hotel discourse were coexisting images or discourses of the various departments, often marked by ethnicity, job type, and status in the hotel. The relationship among these many discourses was often played out through literacy practices, as we will see.

The appearance of the hotel's most open, public spaces illustrates this ideal discourse. The spacious main lobby was well designed to mask its box-like shape with shop and restaurant areas, strategic interior decoration, and placement of guest facilities. The high-ceilinged room was decorated with beige tile floors, matching walls and trimmed throughout in darker polished wood. It contained two check-in counters and a concierge desk. In various directions off the open lobby, guests could access the restaurants, small shops, banks of elevators, exits to streets, a parking structure, business center and a wide staircase leading to the meeting and banquet floors. House phones and public telephones with stationery supplies could be found in the less trafficked corners. Large plants, fresh flower arrangements, and clusters of low tables, upholstered chairs and chesterfields on patterned carpets of muted colors were placed throughout the lobby away from the traffic flow. Posters, signs and art were framed on the wall or placed on metal stands, often softly illuminated by wall-mounted light fixtures.

Managers of departments, particularly the executive group, strove to embody the ideal Urban Hotel identity, and they served as models for the staff. They were impeccably dressed and groomed to conform to typical media images of attractive, successful people. Neither the men nor women tended to be overweight or appear unhealthy. The men all wore dark suits and ties; their hair was fashionably styled, never out of place. The women also wore dark suits, and in addition subdued makeup—always at least lipstick. Body language contributed to their image. I never observed lack of composure; even when staff were confronted by angry, difficult guests, their faces and posture remained poised. They smiled as they spoke, or adopted a look of concern when told of a problem. They engaged others with eye contact, turned to face people speaking to them directly. I never observed them slouch or rest their heads on their hands. Their overall manner was enthusiastic, positive, and interested in both guests and employees. Even their language was positive. Problems were referred to as "challenges" or "opportunities," for example. Enthusiasm was expressed by the word "Excellent!"

And if employees weren't aware of the concrete components of this image, much of it was outlined and described in the official grooming standards document, which detailed rules about attire, including footwear and jewelry, hair and makeup. Various other written rules, such as key standards and standards of excellence, described appropriate body language and speech.

Aside from guests and visitors, the lobby was unobtrusively populated with employees; small bronzed nametags identified them by first
name. Although the staff were quite diverse racially and ethnically, their
manner was similarly pleasant and restrained. Although they were not
all stunningly attractive, I could imagine any one of them in a television
commercial, as part of an appealing, personable welcome to travelers.
Doormen, lobby support, bellmen, and guest service agents behind the
check-in desks wore typical hotel uniform jackets or business-style
jackets. Managers dressed in formal business attire. Security personnel, also in business suits, were noticeable only by their casual stance
and watchful expression. Others moved quietly through the lobby on
work-related errands. Even when the lobby was crowded and bustling,
the noise level was muted. The carefully arranged, comfortable decor
and graciously mannered staff of this public face of the hotel aimed for
an overall effect of elegant repose, with attentive, discrete service.

LITERACIES OF WORKING LIFE

A great variety of literacy activities figured centrally in the everyday
work lives of frontline employees in two ways. First, success in the
highly competitive environment of downtown Toronto, the largest city
in Canada, and matching the keen international competition among
hotel chains were at the forefront of managers' concerns. Officially,
success was counted through Key Measurements, which included two
hotel industry ranking awards, employee opinion surveys, service
guarantees, guest comments, and a variety of inspections. The means
to success was translated in the hotel as "Total Quality," described in
the employee orientation documents as "a cycle of Continuous Improvement ... not a program but rather a culture." The hotel was
deemed to be on a Quality Journey. In my observations, the quality focus among workers was on filled rooms, indications of guest satisfaction, and absence of complaints.

Meeting quality goals was integral to top managers' work responsibilities. They conveyed these goals to the front-line hotel employees,
whose work was also monitored, guided and regulated as part of the
ongoing assessment of hotel success. Quality was conceptualized as
tangible, measured work outcomes and behaviors. For example, Room
Attendants' rooms were regularly inspected and scored. And in the
back office of the lobby, the number of compliments that guest service
agents (who did check-ins) received on comment cards was displayed.
Daily house counts, numbers of return guests, numbers and types of
complaints were all compiled and measured. Assessment was then co-
ordinated with continuous revision of policies and practices to ensure
improvement.

All the quality improvement messages, as well as policy and procedure directives, the employee handbook, newsletters, mission and val-

ues statements and official employee documents like accident forms were communicated largely through print. The texts related to quality and policy were meant to outline and manage employees' self-presentation in the hotel and inform them of their rights and responsibilities.

However, in a stressful work environment, the regulatory messages of these print directives became peripheral to actually doing the job. Employees attended to them much less often than managers hoped. For example, one of the Key Standards, greeting the guest with "Good Morning, Afternoon, or Evening" was posted and written in several forms throughout the hotel. Yet a number of employees said "Hi" or "Hello," and reported to me that the official greeting repeated hundreds of times a day sometimes became artificial or wooden. Managers were aware of and concerned about this kind of deviation from the quality standard, for they used "mystery shoppers" posing as guests, and managers sometimes quietly approached employees from behind to observe them work. Nevertheless, they seemed to turn a blind eye to such deviations, especially, I surmised, if the employee was otherwise competent. This aspect of hotel literacy practices, in which texts officially served as messages from managers to staff, seemed to have had inconsistent effects among employees. When facing the immediacy of guest demands, employees may have acted to satisfy the guest based on their own interpretations of the situation at hand. Also, they may have resisted what they considered excessively regulated directives that didn't reflect the conditions of their work life. Or they simply may not have paid attention to texts outside the everyday discourse of their immediate work group.

At the same time, literacies were also vitally important to employees. They served as a memory and organizational tool to keep track of guest status and work completion and to coordinate this information in the various hotel departments. The size and complexity of the hotel meant that there wasn't just one form of literacy practice. There were "multi-literacies."[4]

Employees' literacy activities involved a range of technologies from pen and colored highlighters to working at computer stations and operating faxes, beepers, and telephones. They filled in databases, hand-wrote lists of information on paper, filled out worksheets and sent work status messages by punching telephone codes. They read and modified computer reports; passed them on and modified them further with pen and white-out; sent faxes, beeper signals, and emails. They responded to and recorded voice and voicemail messages, communicated orally by phone, radio and face-to-face. And they engaged in these many kinds of communication as they performed their work activities, and talked to each other and to guests. Their literacy practices

---

[4]In the same sense, Cope and Kalantzis (1999) refer to a "multiplicity of communications channels and media," (p. 5).

facilitated their work and the work of others who dealt with guests moving through the hotel and calling on services of the various departments. Some of these working documents were highly regulated and standardized; others were developed by coordinators or managers and used only within particular work teams. Other kinds of documentation were personally designed, used mostly as individual memory aids to be later passed on through other means. Together with the pressures of actually performing service tasks, employees also had to record their work accurately and on time.

For the most part, employees were competent and willing to write, read, record and transfer data in the ways that were required for their jobs. They did this so readily, I believe, because their literate practices enhanced their work and their autonomy. That is, many had a sense of ownership of their jobs. They often interacted individually with guests, and even though their work behavior was regulated, they couldn't escape the need for spontaneous decision making and action at times. In a climate where guest satisfaction was the most immediate, concrete feedback on service, regardless of the ways it was measured by the hotel or the larger corporation, the employees I met most consistently tended to use literacies that enabled them to fulfill their sense of responsibility to the guests.

THE VIEW FROM THE TOP: THE QUALITY JOURNEY

As mentioned earlier, a driving force behind The Urban Hotel's successful competition was the Quality Journey, initiated in the mid-'90s. It figured prominently in everyday print communication to employees, training, and administration. Every member of the managers' team that I interviewed referred to some aspect of the Quality Journey. What drove it was summed up by the Hotel Manager: "One can never be too successful … no business can say, 'Yeah, this was it and we were happy.'"

The Human Resources Director, Gino, explained the Quality Journey to me as "a structure system for operating your business … keeping you focused on the integral parts of your operation." His commitment to the program was linked to what he considered its success in other companies and its broad application throughout an entire company:

> I think when you look at organizations that were on a Quality Journey you can definitely relate the results that they've had, whether it's with guest satisfaction, employee satisfaction, improved bottom line, somehow [these are] linked to their Quality Journey. Because when you look at the Quality Journey framework … the criteria that companies are focusing on have to do with your entire business, your people focus, your suppliers, your customers, your performance of your organization. Like I said, the suppliers and people and managers and leadership. So there's seven criteria [leadership, planning, customer, people and supplier fo-

cuses, process managers, and organizational performance] ... that make up the Quality Journey.

Aveena was the Director of Housekeeping and Quality, a position that split both responsibilities. She worked closely with Gino, and in my interview with her, she confirmed Gino's perspective. Her interview also shows how seriously the hotel took the quality plan and how much time and effort managers placed on it. She explained that the company compiled the seven categories of quality for an annual assessment. From the results, the hotel measured its "strengths and opportunities" and put together a Quality Improvement Plan that guided it for the year. She told me of upcoming work:

> Next week the leadership committee are going on a retreat ... where we will ... be revising or examining our current strategic plan, our total quality improvement plan, our customer satisfaction plan and employee opinion survey action plans. And we will try to put those together into one concerted document that we can work from that encompasses everything, as well as most critically, produce the results.

In other words, the executive managers' group not only spent time overseeing the everyday running of the hotel; they also devoted a great deal to planning and reviewing plans for quality improvement. The framework that structured managers' quality responsibilities was highly formalized and documented in its language and process. As other researchers like du Gay (1996) have noted, quality in the service industry is measurable. The actual outcomes produced by the executive group were theoretically available to all the employees. I observed them sometimes posted on the backs of doors, at Quality Fairs, but also sometimes carefully selected, arranged and designed to be eye-catching. Several of the directors I spoke to referred to the Quality Journey as an important communication challenge.

Gino identified two challenges managers face in what he sees as communicating and implementing the Quality Journey. The first was the size and diversity of the hotel. Aveena echoed and amplified his point:

> This was three times the size of a typical hotel that I've worked with. And I've always said that everything we do here we have to multiply by three because this is three times more difficult. In a smaller environment you can afford more time; you can afford the luxury of working, of spending more time on a certain standard, a policy or certain procedure. You can do more fun things as well because fun things help in motivation.... Here it's more mechanical, it's more volume, volume, volume, and so it's that much more challenging to create more of a fun environment where it's easier for learning to take place. Can it be done? Absolutely, but there's so much more to emphasize.

The second major challenge, in Gino's words was "Convincing employees that it's an ongoing 'continuous process' rather than a project." At the same time, he expressed optimism and enthusiasm, just as Aveena did, stating, "We will continue to get better, we'll continue to focus. We'll continue to fine-tune so that it almost becomes part of the culture." In fact, throughout his discussion with me he repeated and emphasized the importance of continuation.

From my interviews with top managers, I was impressed by the conviction and commitment of the hotel administration to the Quality Journey. They followed a predetermined measurable formula for review and improvement, and they problem-solved together to improve their quality "scores." They embraced this scheme, I believe, because it made an abstract, intangible element like quality more concrete and easier to manipulate. They seemed to easily equate the documented measurement with the actual quality. And to measure hotel quality, they organized the work routine to entail the capture of appropriate data and to convey their goals to employees.

THE NATURE OF THE QUALITY MESSAGE

The Emphasis on Customer Service

To the managers' group, communicating to employees seemed to mean an emphasis on customer service. Gino in Human Resources saw the message as clear and direct. He told me that key standards were the "basics of customer service." He described them:

> Smile, make eye contact, and greet every guest. Very simple, it's not rocket science. Answer all calls within three rings, with a smile in your voice saying "Good morning, good afternoon, good evening," whatever it might be. Again, nothing, everyone can do it. Use the guest's name at every opportunity and thank every guest for choosing the Urban, very simple. And if we maintain this, and again remembering that we've got to operationally take care of making sure that all the beds are all made, you know the rooms are neat and tidy, that we execute good meals, I mean those are the basics. But if we can do this with every employee, we will be successful; we will be successful because it's customer service that's really what makes us a part of a hotel. Every hotel in Toronto has the same thing we have. Rooms, restaurants, business zones, a pool probably, parking; they have everything we have. So what's going to set us apart is really the customer service.

This message was posted, carried by each employee with their identification cards, spelled out in employee books, and reinforced orally at meetings and through managers directions. It was monitored by colleagues and others, encouraged by incentive and reward plans, measured in graphs and charts and displayed in the hotel.

Managing Employee Identity

One essential component of customer service was the image the hotel projected through the employees. Although appearance and self-presentation had long been important in the hotel industry, their importance as a manifestation of the ideal hotel identity meshes with current analyses of the new workplace. Du Gay (1996) speaks of the turn to an emphasis on culture in the new service sector, "because it is seen to structure the way people think, feel and act in organizations" (p. 130), and it will lead to greater "productivity through people" (p. 130). And Gee, Hull, and Lankshear (1996) discuss "the new capitalism's" overtly promoted "need to socialize people into 'communities of practice' ... to be certain kinds of people" (p. 21). As noted earlier, The Urban Hotel espoused the notion of hotel culture as an underlying approach to quality improvement. In his research on the retail sector, du Gay sees a culture of employees identifying with the customer, but the hotel image was much more an attractive, congenial, competent servant whose pleasure was serving guests.

This identity as attractive, competent servant in a culture devoted to guest satisfaction was officially laid out through print. At the same time, the demeaning connotations of servitude were often offset in several ways through the language of the documents. Certainly, the employee image of being professional and a servant was modeled by the top managers in their dress, behavior, and speech, and it was reinforced in meetings and face-to-face encounters, but its status as official policy lay in hotel documents. These documents were first introduced to employees at orientation; they were placed in department offices for easy access and reinforced in training materials. Standards of behavior, attitude and appearance were repeated and rated on employee review forms. For example, employee appearance was explicitly dictated through written rules of dress and grooming. Rules of grooming included limits on men's hair length to above the shirt collar, moderation in the use of cosmetics, prohibition of "long chains and bracelets ... visible tattoos, body piercing and voluntary branding," and coordination of lipstick and nail polish colors with uniforms. Meeting dress code requirements and maintaining a professional image were two rating items on the hotel employee review form. Grooming and dress rules like these helped ensure that employees conformed to a conservative style, and that their appearance was unremarkable, inoffensive and pleasant. Likewise, employees were expected to "project a positive attitude and personality," according to the employee handbook. That meant their gestures, facial expression, tone of voice, posture, movement and language choice had to conform to hotel standards.

Further, particular personal characteristics, rather than work knowledge or technical skills, were considered most desirable in the hiring and promotion process. This preference for selecting employees less on their professionally-related qualifications than on their personal characteristics was also reported in research in the manufacturing sector. Laurie Graham (1995), for example, describes an extensive prescreening process where applicants were assessed interacting with each other in an auto manufacturing plant. The Human Resources Director at the hotel told me that "when you look at an effective manager, it's their ability to deal with people.... When we're looking for people, it's ... for exceptional guest service and people skills, and The Urban is committed to train you on all the technical skills to teach you the business." The manager of conference and banquet sales told me that she looked for a "certain eloquence" in communication. The Front Desk Manager was more specific:

> The first thing I look for is personality ... somebody that comes into my office and sits down and if he or she didn't smile in the first minute ... I won't hire them.... The reason, is, it's a little thing, but when you're out there, and you're dealing with the stresses, and interviews are very stressful, but you're dealing out there, you're always out there and dealing with guests.... It's very difficult to train somebody to smile. You know, to train somebody to look pleasant.

In other words, the hotel aimed to screen for pleasant appearance in the initial hiring process. Appearance, along with an outgoing, friendly personality, was seen as essential to project a positive hotel image to the customer.

Smiling was encouraged in several ways throughout the hotel. It was one of the key standards for greeting guests, and was posted on walls and carried along with identification cards. A "smile patrol," a person with a camera, sometimes wandered around the hotel work areas taking spontaneous photos of employees as they worked. Their photos were posted in the basement hallways with brief captions like, "Jane has a great smile for all the guests." A posted letter to employees in the kitchen area behind the café stated that attendants "will smile and appear friendly as they clean tables and ... possess a genuinely friendly attitude when dealing with guests." At the top of the basement stairs, just before the entrance to the front of the house (the public areas), there was a large full-length mirror for employees to check their appearance before they returned to work from their break or lunch. Beside the mirror was a cartoon blow-up that changed several times a week, usually with a work theme, strategically placed, I presumed, to provoke one's sense of humor, to "look on the light side of life." Indeed, one employee told me he appreciated that cartoon, for it put a smile on his face when he left the basement for the front of the house.

Alongside the prevalence of explicit directives on employees' self-presentation, the hotel also promoted an employee empowerment program. Gino, the Human Resources Director, described it:

Empower yourself to satisfy your guest. So if a guest comes to you, regardless of whether you're a Room Attendant, regardless of whether
you're the manager, regardless whether you're the VP, you have the ability
to satisfy a guest. If they say, "Look I came into the room," and the person
could be referring to a Room Attendant, "I had a very bad dinner." The
Room Attendant has the ability to empower themselves to say, "You know
what, why don't you have lunch on me today, you know I'll make reserva-
tions for you and please go enjoy yourself." They have that ability.

In one sense then, it gave employees the right to "satisfy" a guest who
approached them with a complaint by offering a gift or complimentary
service. Of course they needed to document and record their initiative.
During my research in the hotel, I only observed one instance of empowerment, by Guest Service Agents at the business desk. Two employees with several years' experience consulted each other about
sending a basket of flowers to a wealthy repeat guest for an error in his
room profile preferences.

Although several directors spoke of the empowerment plan to me, it
seemed rarely used, and managers were unsure why. One director acknowledged what he saw as employee hesitation. Although he recognized fear of recrimination from superiors as a cause, his solution was
increased training, as we have frequently seen when employees don't
conform to procedures. He explained:

They feel disempowered because they don't understand. So we need to
educate them on empowerment. That's part of the orientation process
here at the hotel.... But we also need to put a dollar value maybe on it.
Just so they say, you know, "I don't want to get in hell from my boss because I gave them a $50 breakfast coupon or dinner coupon. You know
it's going to come back and haunt me, I know I'm going to get it." No, if we
map this out, we call it the "wings" program—"mild," "medium," "hot,"
"suicide"—the different levels of complaint. And then next are the reme-
dies, so tell us what the complaints are from a "mild" to "suicide" guest
complaint.

Managers did produce a document categorizing complaints and
possible responses to guests, and although I was given one on request,
I never saw an employee read one, nor did I ever see one posted.

But the director's assessment of why employees don't use their empowerment program does not recognize the complexity of the situation, taking into account status and identity. Consider the case
involving the two employees at the business desk who sent flowers to a
guest who received a different type of room than the one he reserved.
Both employees who "empowered" themselves at the business check-
in were already firmly established, long-term employees. Working the
business desk accorded them greater prestige than their counterparts
at the regular check-in desk. Only those who were considered "able to

handle the pressure" were promoted to the business desk, for the re-peat business travelers were more demanding and temperamental. The error was clearly not the fault of the Service Agents who sent the flowers, for the room had already been assigned. When the guest checked in, their designated room appeared on the screen only for the agents to confirm. Furthermore, the decision to send flowers was made through consultation, not individually, reducing the risk of pos-sible blame on a single employee.

These two employees, then, were in a relatively safe position com-pared to many other front-line workers, and there was almost no risk that they might be blamed for the guest's dissatisfaction. Instead, the guest might note with pleasure that they had sent flowers and com-ment favorably on the personal service they provided. Thus, although managers acknowledged that fear of blame inhibited use of the em-powerment program, status, identity and risk may have played an im-portant part in the program. And as we will see, the meaning of "empowerment" professed by hotel managers as a form of worker au-tonomy was limited and risky. The kind of autonomy employees fa-vored was broader in scope, but closely interwoven with the tasks they performed daily. It was less risky because they knew their jobs more intimately than managers did.

Although managers' most explicit acknowledgment of worker au-tonomy was the empowerment program, the hotel also expected em-ployees to identify with the hotel, to be unquestionably dedicated in their work, to "go the extra mile." The Executive Director, Harold, ex-plained its importance to me as he described Quality Teams (commit-tees) in the hotel:

> A lot of the front office people were educated, and so their expectations ... [were] way above a lot of other people like housekeeping. Otherwise we have a lot of mothers and single mothers in the housekeeping depart-ment that you know, "I only have eight hours, I have to get in, I have to get out, I have to do my work and I have to get home." So their level of enthu-siasm on participating in some of these spin-off teams isn't that great. Nor do they think it's important to them. So there's a buy-in there that's just not there, but we need that. So we need to find and solicit a select bunch of those people that will want to participate. So we make it alluring and important, and part of their progression is in the personal develop-ment. We need to position it that way, which we do.

Harold compared "educated" workers with workers in housekeep-ing, and he measured their enthusiasm for their jobs as the amount of extra work they were willing to do. He seemed to discount the difficul-ties of motherhood as irrelevant to the hotel. What's more, he seemed to be equating promotion on the job with personal development. The kind of connection Harold made between dedication to work, advance-ment and personal development echoes the findings of other workplace researchers (du Gay, 1996; Gee et al., 1996; Graham, 1995). Ironically, although the new workplace expects wholehearted identification with corporate goals for everyone, not just an executive elite, it marginalizes those whose family lives get in the way of total devotion, particularly women, a stance that is far from new. From my experience observing in the hotel, I would disagree with Harold's interpretation for the lack of "buy-in" on other grounds as well, which I discuss later in terms of employee views of their working life.

COMMUNICATING THE MESSAGE

For the top managers in the hotel, the challenge of persuading employees to buy in to the quality program was framed as communicating information, feedback on performance, and incentives. They envisioned a "culture" of quality they wanted to establish in the hotel, and to accomplish that goal, employees needed to adopt the culture. That is, they needed to participate as members of the ideal hotel image or discourse. Aveena, the Quality Manager, and Harold, the Executive Manager, saw the challenge as communicating clearly and simply across the hotel hierarchy. Gino from Human Resources also believed one of the keys to effective communication was using distinctive language. Most of all, the hotel saw its job to ensure total quality as one of communication.

We have seen that the hotel relies heavily on print material, backed up by modeling and talk. In this section, I elaborate on these three managers' directions to staff. Then I describe the texts used to "communicate the message," but I'd also like to look more closely at these texts as embodiments of the hotel discourse. To do that, it's necessary to examine the language used in the texts and its implications in the social context of the workplace, as well as to examine the social practices around the texts themselves.

Adjusting the Message to Meet Employee Competencies

If workers didn't seem to attend well to the messages of the Quality Journey or incorporate them into their consciousness, managers' response aimed to adjust how the message was delivered, revising the language of instruction and reporting for workers whose language and literacy competence was more limited than others. Although they never referred directly to literacy, managers' understanding of how comfortable and competent employees were with the official written style of hotel documents shaped their concept of how communication was central to achieving the quality goal.

Aveena, the Quality Director, pointed out some of the varied approaches the hotel took:

We've made large posters in every department … we've given all our employees one of these key standards to put on their name tag, and we've tried to enforce it and reinforce it at our ongoing meetings. As part of our games at the end of the all-employees meeting, we kind of ask questions about key standards, and make sure people understand them, and try to enforce them at all times.

"Key standards" were five specific behaviors for each department that employees had to follow in their interaction with guests. They were more concrete than statements of hotel philosophy, and were reinforced both in print and verbally. Signs were posted on the inside of doors to public areas, employees carried them along with their identification cards, and employees told me they were reminded verbally in meetings. For example, in the dishwashing room behind the café, the standards for greeters, hostesses, servers, and managers included "Smile with your eyes; welcome every guest on arrival, using their name if known…. Ensure newspaper availability; offer one to all single diners. Converse with the guest to ensure their satisfaction and enjoyment." Although they didn't often remember them for quizzes, one café worker told me it was clear the hotel considered the key standard behaviors to be important. Nevertheless, I did not often observe the standards consistently acted on in the café.

The Executive Manager, Harold, explained that the hotel tried to reach all employees:

> We need to include a lot of stakeholders and that's not only the leadership committee like myself and the VP and General Manager. But that includes the dishwasher, potentially the dishwasher, the Room Attendant, maintenance people, communications people, parking garage attendant. We all try to include them in the outcome. So they're part of the solution, always part of the solution.
>
> One of the challenges that we have when we get to that level is their knowledge and their interpretation of all these new initiatives coming down the pipe. They've got their own job to do, and all of a sudden wow, here comes the 18-page document that has all these wonderful timelines and critical paths and little icons all over the place. And they're going "This is overwhelming, what do I do with it? I don't understand, what did this word mean, what did 'facilitate' mean?" you know. And that's some of the challenges we have. So we need to get back to the basics, and when we get to that level we need to change the document … so it's very legible for them and they say, "Ah, I understand"—if it means drawing pictures, it means drawing pictures.

Unlike managers in many workplaces, Harold took a position that seemed not to blame workers' literacy levels for failing to understand official documents. He took on the responsibility for making sure that the hotel messages were comprehensible to everyone.

Aveena saw a somewhat more complex picture, for in her interview, she spoke of other influences on quality delivery. However, in her mind, these all related to employees:

> So can we put it all in a book and say, "Hey, you read it, take it home read it and understand it"? No, it will not work for us. Daily reminders, daily delivery of messages, daily checking for accuracy, daily checking for comprehension was an ideal state of being, but it didn't always work like that. Room Attendants come in or employee communications with guests, some do it really well, some don't do it at all.... [It depends on] personalities, introverted, extraverted behavior, disposition, mood of the day, priorities, various focuses.... Are we confident that all of our employees were always delivering the message or portraying the behaviors we've trained them, that we want them to practice with guest interaction? We couldn't guarantee that. What works, what didn't work, it requires focus and prioritizing to ensure that it will always work.

Aveena continued, though, along the same track as Harold, framing the solution around communicating a message that employees could understand:

> We still have only just surfaced the top ... we have yet so much to do in terms of educating our employees and educating ourselves. And again, it's how we communicate, how easily can we break down the amount of information that has got to be delivered.... How much they read them, how much do they understand, are we really capturing all of the things we want to tell them, or is it as much print on paper that we can provide to them and hope for the best? Were we giving them the right information, could we have given them something different that would make them understand so much more.... Besides that, the information ... the participation, how do we get involvement from our employees, how well can we include them, how long did it take for them to understand, how much time can we afford to work on any one aspect of the entire journey?

These conversations with Aveena and Harold showed the extent that the hotel managers were concerned about ensuring that the great diversity of employees understood and took up the quality and other messages from the top. Their awareness of the need to shape the message to meet employees' needs was important, for the hotel had many employees whose English competence was limited and some who had much less education than others.

Managers seemed to assume that the bulk of their responsibility was to convey their messages clearly, and that compliance or non-compliance was the employees' responsibility. Even Aveena, who recognized that non-compliance may have been related to questions other than communication, did not seem to acknowledge that other employer-controlled factors may have been at play. But the managers' solutions were implemented inconsistently, a continuing challenge that they recognized. From their framing of the needs, and even from my perspective as a language teacher, sign-off sheets for job training in orientation sessions were not accessible to all, written in language that was often similar to quality messages. For instance, in Housekeeping, where many of the employees spoke limited English, some items requiring employee sign-off were concise ("no colored nylons"), but others were worded with greater difficulty for English learners ("Employee Identification Cards must be worn at all times").

What might account for this inconsistency? I interpreted the managers' assessments of the situation as sincere. It seems most likely that hotel managers, working under as much stress as front-line employees, simply had other, more urgent priorities than revising the language of print documents. In addition, this kind of language was natural for them, part of the corporate culture of managers, and it may have been difficult for them to realize exactly how opaque it was to others. They themselves may not have been proficient writers or sensitive enough to language accessibility to meet their own goals.

Part of the reason for this inconsistency may have been the perspective that Gino, in Human Resources, took in promoting specialized language for the quality message: He believed that their "official" style of language marked the messages as important. So perhaps the attraction to retaining the complex style competed with impulses to change it. Much more obviously important things to communicate clearly were job responsibilities, where lack of communication would be more concretely and immediately apparent. Managers and supervisors were able to conduct the most crucial departmental training and instruction orally when they found it necessary. The hotel did operate with a great deal of face-to-face interaction on a daily basis.

Distinctive Discourses: The Language of the Hotel Image

What was the style of language that managers recognized as inaccessible to many employees? "There's a lot of terminology and jargon that's used [so] you know people understand we're on a Quality Journey." As Gino emphasized, distinctive, standardized language characterized much of the message that the hotel sent to its employees outlining the Quality Journey. This included the language that defined the hotel's image, that identified and categorized people, and that was used by employers during the work day. Most of this language was characteristic of written rather than oral language, and was most apparent in the hotel's print materials.

The language of the hotel image, repeated phrases and words popular in current business discourse, was presented on wall posters, in handbooks and at the Quality Fair in the table-top displays and written quizzes. The employee handbook contained many examples. There were separate pages for the hotel's Vision, the Vision Statement, the

Mission, the Core Values, Ten Standards of Excellence and the Quality Statement. The quality section of the handbook contained information on the Quality Principles, Key Processes, Key Measurements and the Diamond Quality Committee.

Each of these was formatted with a large heading and a well-spaced list or phrase beneath. Important terms were capitalized, set apart with bullets or bolded. Much of the information and terminology was repeated throughout the hotel on signage, posters or small stickers attached to desktops and computers. The 4th Standard of Excellence, "We are a team! A group of eagles, who have joined to fly in formation," accompanied by a nature photograph of an eagle, was posted and framed prominently in the back office of the front desk area.

Although the language was chosen to highlight the message's importance, there was so much similar terminology that it was difficult to distinguish them from one another. There were "key" standards, measurements and processes. There were "standards of excellence," "key standards," "visions" and "vision statements," a "quality journey," "quality statement," "total quality," "quality improvement plan," "quality assessments." Several directors expressed some awareness that the terminology might be overwhelming, but at Quality Fairs and in departments, employees still took written quizzes or answered questions about the content of these constructed notions. At the Quality Fair quizzes they competed for prizes; in at least one department, the results of their oral quizzes were posted outside the office along with their pictures with comments like, "Bozena couldn't name the key standards this time, but she'll try again."

Official job titles, as in many current corporate settings, tended to be compound or abstract noun phrases, like Guest Service Agent, Room Attendant, Houseman. The choice may have been to avoid sexism in gender-free jobs, but it mostly denoted status. Words like "janitor," "cleaner," or "clerk," the traditional job names for much of the work done in the hotel, carry connotations of menial labour. The abstract titles may show the employees that the hotel did not see them as merely unskilled laborers, but as quasi-"professionals." The hotel invested training time in each employee, and valued their work. It may also have conveyed a similar message about the hotel to the public: Our employees are not ordinary unskilled labor, but are well-trained members of the hospitality profession. On the other hand, it may have been a way of masking the reality of menial labor, presenting to the workers a constructed image of their identity that was more prestigious than the actual jobs they did.

Interestingly, only the managers' job titles were used in everyday speech, except for "Houseman." Words like "managers," "directors," "assistant managers," "executive managers" were used to refer to managers when they were not mentioned or addressed by name, both in speech and writing. I only saw official job titles of front-line workers in

written form. Room Attendants were referred to and addressed as "Ladies" in speech, and Guest Service Agents as "GSAs." One employee in
Housekeeping explained that the term "Ladies" was a purposeful attempt on the part of everyone in the department to show respect to the
women who cleaned the rooms. She explained that even though their
jobs were demeaning and hard work, the women were still "Ladies,"
and everyone wanted to recognize that. "Room Attendant" was a written abstraction from the workers' everyday experience and social relationships. With the spoken title "Ladies," they captured and affirmed
their identities despite the nature of their work.

Much of the language in the statements and standards included
complex clauses, wordy noun phrases, Latinate vocabulary, and pas-
sive verb constructions. They weren't difficult to follow for those with
postsecondary reading experience in English, but they were less accessible to others. The Vision Statement included seven points, such as
"Industry leadership in the application of technology to maintain a
competitive marketing advantage"; "Operations delivering constant
quality services and products, perceived to represent values to customers and a fair profit to our owners." The Statement was framed on
the wall in several places through the hotel: "We will be the industry
leader recognized for innovative travel experiences in which all stakeholders succeed." The Quality Statement used alliteration in a slogan
to be memorable: "The right people, using the right process to deliver
the right product, at the right price." Core values statements were visible throughout the hotel: "Relentless Pursuit of Customer Satisfaction,
Commitment to Employee Satisfaction, Openness and Accessibility,
Continuous Improvement, Honesty and Integrity, Employee Creativity
and Competitiveness, Partnerships with our Communities, Maximize
use of our Resources."

But this formal, densely worded language was inaccessible to many
workers. Aveena, Harold and Gino all saw it as a simple barrier to full
participation in the working life of the hotel. Most of the language
teachers I know, myself included, would agree with them. The solution
would be to simplify the language of print materials, make them more
accessible and take responsibility for communicating effectively rather
than blaming the workers for having a literacy deficit. That was the
managers' aim, albeit more difficult to achieve than to identify. But an
underlying assumption of this perspective was that employees would
automatically respond to the messages communicated by managers if
only they could understand them. The interview with Aveena discussed earlier suggested she sensed this straightforward relationship
between understanding and buying into the hotel culture was not the
case, but her solution didn't carry it through.

I'd like to look at this issue further in terms of discourses and power.
Recall the opening description of the hotel and its efforts to project an
ideal image or hotel discourse through careful attention to design and

atmosphere. The top managers and their corporate colleagues at head office fit into the picture through their business suits; healthy, well-groomed attractiveness; body language, and the ease with which they used the jargon of enthusiasm and service. They also controlled the regulatory documents: the quality program texts and the messages delivered by Human Resources. These texts shaped employees' behavior and identities in the hotel. But at the same time, like the managers' dress and talk, the texts themselves were models of the discourse.

There were two implications of this for employees in the hotel who were not members of the ideal discourse, particularly the cleaners, food servers, launderers, and others at the bottom of the hierarchy. First, the ideal image was distant from their own. As in the broader society, these "back of the house" workers were more frequently members of non-White racial groups, non-Anglo ethnicities and of the working classes. They dressed, worked and talked quite differently from their managers; their world outlooks were different. Attributes of the ideal discourse had little meaning and little immediate relevance in their everyday work lives.

That included the language of quality documents. It was the language of another culture, opaque, and without resonance for them.[5] Although they worked in the same hotel, their lived experiences were in different cultures and discourses. The local meanings of each were not the same. Second, the discourse of the top managers was exclusive. Unless prospective employees had the right smile and the right "eloquence," they couldn't even hope to work in regular contact with guests. And as I learned in interviews, those who were promoted from within (not just in rank, but also into the ideal discourse) had to show they already had key attributes of the ideal culture: "going the extra mile," a flexible enough home life so that they could respond to irregular work demands, the right "personality." To join that discourse would require much more than being able to read and understand the texts. But the density of the text messages helped maintain their exclusivity. For the texts to be meaningful and engaging in the hotel, readers already had to be the kind of people who were familiar with the discourse. In other words, the texts served as markers and acted as barriers to entry into the ideal hotel discourse. In that sense, they helped reproduce the broader social order.

The Quality Fair: Reinforcing the Message

This section illustrates the different meanings employers and employees gave to the quality message, as well as to the exclusivity of the ideal discourse. It shows how literacy practices, in both the ways people

---

[5]Although I would include Human Resource forms, like vacation and sick-time requests, in these official texts, employees do find resourceful ways of dealing with them; the text content has a clear impact on their lives, so is highly meaningful to them.

dealt with texts and the meanings they gave to them, were bound up with relationships, power, and buying in to the culture.

In the managers' view, one of the highlights and symbols of their dedication to employees was the Quality Fair, held three times a year. I was explicitly invited each time and was told it was a mixture of education and fun.[6] There were games, contests and free lunches for the employees. It was organized and run by managers. I attended the first fair with a Guest Service Agent on her break, so she could only stay 15 minutes but left me to explore. The festivities were spread through the basement work area, in the loading dock, the hallways, the lounge and the cafeteria. The basement was decorated with balloons and brightly colored signs. The area was filled with cruising employees, smiling managers and lots of noise.

In the main lounge area of the basement, large tables were set up with displays of information about various aspects of the hotel. They included displays for Planning Improvement, the hotel birthday, rewards and recognition, health and safety, monitoring, testing and standards, and the action center. Each table had a large cardboard stand with charts, tables, photos and printed information. As employees visited each table or "Learning Activity Booth," they received a stamp on their Passport to Quality, which they then filled in with their name and department and dropped in a draw box, to be eligible for a prize like a free dinner and accommodation at the hotel. In order to get a passport stamp, employees had to read the information on the display charts and free information sheets and correctly answer a short question based on the information in the display. The questions were meant to be challenging. For example, one question on the quality improvement process was, "Once a Process Team identifies a Key Opportunity, they then deploy what type of team to help solve the problem?"

At the second fair I attended, the booths corresponded to the seven categories of points in the Canadian Award of Excellence. Questions were similar, but all were short answers, designed to speed up scoring. Most displays had less dense text and more attractive, brighter displays. For instance, at the Quality booth, colorful slogans decorated the display: "The race for quality has no finish line," "Success in the journey was not a destination." Nevertheless, all the booths also contained difficult organizational flow charts, graphs, lists, statistics and diagrams.

The language at both fairs was typical of the hotel quality language: "Key Processes," "Key Opportunities," "Key Strengths," "Strategic Plans," "Improvement Plans." Information blurbs about various points were often densely worded, with unexplained references, such as "PROCESS IMPROVEMENT has been added to our *Vital* Few so

---

[6]The following description is a composite picture of both fairs, unless explicitly distinguished.

now we have four instead of three. Refer to the poster in your department for a breakdown of all activities and who were accountable" [original emphasis]. As employees answered the quizzes, they dropped them in a draw box and were again eligible for prizes ranging from candy to monthly public transport passes. Employees eagerly picked up the quizzes, but I observed several of them complaining about them. One, apparently a part-time student, came in on her day off and said, "I don't feel like reading all this. It's my day off, and I'm still studying." Another read a bit and announced, "I'm not going to do this." Yet I noticed an eager Tagalog speaker answering all the questions. She clearly did not understand the quiz, for on a suggestion form reading "in reviewing our core Values, I would offer the following changes/modifications/suggestions:" she wrote, "Relentless Pursuit of customer satisfaction," one of the core values.

In the loading area, the Hotel Manager and other executives gave free shoe-shines to employees. Other managers handed out free popcorn and soft drinks. In another area there were free makeup sessions, manicures, haircuts and shoulder massages to relieve stress. Managers served lunch over an extended lunch schedule, so that most people could enjoy it. These seemed the most popular, and employees had to sign up or line up to get the services. Workers told me how they liked the idea of the free services, and I heard some talking to each other about how to arrange breaks or lunch to have the time to get a manicure or makeup session.

This aspect of the fair was an enjoyable way for the hotel to instil its message of personal self-presentation and service. Managers serving the employees modeled the service they wanted everyone to strive for. The free grooming services showed employees how much the hotel believed in an attractive, pleasant appearance. I believe that managers did want employees to learn more about their workplace in a fun environment. Their enthusiasm and warmth impressed me, and seemed sincere. I watched the hotel manager shining maintenance workers' shoes with a flourish and smiling face. Managers in business suits, white aprons and chef hats served lunches, chatted and greeted workers. They were excellent models of the ideal hotelier, to my mind. It seemed to be an appropriate treat for employees in a workplace that valued personal appearance, but at the same time, employees in nearly any workplace might have enjoyed grooming services as much.

When I arrived at the fair, I greeted the Hotel Manager, who was standing beside one of the booths, greeting people and encouraging them to visit his table. He asked me what I thought, and I replied that people seemed to really enjoy it. His response was, yes, but was it just fun, or were they learning anything? Certainly, comments I heard from employees were about the fun and prizes, the free lunch, and the free shoe-shines, manicures, haircuts and makeup sessions, and the fact that managers served *them*. These activities seemed the most often commented on and the most meaningful to employees—that the managers would serve them, the employees, and that the hotel would provide free grooming services. For those on small salaries, achieving the polished appearance of managers would likely be an unaffordable expense.

As an example of enculturation into the ideal hotel identity and world, the Quality Fair, although popular and carefully planned and executed, had quite different meanings for the employees. Overall, it was peripheral to the employees' everyday working experiences, their ways of interacting, use of literacy on the job, and their identities.

We've seen how The Urban Hotel's print communication, its major mode of communicating the quality program, was impenetrable for many employees. The language in the print messages was inaccessible to those with limited English competence, further shutting them out of the hotel discourse. Its very exclusivity helped make the messages of the Quality Journey in general irrelevant and meaningless. As a result, it would be much more difficult for employees on the front line to work their way up in the hotel, not just because of their lack of proficiency in language and literacy, but also because the texts were not meaningful for them. This compromised the hotel's explicit goal of promoting from within. Managers would not necessarily be able to recognize competent employees because they wouldn't display the "appropriate" cultural style. Employees in marginalized positions, like dishwashers, would continue with diminished flexibility, mobility or choice in their working lives.

On some level the hotel must have known that the details of the Quality Journey, the charts, graphs, lists and flow charts were peripheral to many workers' everyday concerns. Their solution was to embed the information in a "fun" activity, on the basis that, as one manager said to me, "learning should be fun." That seemed to be an important goal of the fair, one managers strove to achieve, and seemed to be successful at. However, the unimportance of the style and the content to everyday work life further contributed to keeping workers already economically and socially marginalized even more so.

Solutions to this problem might seem like a case for plain language education for the managers, possibly followed by literacy or ESL training for front-line employees. But plain language might not be the only answer.

Not only was the print communication peripheral to workers' everyday lives, but the service activities were as well. Professional manicures, massages, makeup applications and shoe-shines were not part of front-line employees' work lives, nor likely of their personal lives. Even fringe benefits and goods such as hotel candies were strictly off limits and closely monitored. In fact, a more common part of working life was the unannounced spot searches of employees' bags as they left work. The compulsory search policy was also a posted notice on office doors at sign-in areas. The highly hierarchical nature of everyday work, from dress to decision making, made the role reversals of the fair unusual and fun. But they very fact that they were exceptional then made the experience irrelevant to front-line employees' working lives. In this light, it is easy to understand how employees could see the fair as an event only of fun and free perks, but not adopt its intended meaning as a learning experience. Buying in to the new, ideal corporate work world requires much more than perks, whether the print communication is clear or abstract business-speak.

THE VIEW FROM BELOW:
COMMUNICATION, PROBLEM SOLVING AND MULTI-LITERACIES

The most complex work in the hotel in terms of communication and of coordinating and completing working documents was done by nonunionized front-line workers. These employees often supervised others who performed service tasks directly for the guests.

Floor Managers[7]

Floor Managers were responsible for liaising between Room Attendants on the guest floors and managers in the housekeeping office. Each one supervised 15 Room Attendants and two Housemen, covering three to four floors, or 240–320 rooms. On the floors, they checked the status and progress of room cleaning, inspected rooms and augmented the Room Attendants' work.

One of their duties, for example, was putting triple bed sheets and extra amenities in VIP rooms.[8] No-one I asked seemed to know the reason for this practice. The managers I shadowed all found this task a time-consuming annoyance: They had to get the extra sheet, then take some of the bedding off and remake the bed. The number of VIPs they had to do beds for was never predictable, and they had to squeeze them into their regularly scheduled activities. One grumbled that they couldn't ask Room Attendants to do it because of the union. They regularly complained that if the Front Desk would block (assign) these rooms in advance, rather than "just in time," they could incorporate the extra work into their daily plans.

The number of floors and rooms Floor Managers were responsible for varied, too, because of airline employee guests, who rarely checked out until after the day shift finished, and because of movement in the predicted house counts (overall room occupancies). Rooms that were

---

[7]Some of the descriptions of the Floor Managers and the Housekeeping Department were previously published by TESL Ontario in Hunter, Belfiore, and Folinsbee, 2001, and by the Australian Council for Adult Literacy in Hunter, 2001.

[8]VIP rooms received a range of special amenities, like bottled water, special soaps, a carnation in the washroom, the radio on playing soft classical music, and triple sheets (an additional top sheet placed between the blanket and the bedspread).

vacant and clean only had to be quickly checked if they had been checked on a previous shift. Such rooms were not included in the Room Attendants' 16-room daily workload or in the Floor Managers' loads. Nevertheless, if something happened in any of the rooms on their floors, like a complaint about noise in the hall or a request for amenities, they were responsible.

At the basement-level housekeeping office, Floor Managers reported and monitored room status and special room requests received from other parts of the hotel. They checked the computer-generated status reports for discrepancies from their visual checks of the actual rooms. If a room coded for check-out appeared occupied on the floor, they would check the Expected Departure report on the computer to see if the guest had actually checked out. No-one considered the possibility of disturbing a guest to find out when they planned to check out.

One manager underlined the importance of double-checking. She told me that once or twice a week she came across a room reported by computer as vacant and clean that was actually a check-out, an error she attributed to the Front Desk. It was a potentially a costly error, for if undiscovered, another guest could be checked in to an occupied or a vacant dirty room. That meant a free room for the guest and also potential damage to the hotel's reputation, because word of mouth was considered an important form of publicity. In the basement office, Floor Managers also checked for recent special requests like rush rooms or VIPs, or they received them as phone messages, occasionally via pager. Changes like these occurred throughout the day, not always predictably. The story that follows, which occurred while I was shadowing a manager on the guest floors, shows the care that they took to check their working documents:

> The Floor Manager approached a Room Attendant and asked "Which one you finish?" The Room Attendant pointed out that one particular room was a check-out. Vera, the manager said, "Were you sure, check-out? It says occupied." She looked at the work sheet.
>
> Room Attendant: "Yes, you want to check?"
>
> Vera: "Yes, if [it's occupied], I will kill you."
>
> Vera and I entered the room. She looked in the closet and all the drawers. There's no sign of guest occupancy. Vera phoned the Front Desk: "Greta, do me a favor. Check whether 635 was a check-out room. Yeah, OK. Check-out room. She was right." After another call to the Housekeeping office, she called out to the Room Attendant: "You were right." Then she changed room designations on her work sheet.

The Floor Managers were all in the office together at three times during the day: the beginning and end of the shift, and during the mid-morning clearing and briefing meeting. These were busy, but not clearly structured times, with managers picking up special supplies, double-checking irregularities in the room status reports, answering phones, and chatting and joking with each other. Often a popular music station played in the background. Frequently I saw people in the middle of one task, checking room reports against their lists, for example, interrupted by a ringing telephone or a co-worker's query. Most often the interruption involved a guest's urgent request, which demanded an immediate response. People wrote down notes, spoke on the phone to guests, paged others to fill requests and relayed orders to the Centralized Action Room. Several talked at once; seldom was the exchange restricted to two people. Anyone was free to comment on or answer an open question.

The atmosphere in the office, particularly in the mornings when rooms needed to be turned around, often appeared impossibly pressured. Occasionally sharp words were exchanged, but on the whole, the office was full of vitality, sociability, humor and cooperation. These qualities seemed important ways to cope effectively with the tension of work demands. As shown in the story just related, managers and coordinators joked about each other and trying events, told stories and exchanged advice on everyday problems. People told each other recipes, and gave advice on everything from health to car repairs and relationships. They gossiped, teased, and talked about children, vacations and social plans. Yet this kind of socializing never took up blocks of time; people never seemed to slow down or to just sit and chat. Fast-paced work activities were interspersed with bits of social talk. When something immediate interrupted a conversation, it stopped, usually to be resumed where it left off as soon as the work matters were attended to. Sometimes I even had trouble following the threads of communication and humor. One Floor Manager's comment illustrates the pace and tone of the office: In the midst of an enormously stressful and busy morning, she noticed a song on the radio, and said laughingly, "I should be singing that song, 'I Ain't No Superwoman.'" She added a few dance moves to her work for a moment and carried on.

Floor Managers worked primarily from photocopied forms attached to clipboards that they filled out each day as they completed their work. The worksheets served as organizational tools, memory aids and long-term records, to be boxed and stored for a prescribed number of years. From my observations throughout the hotel, the computers stored information on sales, purchases, personnel and payroll, and guests and occupancy rather than any detailed records of daily work. And unless each Floor Manager was equipped with a hand-held computer, inputting such information would have been impractical when there was already a paper record.

Each work sheet, called the Housekeeping Manager's Report, was laid out horizontally, with blanks for the manager's name and date and the floor number across the top, as seen in Figure 3.1. Below were five columns, one per Room Attendant. Each column was headed with the attendant's name, followed below by a space to fill in total number of rooms, number of minus rooms (i.e., rooms that were already vacant and clean), and number of plus rooms (additional rooms in another area to make up for the minus, also called pick-up rooms). Below that was a numbered list of 16 rooms in each column, with blanks for the a.m. check, the p.m. check, and "notes." The form reflected the work organization for both Floor Managers and Room Attendants. Each column of 16 rooms was a section, one per Room Attendant. Each sheet held five sections, covering all the rooms on one floor. Informally standardized codes were used to indicate room status for the a.m. and p.m. checks. VD represented "vacant and dirty," CO "check-out," VC "vacant and clean," O "occupied," and VP "vacant pick-up" (a room that needed to be checked, generally because a guest had registered in it, but moved to another one).

The Floor Manager's reports just described were one of the key documents in a procedure called "clearing," which took place every morning and afternoon in the basement housekeeping headquarters. Shortly after the Room Attendants' workday started, between 7 and 8, the Floor Managers came in and prepared their own worksheets for the day; they checked the 6:30 a.m. room status reports and special requests, along with the log book confirming their floor assignments. Then they went up on the floors to check the room status and supply needs with each Room Attendant, who had verified their status as soon as she arrived on the floor. Floor Managers then returned downstairs to check and adjust room assignments against the Coordinator's log book. For example, some rooms in the early-morning computer status report noted as vacant and clean may have become occupied in the interim. Or vacant and clean rooms may have become VIP or rush rooms, which Floor Managers would hear about in the office and have to inform the Room Attendant about.

At clearing time, Floor Managers lined up to meet with the Coordinator (usually people did other work until they could claim a place right after the clearing). When each turn came to clear, the Coordinator and Floor Manager sat down one to one, each with their list of rooms, and verbally confirmed or modified each room assignment. When I talked with them about the need to do such detailed cross-checking, they all said it was important not to make any mistakes, for errors could have serious consequences such as a room "comp" (complimentary to guests because of a serious error on the part of the hotel), or a grievance from the vigilant unionized Room Attendants. Their discussion about coordination of the Report sheets and the log book was careful and attentive, as can be seen in the excerpt that follows. They worked together to ensure that each Room Attendant had 16 rooms, that all the rooms needing cleaning were covered, and that both their lists matched exactly. As they talked, they each wrote on their work papers and made changes in what they'd written previously.

A.M. Manager: _____

Date: _____

Floor: _____

Name: _____

Section total

(-) _____

(+) _____

Name: _____

Section total

(-) _____

(+) _____

Name: _____

Section total

(-) _____

(+) _____

Name: _____

Section total

(-) _____

(+) _____

Total Rooms: _____

AM	Rms	PM	Note
	01		
	02		
	03		
	04		
	05		
	06		

HSECLN

Total Rooms: _____

AM	Rms	PM	Note
	07		
	08		
	09		
	10		
	11		
	12		

HSECLN

Total Rooms: _____

AM	Rms	PM	Note
	13		
	14		
	15		
	16		
	17		
	18		

HSECLN

Total Rooms: _____

AM	Rms	PM	Note
	19		
	20		
	21		
	22		
	23		
	24		

HSECLN

Total Rooms: _____

AM	Rms	PM	Note
	25		
	26		
	27		
	28		
	29		
	30		

HSECLN

FIG. 3.1. Housekeeping manager's report. This figure is a composite from similar original documents adapted by the authors to preserve anonymity.

FM: Renata, I have to clear now. [She sits down.]
C: 12th floor, 10 rooms [available to clean]
FM: 55 to 83. I have 10.
C: Pick up 58, 82, 78, 75, 71, 73.
FM: [Repeats them back to her with the RA's name, Fima, who will be assigned to them, and writes numbers on her sheet in the RA's "plus" column]. 71, 73, 75, 77, 79, 83. Myna needs 5.
C: On the 5th?
FM: Yes, 55 ... ?
C: Give her 21, 47, 49, 51, 53.
FM: [Repeats the numbers back to Renata and writes them in] ... [for] Zelma, I need 2. You give her 67, 68?
C: 67, 69.
[They both use white-out to make deletions. Otherwise the sheets can become impossible to read.]

This back-and-forth talk and writing might have appeared tedious, but I could see that it seemed to help them both concentrate on the task without losing their places. It also helped them catch errors. And considering the amount of distraction and interruption in the office, it would have been easy to lose track of the details.

Besides the daily worksheets and extra print materials such as Do Not Disturb signs, on their clipboards Floor Managers also carried room inspection forms that they were to fill out before their shift ended. Of course they checked rooms after the Room Attendants cleaned, but generally on an informal basis because they were rushed to complete all check-outs by 3 p.m.

Floor Managers, like other front-line employees in the hotel, were subjects of recorded evaluations. Some were regular reports by their supervisors, but there were also charts on the inside of their back office door, with all instances of rooms "comped," the reasons and the names of Room Attendants and Floor Managers responsible for the rooms. I was struck by a chart that displayed names of workers responsible for guest complaints and lost revenue. But little attention seemed to be paid to it. Finally I asked. One Floor Manager told me they didn't care. They did their jobs the best they could. Another said she knew her job and others who didn't know the pressures they worked under shouldn't evaluate them. One time in a briefing meeting, a recent room comp was mentioned and some looked over at the chart. But the attitude among the employees seemed to be that there was so much pressure, mistakes couldn't be helped. Everyone made them occasionally. One of the Coordinators volunteered to me that she made errors every day and couldn't live without her white-out and the others to catch things for her. For the first 3–4 hours in the morning she was unable to leave her desk, even to visit the washroom. Generally, the

Floor Managers and Coordinators who worked in the Housekeeping Department were not intimidated by evaluation documents. They may have been resentful when they felt they were unfairly given a negative evaluation, but they knew that stress leads to errors, and they did their best to avoid them.

The reaction of the Floor Managers could be interpreted in several ways. At first glance, it was unexpected. A display of individual errors for coworkers and others to see would seem to be humiliating. I imagined that the managers' intention in displaying this chart would be to pressure employees to improve, to avoid such humiliation. If the intention were to correct mistakes, rather than blame individuals, I would not expect people's names to be highlighted, as they were; instead the nature of the problem would be emphasized. Yet in this case, the Floor Managers turned the managers' power and control on its head. They refused to engage in the blame, for they knew that errors were inevitable for all of them. But their resistance may have come with a price. Top managers still had the power of individual job review, and in at least one case I learned of, they used that power in ways the Floor Managers saw as unfairly negative. An atmosphere of uncomfortable resentment and uncertainty arose in the presence of the top department managers, one that could not have enhanced the work conditions.

Room Attendants

Room Attendants, or "Ladies," were unionized workers who cleaned 16 rooms a day. They were trained to clean rooms following a particular order, according to certain standards. Nearly all of the training was "show and tell," as the hotel described it. They had to keep the supplies on their "jeep" stocked, document their work, call in room problems and room status changes, and keep their Floor Manager informed of the state of the rooms covered. They did a thorough "housecleaning" of one or two rooms on a rotating basis, and their work was inspected every day.

Many were not native speakers of English, and in fact their English was limited. The hotel was aware of the Room Attendants' English difficulties and what they saw as limited educational backgrounds. Accordingly, they incorporated little print material into their work responsibilities. Room Attendants signed in and out when they began and ended their shifts. They received a list of rooms to clean each day, with coded jargon representing room status that they had to learn. As they cleaned each room, they punched in a telephone code that input directly to the central computer. In addition, they checked off the rooms they finished on their assignment sheet.

However, they were the subject of much documentation. Floor Managers checked Room Attendants' progress and work several times a day and did random formal inspections, according to checklists of items with predetermined scores. Scores were tallied, and each month Room Attendants with low scores needed to be "retrained." However, when I asked one Room Attendant about the monthly scores and the graphs displayed on the wall in the back room of the office, she appeared not to know. She said she'd never seen or heard of it, and it never affected her. When there were changes in procedures, and training took place or information was given, Room Attendants had to sign off on a document that confirmed they had received and understood their instructions. Sometimes they were straightforward: "Clean drains, tiles and fan." Other times they were more complicated, with less everyday language: "Professionalism. Cream of the Crop. We expect it from all our employees to act in a very professional manner at all times" [sic]. If employees didn't fully understand what they signed off, they were placed at a disadvantage.

Even though literacy activities were downplayed as part of Room Attendants' jobs, texts became objects of power in the tensions between the supervising Floor Managers and Room Attendants. Every Room Attendant I spoke with alluded to or spoke openly about the physical demands and heavy workload of their jobs. Indeed, when I shadowed these workers, I was impressed by their speed, efficiency, and endurance, and the need for these attributes to do the job well. At the same time, everyone in the hotel was aware of the demeaning nature of the work, and I frequently heard acknowledgment of their hard work and contribution to the hotel. But they seemed to get little concrete support.

In everyday interactions, the higher status of the Floor Managers who closely monitored them was evident, their notebooks one mark of their power. Room Attendants also had working checklists that they were supposed to fill out, indicating which rooms they had finished and their status. Yet when I shadowed the Floor Managers, I frequently noticed that Room Attendants hadn't marked their checklists. Floor Managers would approach the attendant's jeep, parked across the doorway of the room being cleaned, look for the checklist, and call out to the attendant to come and talk. The manager asked for the checklist if it wasn't visible, and often commented on the lack of information filled out. Some managers placed the list on their notebook and filled it out; others directed attendants to fill it out in front of them. Meanwhile, they discussed the status of all the rooms on the floor, and in this face-to-face interaction most of the information was exchanged.

In other words, checking off the Room Attendants' checklists seemed almost superfluous, for most information was exchanged orally, and then noted on Floor Managers' report sheets. Room Attendants also punched telephone codes into the computer as they finished each room, later checked by the Floor Managers. Floor Managers also used room checklists to write in additional jobs, such as "housekeeping rooms," which had to be fully cleaned on a rotating basis. And attendants often responded by telling supervisors they were missing supplies, or that there were room problems that hadn't been fixed, which gave Floor Managers additional work. I observed these kinds of turn-taking responses, where each added work for the other or in some way controlled the other, several times. Where the Floor Managers had the power to control through paperwork, the Room Attendants had the power of resisting paperwork and claiming the need for resources to do their work.

Floor Managers sometimes also helped Room Attendants fill out accident forms. I observed one instance during my stay in the Housekeeping Department. The Floor Manager held the form while interviewing the Room Attendant across a counter. The attendant had bruised her arm, and the manager was asking questions to fill in answers on the form. When the question about seeing a doctor arose, the attendant said she didn't know; she might see a doctor if her bruised arm didn't get better. The form had boxes to check, either "yes" or "no." The manager checked "yes." Clearly the form couldn't capture the answer, but the manager's answer was her own interpretation of the attendant's response. It may not have been the attendant's choice. The point is that while The Urban Hotel carefully worked to ensure minimal literacy demands on Room Attendants as they completed their everyday tasks, other documentation important to their work conditions and their evaluations were less accessible. As a result, they had less control over their working lives and less opportunity to promote themselves than others did.

Guest Service Agents

Guest Service Agents worked at the check-in desks and were responsible for checking in and checking out guests. GSAs were mostly young, mostly women, mostly single and recently out of postsecondary education, but they were diverse ethnically and racially. Their jobs were recognized as highly stressful, for they made the first impression on guests and they tended to "take the brunt of everything," as the Executive Manager put it. The GSAs told me they learned through training, shadowing others and practice. It was confusing at first and took some days to understand, then a few weeks to feel comfortable. Several told me the training wasn't sufficient. It had recently been cut back from 2 weeks, and even that wasn't enough time to learn everything they needed to know.

GSAs stood for their entire shifts at a wicket facing the guests. On their side of the wicket, at a long work counter below the level of the guest counter, was their equipment. Guests saw none of this unless they stood up close and leaned over the wicket. All they saw was the smiling face and upper torso of the agent. The agents stood directly in front of a keyboard, with the monitor placed slightly to the side, so they could look at it and at the guest only by shifting their gaze. Within their reach were a telephone, a keypunching machine to magnetize room key cards, a credit card swipe, small information sheets with mini-bar price lists and parking rates, a list of recent changes in computer commands, small pads of paper and pens. A file facing them contained brochures and fliers to give guests, such as sales tax rebates for international tourists or parking chits. A printer was located between each station just below the desk, so that the agents only needed to bend slightly and reach down to retrieve a guest invoice or check-in "folio." In other words, an uncomplicated guest transaction could be completed without losing eye contact with the guest.

When I first shadowed GSAs, standing slightly behind them and to one side, I was stunned by the speed of their computer work. Figure 3.2 shows one of the many screens the GSAs worked with.

Screens seemed to flash past; the agents entered data while talking and smiling at each guest. They barely looked at the screen. They were poised and attractive. As a guest approached their wicket in the line, they leaned forward slightly, caught the guest's eye, and smiled, then

	CHECKOUT		Date: _____
			Time: _____
Hotel _____		Arrive Date _____	
Room _____		Depart Date _____	
Guest Name _____		A/R _____ Voucher _____	
Group _____		Cr Avail _____	
Company _____		A Balance _____	
Guest Status _____		Other Balance _____	
Posting Status _____		Balance _____	
Settlement Type _____ Car Number _____			
Fast Checkout _____	Departing from Room _____		
Type	Description	Card Number Exp	Cardholder Name
____	_____	_____	_____
F Ctry	Amount Owed	Amount Received	Amount Applied Change
__ ___	_____	_____	_____ _____
__ ___	_____	_____	_____ _____

FIG. 3.2.   Hotel checkout form. This figure is a composite from similar original documents adapted by the authors to preserve anonymity.

greeted the guest, quickly ascertaining whether it was a check-in or check-out. They asked the name or room number, entered it, and then began a ritual "conversation" as they filled in information on the database screen in front of them, culminating in a print-out of the bill or a check-in card, which they folded precisely so that the hotel logo was displayed right-side-up to the guest. They explained each bit of information to the guest with the same smile, slight forward lean, and often slight tilt of the head. Although standing so long was extremely painful, they were not allowed to twist their feet around, lean on the counter, or slouch. When I left for a break to sit down early in my observation, they knew immediately why, and told me to wear support stockings and try to stand on the thick rubber mats placed at each station.

During the first week, I was certain that mastering the computer was the most challenging part of the job. Not only was I unable to track their keyboard action, at the same time they frequently asked each other for advice if they needed to do something out of the ordinary. Such occasions might be if they needed to split a bill for people sharing a room, if they had to calculate extra charges accumulated just before check-out, or when a guest arrived with a coupon and the GSA didn't know the code to punch in to subtract it from the bill. One complained that the system was constantly being improved, and that meant there was always something new to learn about the computer. Sometimes they received notices, but sometimes not, and they relied on each other to share knowledge of how to do things.[9]

But when I asked the GSAs what was most challenging, they said that the computer was actually an organizational aid. It cued them as they followed through the procedures for check-in and check-out. They said their challenge was difficult guests. Once I observed a woman check out with a movie charge that appeared on her room screen. The GSA printed out the bill and the guest objected. When the agent asked if her roommate had watched movies, or if she had inadvertently put one on, but failed to cancel it before going out, she became adamant and angry. The GSA was apologetic, but wondered why it appeared on the screen. Could the guest ask the roommate. The guest became angrier when the roommate appeared. The guest asked her if she had watched movies, and she cheerfully answered that she'd seen two late at night when she couldn't sleep. Afterward the agent told me she feared that the woman would demand to see the manager, and if she did the manager would always please the guest, but that she was only trying to protect the hotel,

---

[9]Gee (2000) discusses this kind of collaborative distribution of knowledge among workers as feature of the "new capitalism," adopted by business and industry and promoted as part of building "communities of practice," a concept he maintains has been exploited to ensure that workers are replaceable and flexible. At the Front Desk I observed workers helping each other do their jobs, but none of them were replaceable. I believe the hotel promoted sharing knowledge to save on training, as several employees implied to me. Saving on training does not seem to be a new feature in the workplace.

her employer. She and others mentioned this frustrating difficulty. One told me her strategy was as soon as the guest asked to see the manager, she would give them whatever they wanted.

Others told me of the conflict built into their jobs, that hotels, like airlines, overbook rooms because people frequently cancel at the last minute or just don't show up. Specific rooms were also not blocked in advance. That meant that agents could be faced with a guest who had reserved a particular type of room, asked about room preferences by the reservation desk, but the room might not be available on arrival. The room might also not be available if the guest arrived before 3 p.m. because the Room Attendants had not had time to clean it. In any of these cases, the GSA had to find an acceptable room for the guest. They called up a room status report screen on the computer, and scrolled through the lists of available rooms, until they found one the guest would accept.

In these ways, computing as a literacy practice supported the GSAs' work. It helped them to solve problems and to keep track of their tasks. There was another side to the computer as record keeper, however. It automatically recorded each GSA's entry in a guest transaction by name. Some GSAs told me that if there was a question about any aspect of a guest's stay, they could look through the records and ask the GSA involved to clarify it. Additionally, managers were able to track the work of each GSA. They could monitor the number of guests each GSA processed, calculate averages and compare them to their coworkers. GSAs thus contributed to policing themselves as they entering data into the computer, as has been noted in other of our worksites studied. Yet it seemed to be far in the background of the working day at the hotel. No-one mentioned it or even seemed aware of it. Immediate concerns about handling guests seemed consistently to take precedence over all else. When there wasn't a line at the check-in desk, GSAs had several other duties, like filing room stubs and placing guest brochures in slots at the desk. What's more, "house counts," the number of rooms occupied, were calculated for each day and for several weeks in advance, so that numbers of employees working at the desk varied according to house counts. Flexible work schedules enabled the hotel to adjust the number of GSAs on any given shift so that there were always just enough.

Delivering Quality: Employees' Interpretations of "Empowering Yourself to Satisfy the Guest"

Although managers expressed concern about communicating the quality message by simplifying it and using multiple modes of indoctrination, the message delivered to employees tended not to be taken up as wholeheartedly and precisely as they hoped. In fact, the more determined the message, and the more rigidly behavior and identity seemed to be regulated, the less the employees seemed to follow it.

At the Front Desk, for example, I noticed that several key standards were regularly ignored. Certainly the employees knew about them. Their ID cards all had the standards written on them. The key standards were posted prominently in the back office, and a manager individually quizzed Guest Service Agents on them. No-one mocked the standards or openly resisted them. They simply didn't use them.

The least used standard was mentioning the guest's name. Almost no-one did so, unless they were verifying the data from their terminal. Several times I mentioned to a GSA during a lull that I noticed few people used guest names; they usually answered for themselves, in such a forthright way that I got the impression they didn't feel they were really doing anything wrong. The consensus seemed to be that working under extreme pressure, they didn't want to mispronounce a name or use the wrong name, because the guests came along so fast, they all became a blur after a while. If it wasn't too busy, they often said they'd make a stab at a potentially difficult pronunciation, with a question in their voice, and ask for confirmation from the guest. However, when I was with a small group, one agent said she found it artificial to use a guest's name three times, and that in her judgment, some guests could become annoyed if you kept repeating their names. The others in the group agreed.

The Key Standard greeting throughout the hotel was "Good Morning" (or "Afternoon" or "Evening"). It was documented and posted as signage in many places. It was written as part of the formulaic greeting required when answering the phone or recording phone mail greetings and it was mandatory when greeting guests face to face. Yet it was only sporadically followed at the Front Desk. When I observed Front Desk training for Guest Service Agents, on our second day, the trainer asked the women what they'd noticed when they observed the GSAs at work. One pointed out the different personalities and styles of interaction with guests, noting there were "lots of 'Hi's." Another nodded and added that greetings were not always according to protocol. The trainer was disturbed, and replied that it was more than a word. "Hi" may be friendly, he said, but it was not up to hotel standards. Standards demanded "Good morning, afternoon, or evening. How may I help you?"

When I later spoke to GSAs at the desk about the greetings, the answer was generally that the hotel greeting didn't seem natural, especially when it had to be repeated over and over. They spoke without rancor, but in a confident, matter-of-fact tone. Ironically, according to Harold, the Executive Manager in charge of rooms, the feedback from guests in the past had been that hotel employees weren't friendly enough; they seemed too robotic. Moreover, the hotel was clearly interested in screening potential employees for their personalities, instead of just their technical skills. The GSAs may have been responding to that guest complaint, but my sense was that they were empowering themselves to please the guests in their own way. And their application of empowerment went far beyond the limited measures defined by managers. They felt they were using their best judgment and flexibility in handling the pressures of their work, while still ensuring guest satisfaction.

Near the end of my study, I saw a large wall display at the basement stairs with employee photos mounted on cut-out paper stars. Their names were printed below the photos, along with a number. Throughout the hotel, when employees expressed frustration about their managers or resisted some specific work or policy, they identified the issue as "guest satisfaction." When they deviated from official written procedures, they justified their action with reference to their own experience and expertise at doing the job to ensure guest satisfaction. In other words, what may have at times appeared as resistance often seemed to have another meaning for front-line employees. I never observed employees who had not invested some pride in their individual work or who resisted work, although they may have existed. Actually, in the Housekeeping Department, the most serious insult among co-workers was laziness. I interpreted any resistance as an underlying desire for autonomy, the freedom to be self-governing on the job and to be valued for performing the job well rather than being owned by the hotel. Employees were not averse to satisfying guests' needs; they seemed genuinely to take pleasure and pride in it.

Several examples will illustrate this. First, turnover at the Front Desk was very high, which the directors I spoke to recognized as a problem. They attributed it to the high stress levels of the job. When I was observing at the Front Desk, only two of the GSAs hinted that internal problems may have contributed to the high turnover rate. Much later, in another department, a unionized employee told me it was the irregular, unreasonable hours that Front Desk employees were expected to keep. In the context of appreciation for her own regular work hours, she pointed out to me the high proportion of young, single GSAs. She said it was nearly impossible to have a family as a GSA because of the unpredictable hours. As nonunionized workers, they had no specific contract as the unionized employees did. The Front Desk managers, faced with changing house counts, juggled hours and personnel to meet projected and last-minute check-in and check-out needs. Sometimes young women unexpectedly had to work till one or two in the morning, and were not given cab fare home. When she told me, I recalled GSAs jokingly mentioning that they had come into work on the wrong day, or having to come into the office during off times to see what their work schedules were.

How could this high turnover tally with the notion that employees want to do a good job? I'd surmise that those who quit see working conditions as overwhelming, and leave with the hope they can find better conditions elsewhere, where they can apply themselves to their work.

In each of the other departments I observed, I saw evidence of resistance to these kinds of expectations. In the Housekeeping Department, I observed a very experienced Coordinator resist a directive from her manager in order to protect Room Attendants. Once at midday, when there seemed to be a shortage of Room Attendants for a rising house count, the manager ordered a Coordinator to call one or two from the seniority chart for work immediately. After the manager left the room, the Coordinator called, asking for attendants to come at mid-afternoon, explaining the house count situation. When a nearby Floor Manager asked if the Coordinator had called for them to come in right away, she answered that Room Attendants had lives, too. They couldn't just stop everything and come in immediately, especially when some of them lived far away. They might be in the middle of preparing dinner, or something else. Yet when her manager questioned her, she stared silently for a moment, and then answered that she hadn't, that she couldn't reach them to come immediately. The expression of irritation on the manager's face suggested to me that she thought little of the Coordinator.

This event was particularly poignant to me because the manager was a White Anglo-Canadian woman, the Coordinator an older Afro-Caribbean immigrant. If the Coordinator had argued with the manager, she could have appeared insubordinate or been vulnerable to accusations of jeopardizing the hotel's needs. In settings like this, where there were local tension and power differences between racially distinct groups, racial stereotypes and discrimination were potentially intensified.[10]

The third example took place between a unionized Table Attendant and the Café Manager. Jill, the manager, approached Keri to ask if she would work until closing (midnight) because she'd just found out that the house jumped by 700 that night. Keri agreed to consider it, but later said she thought about it and would not work late. She didn't like when it kept happening so often. She had no time to arrange for someone to pick her up and didn't want to go home alone so late. At the same time she told Jill she felt very guilty because it meant she let down a co-worker who would have to close alone. (Managers went home about 10 or 11.) But Keri added that these kinds of requests meant that in the hotel's view, she didn't have a life, that her life didn't count. She continued saying that it happened too much. Once in a while was okay. It hap-

---

[10]I hesitate to point to racism in this example, for my interpretation was based on a small event, subtle expressions, and a knowledge of the racism present in our broader society. In present-day Canada, and in the hotel, it was no longer socially acceptable to speak or act in overtly racist ways. Yet racism and racial stereotyping do exist, and appear in a much more subtle manner than in the past or in other societies. Several people in the hotel told me of quiet slurs and thinly veiled derogatory remarks. I observed this in two departments with workers at the lower end of the job hierarchy, but it was generally hidden, so that no-one could be accused. And as in the housekeeping office, it was often interwoven with tensions among culturally based discourses and status and power in the hotel.

pened to others, too, but she was sick of it. Keri said all of this unemotionally, in a matter-of-fact tone to Jill, in the presence of another attendant and me. She gave an example of the last time a guest came in just at closing, and wanted one small thing, but then she had to get take out supplies and it all took her over 20 minutes, so she was much later. There was then some disagreement about promised policy changes, with Keri reminding Jill that it had been agreed at a recent meeting that two people would always close together.

Jill began to explain that the hotel needed Keri because of the sudden jump in the house count, a development the hotel didn't know beforehand. Jill assured her they would have told her if they knew. Keri repeated the need for two people regularly. Jill began to appear annoyed and said, "Okay, we can call people in and then let them go when it's not too busy, let a person go who has less seniority; they won't get their hours. I'll talk to Dave [the senior manager]." As Jill and I left, she told me that now I could see that "they just don't get the big picture, we should go into the minus situation? We can't do that."

The first example was general turnover, the second telephoning, the third working overtime. Yet I see them all as illustrations of the context of literacy practices in the hotel, underlying issues of power and autonomy, respect, dignity, and engagement in one's working life. The following story of conflict over literacy practices in the Housekeeping Department shows more clearly how these issues were interwoven with literacy issues.

OUTSIDERS, JOB AUTONOMY AND OWNERSHIP[11]

When I first arrived in the Housekeeping Department, the atmosphere was warm and friendly. I quickly met and spoke to many people. However, Mark, a White man in his 40s, seemed apart from the group. He wore his own black suit, shirt and tie, indicating manager status, but no name tag. When I asked one of the women, Adrian, who he was, she answered that he'd worked in the department many years before as a manager, left, and recently returned, but it wasn't exactly clear why. Adrian, a Room Attendant and ex-union steward temporarily helping in the office because of an injury, told me he had not been popular. She said Mark had accused another Room Attendant of not vacuuming the carpet, when Adrian herself had been on the floor and seen the job completed. Mark applied sticky tape to the carpet, and when it picked up a hair, he claimed that as evidence the room hadn't been vacuumed. But Adrian, having witnessed the vacuuming, told him to get a better vacuum.

---

[11]Some of the descriptions of the Floor Managers and the Housekeeping Department were previously published by TESL Ontario in Hunter, Belfiore, and Folinsbee (2001), and by the Australian Council for Adult Literacy in Hunter (2001).

I later learned that Mark was an external consultant, hired by the Executive Housekeeper to recommend and oversee job restructuring in the department, particularly the Floor Managers. When offered the job, he took it on eagerly, and as he said to me:

> I'm sort of getting things straightened out, which I'm more than willing to do ... [the Executive Housekeeper] knows me as a straight shooter. If the pipe was red I say it's red, I'm not going to tell you, "Well it could be red, it could be orange, what do you want?" I'll tell you it's red. If you got a problem with that, well.... Her role was that she can take [my recommendation] as feedback and do what she wants with it, or not take it, which makes it kind of fun.

He compared Floor Managers' jobs in his day to now: "It wasn't perfect in my time, but there was a lot more responsibility as a manager."

In the weeks that followed I observed Mark closely shadowing the Floor Managers and Coordinators, working in the office, and becoming the object of great resentment. He tried to participate in the everyday banter of the office, but his jokes and commentary fell flat. No-one responded. He was the object of joking, as I overheard between Caretta, a Coordinator, and Robert, one of the Floor Managers:

R: How's your friend here?
C: My friend was here. My friend was keeping watch, like the wise men keep watch over Baby Jesus.
R: He's from Russia, From Russia with Love. He's Dr. No.
Caretta and Robert laughed and moved on to other work.

Mark's position as an outsider was not just a result of his official job or employee resentment at being so closely monitored. His reputation was built as much by his own actions. In an interview with me, he referred to several of the women office workers in ways that diminished their job experience and expertise. He referred to Lily, the woman who was in charge of Housekeeping payroll (the only department with a separate payroll office), as "a very good file clerk." He referred to the middle-aged Coordinators as "young ladies who've been doing the job for 20 years ... [who were] not going to change." He physically intervened in work activities, including documentation practices. One time I observed him place his hand on Robert's to stop him from writing, saying "No" as Robert was about to check off an item on his Housekeeping Report. Apparently Robert had forgotten to ask the Room Attendant a question. Floor Managers complained that he grabbed papers out of their hands.

Resistance to Mark and Marg (the Housekeeping Manager) as managers seemed to peak around changes in documentation practices that Mark initiated and Marg attempted to enforce. Mark restructured Floor Managers' and Coordinators' paperwork so that the Floor Managers could be more involved on the floors, rather than in the basement housekeeping office. I believe the resistance arose partly from their being outsiders to the community of employees. It wasn't so much that the managers were outside an ethno-cultural boundary; they may have seen their distance as part of a natural hierarchy. The workers, however, interpreted it as disrespect and ignorance.

The Room Standards Problem

Mark had been called into the hotel to help solve a problem of "quality control" that managers had pinpointed stemming from Floor Managers. Others besides Mark had alluded to such a problem. One of the Coordinators, Caretta, who had worked up from Room Attendant through Floor Manager to her current position, told me something was wrong, but it wasn't clear to her what. The rooms were "not up to standards." When she was a Floor Manager, they were called "supervisors" and their jobs were spelled out in much greater detail. She added that they spent more time on the floors working. In addition, she made a comment that I took to be a reference to Marg as well as to some of the Floor Managers: "You can't have people just out of school telling people who've worked here 10 or 12 years how to do their jobs." One of the Floor Managers told me that they'd been accused of "wasting time" on the job, insisting that they worked hard.

One of the sources of problems that Floor Managers themselves identified was VIP rooms because they had to spend extra time to set up the rooms, and collect and deliver the extras. The VIP rooms could not be neglected, and they were seldom blocked (assigned by Front Desk) in advance. So throughout the day, Floor Managers had to monitor upcoming VIP rooms and prepare them in time for the guests' arrival. Another responsibility that took a large part of their work day seemed to be the amount of paperwork they were required to do, which took precedence over the time they could spend inspecting rooms and supporting the Room Attendants. The paperwork was not superfluous. If room cleaning was inaccurately documented, or inaccurately put into the computer either by Room Attendants or Guest Service Agents, consequences could be costly for the hotel. Floor Managers had to double-check the room status reports, by visual inspection and by Room Attendant confirmation. Room conditions were taken seriously; as mentioned, if the hotel was seen as responsible, guests received various compensations.

Two Solutions to the Problem

Onc of thc kcy papcrwork tasks was the "clearing" process described earlier (see "Floor Managers"). When I had talked to Floor Managers about the need to do the detailed cross-checking they did, they all said it was important to prevent mistakes, for errors could have serious consequences such as a room comp or a grievance from the vigilant unionized Room Attendants. Shortly after I arrived, Mark redesigned the clearing procedure. According to Marg, it had been taking as long as 45 minutes. Mark's plan would eliminate the waiting time for clearing and the laborious face-to-face oral cross-checking. The new way was for half the managers to come downstairs promptly at 9:15, drop off their reporting sheets with the Coordinator, take their break, attend the briefing meeting, and pick up their modified sheets on their way back to the floors. The other half would take their break at the end of the briefing meeting, thus staggering the times for the Coordinator to check them over and make sure her statistics matched the Floor Managers'. There would be no more face-to-face interaction with the paperwork. Widespread anger resulted. Some seemed to ignore it. Others, like Robert, muttered, "We have to have communication."

Generally the Floor Managers told me the new system wouldn't work, that it would cause mistakes. Everyone had slightly different ways of writing in their notes, for they wrote their notes on the reports mostly for themselves to use as working documents. And Caretta wouldn't be able to decipher everyone's records. For example, I noticed that Caretta sometimes used sets of dots rather than letters to indicate room status. One dot represented an occupied room, two dots a check-out room. She sometimes tallied up types of rooms at the bottom of the forms with these marks, or she entered the dots, expecting the Floor Managers to tally the counts beside them. However, not all the managers made use of the system. In fact, I once asked a Floor Manager what the dots meant, and he replied that they meant nothing. Other objections related to the constant distractions of the office. The managers and Caretta knew that it was easy to make mistakes when work was rushed and frequently interrupted by people, telephones and beepers. Only one Floor Manager, Slabodanka, an East European Canadian woman, said loudly in the office that she liked it because it saved time. Yet she was also frequently at odds with most of the other Floor Managers. Whether she pushed past someone without excusing herself, or made a sharp, insulting comment, she was also often on the edge of the group. All the other Floor Managers I spoke to said it wasn't practical.

Anger was high at one briefing meeting I attended. The Floor Managers were unusually quiet as they got ready for the meeting. But when they found Mark was absent, they spoke out angrily about his rude, arrogant working style and the impracticality of the new procedure. They objected to the rigidity of the timing as the first issue. Carol spoke first, her posture tense and voice louder than usual: "I find [if] I have more rooms, I can't get downstairs in time. If I go upstairs and it's a split section [rooms on different floors], you don't know." Marg asked why. Another answered, "Because we don't know." Several others spoke vehemently about Mark. Carol said he treated them and talked to them "like pigs." Slabodanka said he told her to "just get started" when she arrived in the morning, rather than greeting her. Estelle reported that he "grabbed" her report when she brought it in, saying, "Give it to me."

Marg gave them all a chance to speak, but she was firm. She seemed to be referring to Carol's objection as an exception when she responded, "Let's not talk about things that happen once in a while, like pick-up rooms [rooms from other floors added to Room Attendants' assignments to total 16]. Let's talk about the regular things and then deal with exceptions. We can't organize for exceptions." She reminded them that "Change is part of life. You can't be negative and not say it won't work, but talk about how you can make it work.... It's going to take some time to adjust. For one, you need to come in on time ready to work, be more organized." She compared them to the Room Attendants, who were required to be in uniform and ready to go on the floors at their starting time. She added, "Change was inevitable. If you don't like it, maybe this isn't the place for you to work." At 10:00 she looked at the clock, broke off the discussion, and said she was due at another meeting. As they left the room, I heard Carol say, "With this attitude, people will rebel." Someone else said, "Maybe they don't want us here."

I began observing on the floors and didn't see the clearing process for a few weeks. When I returned to the department, no-one was following the new procedure. Giselle, one of the Floor Managers, told me "nobody did it." According to her, Mark was just showing off. Estelle told me it wouldn't work; it would have caused too many mistakes.

Some time later, Giselle also designed a new work form to overcome some of the ongoing problems with common types of room complaints. She first presented her form at a briefing meeting, arranged in advance with Marg. She took the floor at the beginning of the meeting and passed out the photocopied forms. She had researched the kinds of complaints that occurred most often, and made a chart to create a rotational cleaning scheme, titled the "90 Day Rotational Cleaning Program." She presented it for feedback at a morning staff meeting. The chart was a checklist, laid out horizontally on a legal-size sheet with 40 single cleaning tasks listed in the left column and dates following along to the right. The idea was that Room Attendants would add one task to their regular room cleaning chores, go through the list until all the tasks were finished, then begin the cycle again. The rest of the Floor Manager staff received her new document favorably, some offering small corrections, for example, that the Housemen took care of the balconies. They all agreed to try it out. They would try one task a day. Carol suggested they begin with the bathtub drains, where she had "seen some big old frogs." The following week I asked how the program was going, and was told it was working fine. Giselle was not happy, though. She said she "put lots of time in" working on the chart. It was "good for the hotel, good for everyone," but Marg had rated her only 4 out of 5 points for her work. She repeated what others had said about

Marg as lacking job knowledge with regard to the annual "incentive plan." She said they were rated at the end of the year by someone who didn't understand the job.

Like Mark, Giselle used documentation practices to address the problem of room standards, but approached it from a different position. Mark was an outsider, not liked or respected, who didn't understand how closely tied the office literacy practices were to the work they were doing. They had established a system of working with their documents to minimize errors. The Coordinators' and Floor Managers' clearing procedures, although time-consuming, were effective at quality control. The employees knew that from their shared experience on the job. Giselle, on the other hand, was an insider, worked the floors, knew the others, and was close to them and their ways of working with the documents. Mark streamlined the process of clearing, but he also compromised the quality of the task, and he compounded an "us versus them" mentality in the department. As Giselle told me, they had low morale.

Mark and Giselle also framed their solutions to the problem differently. The problem was the same: quality of room standards. Mark's solution focused on reducing time spent on paperwork so that the Floor Managers could spend more time on the floor with the Room Attendants. Giselle's solution was directed explicitly at the rooms. On the surface it seemed a logical, straightforward approach. But in implementation, she increased the amount of paperwork for the Floor Managers and increased the workload for the Room Attendants. Her solution reinforced the supervisory status of the managers, and the subordinate, cleaning status of the Room Attendants. In addition to doing more work, Room Attendants were formally told their new tasks and had to sign off that they understood, and by implication accepted, the new responsibilities. At that time I was just finishing my observations in the Housekeeping Department, and didn't have the opportunity to see the effects of Giselle's plan among the Room Attendants. However, this small twist in the outcomes of this story shows that issues of power in the workplace were never simple, but complex and dynamic.

Local Meanings, Power, Identity, and Autonomy

This example of contested local meanings and successful employee resistance differs from those in the manufacturing sites where quality control is achieved through standardized documentation. There, local meanings of documentation can be seen as superfluous and risky to line workers. Quality control through document practices in the Housekeeping Office was considered essential to those most intimately involved in documentation work. So in this sense, the Urban Hotel experience was often the flip side of the resistance in our manufacturing studies. However, the issue of contradictory or contested local meanings seems common to all our studies. Employee subversion of employer policies has also been seen in other research, when workers' local meanings and local knowledge of the job conflict with official policy (O'Connor, 1994, as cited in Prinsloo & Breier, 1996). Importantly, in the hotel, workers' own established practice assured quality control, whereas in their view, Mark's meant "showing off." Mark's solution, on the other hand, was his answer to an efficiency problem, a means of reducing "wasted time." I'd like to outline several forces underlying these local meanings.

The first was identity. The Floor Managers and Coordinators were all working class but, through education or promotion, had positions above the lowest ranking unionized workers. Their dominant racial identity was African; most were African Caribbean, but others were African Canadian and African European. Although I never heard allusions to race, they shared a social identity of otherness in the white Canadian Euro-dominant society. But they had much more in common than race and class. They shared the local discourse of the Housekeeping Office. In addition to their common dress, their clipboards and white-out, and the daily responsibilities imposed by the hotel, they shared greeting conventions, an easy interactive style, a degree of openness about domestic life and a sense of humor that helped them manage stress. They shared a sense of history in the hotel that materialized through stories and knowledge shared by the long-term employees in the group. Their collective knowledge of hotel operations, past problems and solutions gave them an edge over the more recently hired Executive Housekeeper and Housekeeping Manager who enlisted and supported Mark, both of whom belonged to the more elite, idealized discourse of the top managers. They also seemed to share a resentment of what they saw as an excessive workload and an unappreciative manager. Mark was clearly not a member of their discourse; he was a White Anglo-Canadian who dressed differently, spoke and joked differently, and acted in an aggressive manner with the others.

Other features in their working lives buttressed the solidarity enabled by race, class and their housekeeping discourse. The office location in the hotel, in the middle of the basement, could be seen as marginalizing, particularly in an industry where the "back of the house" can carry connotations of menial, low-status labor. Yet this location also offered housekeeping staff a degree of freedom from the constraints on public appearance and behavior dictated throughout the hotel. They were free to joke and laugh, to make noise, and even to speak sharply to each other. Furthermore, they were not resented in the hotel, but seemed acceptably construed as a pressured but affable work group. Executive managers all spoke of the stress of hotel work, the importance of humor and a consistently positive attitude toward guest satisfaction.

Autonomy and power were also interwoven in the story. Ironically, although the housekeeping workers engaged in an act of resistance, they demonstrated many of the qualities so highly promoted in the new workplace discourse. In the jargon of workplace practice, we might look at it as "occupying the contradictory space in the discourse of the new work order," similarly to the way Katz (2000) did in her research on immigrants in the electronics industry. She maintained that Mexican workers' culturally preferred silence despite managers' expectations for them to speak out was their way to straddle the company's "slippage" in articulating its own values about group membership. Although the company valued group work, it was not clear about what the groups were: the entire company, managers, or workers. Taking this space may have reduced the risk they took in resisting. Likewise, in The Urban Hotel, the workers invested in quality assurance, so highly valued and relentlessly communicated, at the same time as they defied the hierarchy. They could have continued grumbling but followed orders, a less risky path. Yet their steadfast resistance to the new procedure, not formally organized but arising from common local knowledge, suggested a deep investment in the goal of guest satisfaction and in the social solidarity of the group discourse. Their comments that "We have to have communication" and their repeated references to "causing too many mistakes" used the values of the hotel to support their resistance.

The housekeeping group had created an autonomous workplace culture, one that adopted some of the official hotel corporate image and values, but fashioned them in their own local discourse. Moreover, they exercised the power of their group to resist the hierarchical directives of the official hotel managers. I do not believe they "won" only because of their power and solidarity. Managers must have recognized that they were right, that mistakes would result from the more streamlined clearing practice. For in the end, corporate managers in the new workplace have much greater power over workers' lives, when they choose to exercise it.

WORKPLACE LITERACY AND LANGUAGE EDUCATION

As stated early in this chapter, The Urban Hotel was proud of its commitment to education and training, guaranteeing every employee 12 hours of paid education per year. In the area of literacy, it sponsored seminars and mini-courses for managers to improve their business writing, as one manager proudly told me. It has also sponsored many other kinds of workplace learning programs, including for speakers of other languages. Every department has a designated manager whose responsibilities include training. Both of the managers I observed as trainers had worked their way up from the jobs they were training employees for. They knew the work firsthand. Most of the training I observed was on how to do the job, how to follow new procedures, or for those who didn't measure up on their daily inspections, how to improve performance.

New employees were given general hotel orientation and several days to a week of departmental training. They then spent time shadowing an experienced employee before working on their own. I spent two sessions in Guest Service Agent training for the front desk. Each day, they met first in the café for coffee and a brief, informal discussion of the previous lessons, and then moved on to the new day's agenda. The first day, the trainer showed and explained important features of the hotel, then handed out booklets of hotel information summarizing the tour, saying that he would quiz the four new GSAs on the information the following day. The atmosphere was informal and friendly. We had lunch together in one of the hotel restaurants, and were joined by another manager. While they made small talk with us, they also retold entertaining stories of past hotel Christmas parties or unexpected encounters with guests.

A large chunk of training time was spent in the small basement classroom on the Rooms database, which they would have to operate as they engaged face to face with guests. They received both keyboard command information and practice simulations. Once on the floor, all the employees said they found the basement time invaluable, just like the rest of the training, but they could have used more of it.

Like the new GSAs, I thought favorably of how training was organized. Although their initial time was spent off the floor, they had seen the work site and had some idea of what they were facing. They knew the relevance of what they were learning, and their time in the classroom allowed for unpressured learning. The days they spent shadowing other GSAs gave them time to observe more expert workers "performing" in real time. I believe the social occasions served to initiate trainees into the hotel world as much as the information and practice sessions. In these ways they were carefully guided and supported as incoming members of the hotel community of practice. Literacy and language were a natural, integrated part of that guidance. Ironically, once Guest Service Agents finished their training, they would not be allowed in the restaurants or the café, an issue around limited accessibility to the ideal hotel world that also came up in other ways.

Another avenue for training and learning about the hotel was the Quality Fairs. These events were planned by a committee of managers and organized by other managers in each department. They considered the Quality Fairs a way to teach and reinforce their perspective on the Quality Journey. The workers saw them as fun, but didn't seem to learn much. Although the fairs seemed to improve, the "learning" aspect of both the fairs I observed seemed based on traditional school tests: complex, densely written text accompanied by comprehension questions. There often seemed to be a misleading trick in the answer choices or in the text, for the managers stated they didn't want it to be too easy to win the prizes that went with the quizzes. Overall, those employees who searched the texts for answers to the questions didn't seem to see them as anything more than puzzles. Many were not able to understand either the texts or the questions. Managers generally saw the limited accessibility of texts, especially written directives, as an important "communication" challenge in the hotel. But it seemed they had yet to deal fully with communication in the Quality Fairs.

What might they have done to be more effective educationally? Their first answer was, as with all their communication problems, to the use plain language and increased graphics. I believe these were necessary, but not always sufficient. One modification that could have better increased employee buy-in would be to involve all levels of the workplace in organizing and participating in the Fairs, and thus in the Journey. Learning might include finding out about everyone else's responsibilities. Literacy engagement in the hotel discourse could then be more meaningful, and even more characteristic of what's now talked about as the "smart workforce" (Gerber & Lankshear, 2000). This would draw on employees' intimate knowledge with the challenges of their work, and it could draw out creative approaches to problem-solving from a greater range of resources than just the managers' group. Moreover, it could serve as an impetus for greater participation in literacy and greater accessibility to the ideal hotel discourse for all.

How could workplace educators best help improve the language and literacy competence of the kinds of employees we've met at The Urban Hotel? Two principles might guide their approach. The first would be to engage learners in participating in their own learning, in context with their work responsibilities. They might teach, explain, or evaluate their own work. They might write their own job descriptions, peer-designed training materials, job manuals, reporting documents and evaluation schemes. The second principle would be to educate employers on the nature of literacy as a social practice. For, as we have seen at all our work sites, a narrow view of literacy as simply being reading and writing skills does not include how people interpret and act on texts, because of the many meanings that texts hold in the workplace.

CONCLUSION

As at the beginning of my study, I saw The Urban Hotel as a vibrant, thriving competitor in the globalized corporate world. Like many other multinational corporations, the hotel had adopted a Quality Journey. It aimed to meet the challenges of global competition by restructuring the hotel culture and engaging employees in "buying into" the idealized image, values and goals of the hotel. Like other corporations at the turn of the millennium, many forms of literacy were central to the hotel operation. Popular notions of the demands on literacy in the workplace define it as a need for enhanced skills of reading, writing, computing and using other technologies. But this study of hotel literacy practices has shown that literacy is multifaceted, interwoven into the fabric of work activities, relationships, issues of power and identity, and conflicting meanings.

The public face of the hotel was impressive in its attractive, restrained welcome, populated with confident, enthusiastic "hoteliers." Just beyond the public face of the hotel, in the "heart of the house," the many kinds of employees who work in the hotel were visible by their attire. Likewise, beneath the surface appearances, these differences in dress and manner indicated a range of local cultures, or discourses. Although I was impressed with the dedication of nearly everyone I met across the hotel, each local discourse had a distinct style of interacting, a particular up-close knowledge of the fast-paced, stressful jobs they do, and a slightly different way of acting out the Quality Journey. And in each of these local cultures, literacy practices were also distinctive.

Overall, however, literacy practices in The Urban Hotel had two functions. The meanings of texts and the ways they were used varied within these functions. First, the hotel managers used texts to officially manage employees, to bring them into line with hotel culture. The large numbers of forms, policy documents, job descriptions, training documents, worksheets, inspirational posters and wall displays all served this function. Generally, they were written in an abstract, dense style familiar and meaningful to the managers' culture, but less meaningful to employees. Some of the texts, like sick-leave forms or daily work assignments, did have immediate relevance for employees' working lives, and they read and attended to them on their own or with help from co-workers. Other texts were intended to communicate the Quality Journey, to regulate employees' attitudes and behavior as members of the quality culture. But when they were not seen as immediately meaningful, they received much less attention than other texts. The company's hoped-for enculturation was diminished, as was the employees' potential for upward job mobility. When employees faced various guest demands, they acted somewhat independently to provide what they saw as quality customer service, based on the situation at hand. They didn't seem to break the boundaries of what would be acceptable behavior, but they may have pushed the boundaries of regulated behavior.

Second, work documents enabled employees to keep track of their work and communicate guest and room status to others in the hotel. These were tightly intertwined with the variety of tasks and decisions workers had to handle as they fulfilled their work responsibilities. All the workers I observed, no matter what their job was, had to know not only how to do their jobs efficiently and effectively under pressure, but also how to integrate a variety of literacy practices and technologies into their work in order to do it well. The size of the hotel and the immediacy of feedback they received from guests, along with their local knowledge of their jobs, contributed to their buy-in to documentation. It served an immediate, meaningful need in their own enactment of quality control and guest satisfaction. But when imposed practices had little relevance to their lived experience on the job, employees tended to resist.

What are the implications for understanding literacy practices in terms of The Urban Hotel's Quality Journey, or in other hotels and workplaces with similar goals? It appears that simplifying the language of the print messages would reach all employees more effectively. That's what the managers' team thought, and many language and literacy teachers would concur. But that answer also assumes that communicating a message with abstract information about corporate business strategies or lists of regulations is adequate to ensure buy-in. Cleaners, dishwashers, and launderers saw that buy-in entailed on-call working hours and "going the extra mile" (i.e., doing more work than the job called for) for themselves and for managers. But they also saw that while they got toast with jam and hot water in the basement, managers got heavily discounted meals in the hotel restaurants. In such conditions, employees bought in by doing their jobs with dignity and their best judgment. They bought into literacy practices that meaningfully enhanced their work and their sense of power and value in the work they performed.

4

Literacies at Work
in a Culture
of Documentation

Tracy A. Defoe

Walk with me into Metalco,[1] where a kind of industrial magic takes place, three shifts a day. Bars of solid metal are delivered here along with hundreds of widgets, washers and springs. The metal is cut and precisely shaped, and the bits all assembled into useful products that sit in the guts of machines around the world. If you work mostly with words, ideas or people like I do, the tangibility of Metalco's products is enticing. And the way things happen here is interesting. Metalco is an example of a "new" workplace where literacies and documentation mediate participation in the work, and where external standards and forces ascribe powerful meanings to those same documents as much as individuals do. As we walk around we will see more people and many more documents than you might expect. For every piece of paper, every signboard or chart, there is an unseen world of data and documentation on the company Intranet. For every person there is a complex story that we can only begin to understand. We visit Metalco at the turn of the 21st century, a time of business expansion, purposeful change and optimism for the new millennium.

---

[1]All of the names used in this chapter have been changed to preserve anonymity.

This chapter is about literacies at work, and how people communicate through print in a high-tech manufacturing plant. I have tried to put print communication into the context of the work culture at Metalco to show the place of documentation at work from the point of view of different groups of people, what we call the "local meanings." Through stories and comments from working life as I observed it, from how people interact with print and with each other, we will see how culture and context create local meanings for literacy, and also how new literacies affect work culture. More than that, we will see people learning. And the ways learning is supported here also tell us about the work culture of Metalco.

Compared to the other workplaces used for our In-Sites research, Metalco is farther down the road to being a high-performance workplace. If not yet a learning organization, then it's an organization learning, with the learning tied to literacies. A complexity of issues is interwoven with print literacies in the evolving work culture of Metalco: Growth, rapid change, participation, training, quality and communication are the ones I aim to uncover here. We will also hear from Metalco's managers. Their understandings of the complex issues are important strands in reading work at Metalco. Global business forces are felt in the managers' offices and on the production floor. Metalco is part of a world culture of quality programs,[2] and with registration and compliance with their standards comes a "culture of documentation."

METALCO: HIGH-TECH MANUFACTURING

These stories take place in a high-tech industrial products company striving for status as a "world-class" manufacturer. For Metalco managers and engineers, "world-class" means achieving a list of quality and process improvements and implementing the system to monitor and maintain them. Metalco is a Canadian subsidiary of an American multinational company, independent in some respects, tied to corporate strategies in others. World-class manufacturing goals are corporate as well as local. The Canadian and parent companies are prosperous and growing. The company's products dominate niche markets around the world, but it is not a household name. Like the buildings that house Metalco in the suburbs of a Canadian city, the

---

[2]At the time of this research, Metalco was registered with the International Standards Organization at the ISO 9001 level. The company was also registered and complied with a number of customer quality assurance programs and, even more importantly, had developed its own corporate version of a manufacturing process quality system called MPS, the Metalco Production System. It was designed along the lines of TPS, the Toyota Production System described by Monden (1998) in his book *Toyota Production System*. In adopting this Japanese manufacturing orientation with a focus on eliminating waste and increasing flow with a flexible workforce, Metalco is part of what Gee, Hull, and Lankshear termed the "new work order" in their 1996 book *the New Work Order: Behind the Language of the New Capitalism*.

corporate stance is low profile and modest. About 350 people work in this location, everyone from the senior executives to product designers, engineers, managers, direct production workers, and marketers. They design and make industrial parts and products from cast and machined metal for customers worldwide. Rapid growth, changing technology and ever-higher internal and external demands for reliability and accuracy have shaped the social and literacy systems of this unionized workplace.

Metalco has ongoing adult education opportunities for a range of learning interests. In addition to manufacturing, technical and leadership training, company managers support formal and informal adult education in many forms. This includes spoken communication, writing and reading, basic computer skills and English language instruction for individuals and groups. Metalco has paid for English language instructors and on-shift training for 5 of the past 10 years. As part of the current mandate for learning support, skills for teaching and learning, together with an emphasis on understanding, are part of the Metalco concept of workplace education.

THE RESEARCHER

As a workplace educator turned researcher at Metalco, it was not easy for me to blend in. I was a White, middle-aged, middle-class, English-speaking, Canadian-born woman in a place where most people would not identify themselves as more than one or two of those characteristics. I adopted a sort of uniform of nondescript clothing, and tried to move with the rhythm of the workday, but my autonomy set me apart. Because I was not actually working at any one job, I was free to come and go or move around the production floor in ways that only managers, engineers and perhaps office workers do. As a person paid for only the work of my mind, not of my hands as well, I was set apart.

I don't think people thought I was the first female manager, though. If you asked people at Metalco what I did there, I expect there would be a range of answers. Some people would say "teacher" because before and after the research period at Metalco I taught clear writing, how to use a computer, and how to communicate more effectively. Other people might say I was a tutor or even a helper, and I know there would be people who would say "consultant." When I was collecting data, I met dozens of people for the first time. They would say I was a researcher perhaps, who had "got a job" and was helping out with training now.

At Metalco, consultants, students and even researchers are commonplace. A third of the people at Metalco who had been there more than 10 years knew me and my colleague Mary as English as a second language (ESL) teachers who had worked with everyone in the company on communications at a critical time in the company history. We were there for two winters and springs in the 1990s when the company was registering for an international quality program. Then, as now, Mary did more of the teaching, and I did more of the curriculum planning and reporting. We have both since expanded our practice beyond communication and diversity. We are such a pair that people not only call us by each other's name, but merge our names into "Terry and Macy" instead of Mary and Tracy.

During the 10 months I wore a researcher's hat at Metalco, I was careful to remind people when I was on site as a researcher, not an educator. I didn't literally wear a research hat, but a gray zip-front jacket with a metallic Ryerson University pin on it. As a researcher I always wore very casual clothing, steel-toed shoes and safety glasses. Most of the time I had a notepad at hand, and a denim bag with my tape recorder. I tried to blend in, and was not surprised when people would walk by without stopping to talk. "I didn't know it was you," I was told more than once. Being in research mode is a quiet observational state. In contrast, as a workplace educator I favor brighter colored clothes and always walk around to say hello to people when I arrive, just so they know I am there if they want to talk to me. This research draws for the most part on my notes and observations as a researcher, but also on my prior relationships, experience and mind set as a workplace educator. My deep background knowledge of this place all surfaces in this tour of Metalco.

For most of my working life I have been an educator, and for the past 12 years an educator who focuses on learning at work. My everyday work involves applied research that leads to curriculum development or programs or support designed for the learning needs of specific workers in a specific workplace. No two workplaces are exactly alike; work cultures are local. I have found little routine in this work of understanding and helping to support those intersections of knowledge, work and learning where people seek something other than specific job training.

At Metalco the "something" was framed as communication. Ten years ago, the engineers and quality-control staff were having a hard time getting the concepts and requirements for a quality program demanded by a customer across to the people in the shop. Few of the shop workers spoke or read English enough to participate easily in the training for the new quality designation, so what began as a request for ESL classes for volunteer shop workers became a companywide communication project: the requested ESL classes, plus writing workshops and multicultural management workshops for people who had supervisory and management jobs. Today at Metalco the "something" is still communication, still tied with participation in a changing workplace and keeping up with the customer demands for quality and standardization.

There are not many classes, though. Mary and I have tried to evolve our practice to fit both Metalco and our understandings of adult learning. We established one-on-one planning as the norm. We also adopted the manufacturing notion of a "pull" system, talking about people "pulling" learning support from us as they needed it. We started working with people at their work stations and experimented with shop floor teaching for individuals and work groups. As before, we work with everyone from machine operators, assemblers and packagers to managers and engineers. We respond to the pull—the needs. We try to be accessible and we report to a joint committee of people who also listen for needs and wants among their networks of co-workers.

In 1990, I almost never went into the production shop. Now I'm there every day that I am on-site. In the "old days" we held classes and invited engineers, managers and others in to answer questions or talk about a topic of interest. Now we attend regular production meetings and take part in planning individual and group learning. We answer requests for help; we mentor people by email and in person. There are groups that meet to work together on writing and editing; other groups work on "speaking up." Today our practice is close to the point of use; workplace education on demand at work. Even our desk is now part of the production area, where in 1990 we had a workspace in the Human Resources office.

Thinking about these changes helped me see a parallel shift in work and in the conceptualization of learner need that I have also seen in other worksites. When workplace learning was primarily a Human Resources issue, the learning sought was to increase people's capacity for technical learning and face-to-face communication. Today, every aspect of production, and especially the incremental changes that make up continuous improvement hinge on literacies and learning between people and documentation systems. As work itself becomes a literate practice, my workplace education practice responded to become a support service for people right at their workstation. It no longer made sense to me as an educator to withdraw people from the place where they needed to learn and take them to a classroom. I joined meetings and tried to support people, learning and literacies right where they were at work.

"A BIT OF A CULTURE"

I asked a lot of people what it was like to work at Metalco and how they saw the place as different or the same as other workplaces. This answer, from a transcribed taped interview with the company president, is one that I kept coming back to read again: "People here are driven to be successful under adverse conditions. We all love building things. There is a pride of workmanship, a work ethic, a mechanical aptitude. As a collection of people we represent a bit of a culture."

What strikes me about this comment on Metalco's essential character is that it is so inclusive. Yes, from the president's viewpoint there are always adverse conditions to overcome in the marketplace and in production. The company has been successful, growing and profitable for years. Essentially though, for the president and I think most of the people there, Metalco is about "building things." His characterization of the collection of people is one that applies to everyone, nodding to the production shop workers and the engineering group as defining the company culture. At the time of this interview, I did not know how many of the people I thought of as managers and office people started with the company running production machines. I eventually learned that senior people in sales, quality and information technology all started in by running lathes and tool and die machines in the shop. A number of people whom I thought of as university-educated engineers turned out to be mechanically inclined and as much self-educated as book-learned.

Pride and Stress: Keeping Up With Rapid Change

The people at Metalco seemed optimistic and took pride in their work. Pride was expressed to me in dozens of ways: pride in the precision and reliability of the products; in working with good equipment, in the "good" company that is profitable and growing. Working for a company that has been steadily growing for 20 years means more than just job security, although many people who have moved to Metalco from failed or downsizing companies value the ongoing expansion. It means opportunities for promotion, for training, and, for hourly workers, a chance to earn overtime. Shop workers are paid better than the manufacturing industry average, but they still value the chance to make overtime pay. People here are also under stress. At the time of my research the company was launching a new line of products, involving setting up new manufacturing cells with new machines, new procedures and new employees. For some people, working long hours and weekends is stressful.

There are other sources of stress as well at Metalco, overfamiliar issues found in many other workplaces. People think the engineers look down on them, and they sometimes do. The managers try to spread their enthusiasm for quality, for profits and for Continuous Improvement with mixed success. As we will see, managing the message and "walking the talk" are part of the quality journey at Metalco. Many people say they feel underpaid, although both the union and the company agree that wages are better than average. Some of the people believe they are responsible for the growth and success of the company, that the history of the company is the history of their own hard work and innovation. They don't always feel this status is recognized. There are conflicts and mixed messages over the importance of quality and production, although people say there are fewer inconsistencies than there used to be.

Change is more than a theme at Metalco; it is a way of life. The philosophy of Continuous Improvement means change is ongoing, through evolving systems and through a series of focused rapid improvement campaigns on one area or department. I experienced some of the outcomes of Continuous Improvement during the research period, when any number of people changed their work and their work locations. I often went to find someone only to be given directions to their new workspace. New production cells were established, two senior managers left and were replaced, departments were redefined, reorganized and relocated. I learned to ask, "Are you still in the same place?" when making arrangements to see someone, and to check for messages and announcements of reorganization. Keeping up and getting information is a survival skill for researchers and workers alike when things are changing fast.

Process and Production Systems

Metalco is distinguished by more than 20 years of experience in carefully keeping records of manufacturing work processes through Statistical Process Control (SPC). People at the company have worked with a series of quality programs and manufacturing philosophies. Registration with the International Standard Organization through ISO 9001 and their version of flexible manufacturing approaches such as developed under the Toyota Production System (TPS) are just the latest for them. TPS means using space and people efficiently, and building products to customer orders in specially designed assembly cells. TPS also means running "lean," with less inventory and overhead. At Metalco, I found a culture of documentation, of taking care, of not making mistakes and of learning from mistakes that happen. Implementing their version of TPS was driving many of the ongoing changes in workstations and in relationships between work groups that I saw at Metalco during the research period. TPS, called MPS at Metalco for Metalco Production System, is not fully in place anywhere in the company. Each department, every production cell is rated on a checklist to show where they are on the path from traditional batch manufacturing to one-piece, made-to-order MPS. One of the managers' goals is to make the data and meetings on MPS implementation accessible to workers.

New Ways of Communicating: The Intranet

In the last 3 years, Metalco has established an Intranet system. All of the important production documents for the company (except at the time of this research engineering drawings) are controlled through electronic originals available only on the company Intranet. Customer orders and the production planning system, the purchasing system and other information vital to the minute-by-minute operation of the company are also only available via computers accessing the Intranet. Metalco has adapted to the computer age to take advantage of the control, flexibility and accuracy the Intranet potentially provides.

With so much information on the Intranet computer system, and even more information spread by email and electronic notice boards and shared files, people without a computer or without the ability to run a computer are left out of the inner circle of information. The information network for those among what one worker called the "computer blind" is oral. In an effort to keep shop employees in the loop, memos, announcements and information sent to all employees by email are also printed for circulation among workers and posted in the lunchrooms on bulletin boards. In this way a written notice-board network works with and feeds "the grapevine." Before this practice of routinely printing and posting all information, leaders and managers were responsible for relaying information.

For more than a decade before the Intranet, office workers and production managers used email as one of their preferred modes of communication. As computers wired to the Intranet are installed in the lunchrooms and on the shop floor, production workers and leaders are joining the circle of the Intranet- and email-connected. To understand the work culture of Metalco, one has to know that a lot of information and interaction happens via email. During the research period, production workers were marginal in those exchanges, as readers or writers of email. I was fortunate to have an email address within the company system to experience it firsthand. Many people received and sent dozens of emails a day. They did not spend a lot of time choosing words or replying to email that they were only required to read for information. Some people told me stories of a misspelled word or a hastily written message taken as an insult by the receiver, but these seemed to be the exception rather than the rule. As is the case in many workplaces, email is imposing hastily written communication on many people who would have previously only spoken face to face to report or solve problems. Email is a relatively new and changing social literacy, an evolving literate practice enmeshed with technology and workplace reorganization.

Growth

Growth is also a factor driving some of the changes reported to me. Ten years ago Metalco employed about a third as many people as today: 120 employees, with only 20 people not involved in production. Those 120 people are almost all still there, an established community challenged to incorporate newcomers and acculturate newcomers at a rate of 2:1. The 1990 employees worked around a cultural divide. The engineers and managers were in the majority educated, Canadian and European-born, English-speaking men. The shop workers were mostly first- and second-generation Asian-born men with a range of languages and mostly limited proficiency in English. Many of the shop workers had completed grade 10 and machining courses. A few, especially the assemblers, left school very early. There were family ties in the office and in the shop that formed other unofficial networks of relationship and authority.

Today numbering 350, the people of Metalco mirror the demographics of their metropolitan area. People from South Asia, Central and South America, and Eastern Europe have changed the mix of workers through the company. New employees from China and Hong Kong are not production workers, but engineers and educated office workers. There are also proportionally more Canadian-born people at Metalco now. The office workers include many visible minority members, some Canadian-born and some new immigrants. In general, the newer shop employees speak English more fluently and have more complete educations than the old-timers. Also in general, the newer employees are younger, and at least some of them are female. They are familiar with computers or at least welcome them; they like the high-tech parts of their job. There are no family ties among the newer employees, who were mostly identified, aptitude-tested and hired through an employment agency rather than word of mouth. This, too, is part of a change in workplace culture at Metalco.

Metalco is like an established neighborhood experiencing an influx of new arrivals. The long-term employees eye the newcomers, most with less than 2 years on the job, with some suspicion. The new ones find some people less welcoming than they had hoped, and even a little set in their ways and their cliques. There are stereotypes both ways, if not totally "us" and "them," then at least "old building" and "new building." The rapid growth resulted in expansion to first one, and later two adjoining buildings that are the same age and look more or less the same. People throughout the company, especially people working away from the production floors, are crowded despite the expansion.

Ongoing Learning

During the research period, as I spoke with the other In-Sites researchers and heard stories from their worksites, we realized that something was different at Metalco. This was a place where the manufacturing tenet of Continuous Improvement translated into ongoing change and ongoing learning for production workers, managers, engineers and others. New ideas came from courses, from visits and from networks of like-minded businesses as well as from the head office. No-one talked about Metalco as a "learning organization," but they were engaged in exploring new ideas, new equipment, new attempts at getting things right. The steady implementation of the production system (MPS) is one example; the new products and new cells established during the research period provide many others. The quality journey at Metalco was talked about and lived as a learning journey of continuous change.

Control and Standardization

As I tried to understand the literacy practices of the work culture of Metalco, I focused on the people using the documentation system, and the document system that shaped and directed the work of the people. One of the engineering managers explained to me his view of why there had to be controls of work procedures and of documents. He said the goal of process control is to find the best inherently error-proof way of doing the job safely, and with the least waste of time, energy or materials. In this explanation from a taped interview, he also stresses understanding and the limits of participation and autonomy:

> There needs to be some control over how the parts are assembled; for instance, people need to understand some basic things. Things like, people don't get to work differently. You know, if there's six people in there [working in a production cell] and they each work a different way, there's probably one best way of working.... Okay, now the team (with maybe an engineering person and a production manager or whatever) ... will agree upon the best way. And then everybody will work that way. Because didn't we just agree it was the best way? It may not be your way, but that's where this idea of these Standard Operating Procedures comes out. The team defines it. You can change it tomorrow. And you can change it the next day. But when the team says, "This is the best way to work ... or the Standard Operating Procedure," then that's the way everybody works. 'Cause you don't want it to get away from certain principles [for error-proofing your work].
>
> It used to be left very much to the [production] supervisor in the old days, ... [but] we just can't work that way anymore. We need to do a lot more planning beforehand. We've got a lot less time to get these things done. And we're very, very conscious of including the people.

So this manager at least sees continuous change and Continuous Improvement at Metalco within an overall agreement that these changes are negotiated with a team, and evolved within tight criteria. This manager told me that they are not trying to do everything the way Japanese manufacturers do, because Metalco has different people and its own goals. The way he described process control and incremental change to a single team standard is in line with world movements to emulate the Toyota Production System as the best way to manufacture products.

All of the stories in this chapter have to be understood as operating within this overriding concern for control and standardization as keys to making reliable quality products. The managers are trying to involve people in order to get their participation within this system. To do this, the understandings they need to communicate include this concept of Standard Operating Procedures.

The "No-Blame" Environment

Another one of the ideas that the managers at Metalco were actively trying to get people to put into action and make their own was the idea of a "no-blame" environment. This approach is promoted in Manufacturing Excellence courses supported by the company and its business organizations.[3] "No-blame" means not pointing fingers at people when things go wrong, but instead looking for problems in the overall business process. Starting from a position that problems and mistakes have sources in the system is supposed to make it easier to move on to solutions. Running "blameless" also promises to keep people interacting on a positive or neutral base, without investing time and energy on recriminations. There were posters on the walls of the production areas with no-blame symbols: a pointing finger surrounded by a red circle with a line through. I heard managers in meetings reminding each other, "No blame" when the discussion of a quality problem strayed into naming names.

One manager said that there still was blame, of course, but he saw the no-blame idea spreading because it worked. When I asked the senior managers about blamelessness another one said that achieving a no-blame environment "might not be likely ... but let it be a goal—it's a good goal." A no-blame environment focuses attention on process, giving managers the strategy to act rather than to lament their people, their equipment or their competition. We will see situations in this chapter where this no-blame philosophy is tested.

Our group of researchers wondered how this no-blame environment affected literacy practices at Metalco. Is there a connection between no-blame and workers participating in literacy practices? As we have seen in "blame" environments, participating in literacy practices through work documentation can mean trouble for workers. In a workplace with an explicit goal of not blaming individuals, but rather looking at the overall systems, what would happen when mistakes were made or there were production problems? I asked a production worker if someone could get in trouble for keeping production charts (that is, participating in the literacies of his job) if the charts showed that there was a problem. He told me: "If the machine goes wrong, then the parts are in trouble. It's not the person in trouble."

And then he laughed. At the time I thought he was a little embarrassed by my question. Later we wondered if his laugh was an ac-

---

[3]Metalco is part of several organizations that promote Manufacturing Excellence and sharing of information between noncompeting companies. Several of these associations promote the "no-blame" approach to management, as does the Association for Manufacturing Excellence. The no-blame approach is described in, for example, Hogg (1999).

knowledgment of the complexity of such a situation, as if he were saying that in theory the parts are in trouble, but things can get complicated. Perhaps he meant to convey that it was unlikely an inanimate part could be blamed, so blame would still fall on the person closest to the fault, the worker. Whatever that laugh meant to the worker, it gave us pause and made us look carefully at the occasions when literacies rubbed against work processes, "no-blame" goals and the degree of participation. We knew by the time I spoke to that worker that things were different at Metalco than at our other sites: Part of the difference was the attitude and actions of the managers.

Managers in a Learning Environment

As a researcher and an educator, I was interested in what people said about learning, and I paid special attention to what they did. At Metalco, people, especially people in positions of leadership, had a lot to say about learning, and most of it was not simplistic. People here seemed to understand that learning is a human activity, something people engage in for social as well as functional motivations. When people at Metalco talked about learning and training, they talked about choices, about feelings. I came to see this as another feature that distinguished Metalco from our other research sites: People had an understanding of learning as more than just drumming information into people's heads.

An engineer who has worked closely with workers on the shop floor said that for him, the key was accepting that it would always take more than one kind of training opportunity to get something new going. He explained that group training, written procedures and one-on-one support were the norm for everyone: vice-presidents, engineers and shop workers. He has come to understand and accept that "You do have to let people, within reason, learn the way that best suits them." I found this to be a powerful insight from a leader in the company, who reminded me that he had learned it 10 years ago as part of our workplace education program.

Another long-term senior manager whom I observed working on new training and getting ideas from people about what learning situations could work for them told me that one of the most important things he brought to his job was a distinction between training and education. Like the engineer quoted earlier, this senior manager did not locate training issues in the literacy levels of his workers. In his thinking, understanding and participation are central to how engaged people are in training, and in all aspects of their work:

> Irrespective of literacy [or other skills], there are issues related to how involved people are in the process and the work. The understanding is the key. If people can buy in to the purpose and see why there is value here ...

in the quality systems, in SPC.... People need that buy-in. They need to understand how they can participate.

The hows and whys of participation hinge on meanings and under-standings, and at Metalco, many people seem to know that. When man-agers or leaders talk about communication as a challenge, they refer to making information, but also background and systems knowledge and goals available to production workers, and the reverse, making pro-duction experiences part of what engineers and managers know. How then do they talk about skills and literacy? Remember Metalco sup-ports adult education and is especially committed to improving oral and written communication. They have had long-term contact with workplace education through colleges and consultants. When people name the challenge facing them, they don't say "illiteracy" or "low skill levels." Some sample phrases I heard include "people who do not read regularly," and "people not too comfortable speaking up." One of the Quality Assurance people, a man whose job keeps him between the production workers and the engineers and managers, offered this comment, which includes both a positive interpretation of learning and a respect for meanings: "When they ask, I teach them, and so every day almost I say to someone: 'Let's learn this together.' It's not really teaching. Anyways, operators need to see the value of it."

Again we see an emphasis on "seeing the value," and the view that this highly technical lab worker is learning with the operators. At Metalco I did not see the Quality Assurance people putting themselves above shop workers in their interactions or in their words.

We will look at a number of situations that showed me the layers of meaning revealed in unraveling a production problem, looking for rea-sons, causes, meanings and interpretations. But first, walk with me through the door to Metalco.

WELCOME TO METALCO

As we walk through the public entrance to Metalco, through a modest reception foyer in the old building, we might notice that the carpets here are new and the walls freshly-painted to make a good first impression. One of the young female receptionists sits behind a counter that has a clipboard and a flower arrangement on it. Visitors sign in on a form held on the clipboard before receiving a badge that allows them either es-corted or unescorted access through the site. There is a large company name and a black sign with changeable letters on the wall behind the re-ceptionist. The sign is changed daily and welcomes important visitors like customers and people from corporate headquarters by name, com-pany and often city. There are important visitors several times a week.

Also in the reception area is a display of metal and plastic products in a showcase, attractively arranged and well lit, like art. The average person would have a difficult time identifying them, though. They are from the insides of machines, the precise unseen parts of mechanisms that make things work. There are plaques and awards, and brief descriptions of the parts in the display. The company's value and philosophy statement is engraved on a plaque over the display case.

As a researcher and not an employee, I always sign in here, and the receptionist gives me a warm welcome and a clip-on badge for unescorted access to the site. Once we have badges, we are free to walk around the office or production areas of this building and one building next door.

On the Production Floor: Parts and Paperwork, Layers of Literacies

To go to the production area, we have to go through a door with a sign on it warning, "You are now entering a Controlled Materials Location." The sign instructs that all material must be identified and labeled. On the other side of the door, another sign reminds people leaving the shop that they are entering an "Uncontrolled Materials Location."

Opening the door to the shop floor is a bit of a surprise. First, the space seems huge. There is no second floor here, so the ceiling is far overhead. Then there is the noise. Above the steady hum of the ventilation and the chug of machinery, there is a hum of speech. Intermittently comes the loud rushing sound of pressurized air, a sound most of us know from the dentist's office. There is also a buzz of hand tools and the sound of radios, tuned to music, news and talk in several languages, so walking around is an unexpected sound mosaic. The smell is distinctly the smell of a machine shop, a metallic oily odor characteristic of metal works. It is the smell of lubricants and metal filings. You can't smell this at all in the office; you can't avoid this smell in the shop. It is not unpleasant. I've heard people say they like the smell, and they like the way it welcomes them to work. I've grown to like the smell, too.

The colors are another surprise. Most of the lathes and machining centers are gray, but others are brightly colored: blue, green, red. One is even pink. Some of the fixtures and shelving is orange, and the staircases that lead to the upper office floors and the lunchroom area are red. The assembly areas have rows of yellow bins. There is a lot of color here, although little natural light. I am told that although color-coding the work areas and the product families might have been a good idea, these bright colors were chosen without a plan. The splashes of color are just punctuation on the gray production floor, each chosen by whoever had the choice.

The production workers here wear blue coveralls with their first names embroidered on a patch over their left breast pocket. They smile or greet me when I pass by. They all wear protective goggles or glasses with side panels. I do, too. I walk within the safe walkway, marked on the concrete floor by green lines. Just outside the green is another line, painted yellow. Once off the safe green path that bisects the shop floor, safety equipment is mandatory. There are shields and guards, and much of the actual shaping of metal parts is done away from view deep inside closed machines. But it is still dangerous here, and people are very careful.

In the months of my research, I spent time over many shifts with men who operated machines that shape the metal parts. Some were experienced operators, some were machinists who could program the computer controls, and some were lead hands with responsibilities for coordinating people and tasks. Two were new employees still learning the job. These operators worked on the day and afternoon shifts in the two buildings.

I have known more than 30 Machine Operators through the work-place education program, but I never really understood their work until I spent such extended time at the side of workers in their machining cells. Although the specifics of running any machine to make any part are different, these jobs looked similar from the outside. The jobs have a rhythm set up by the different cycles of the machines and by the opera-tor's movement around his workspace. Even I found myself glancing at a machine seconds before it stopped running, or seconds before a part popped out. There is a rhythm, too, to the measuring, checking and charting, to the cleaning and polishing, to the work breaks and the times that the lead hand stops by. Reading and interpreting printed data, drawings and numbers on printed pages and on computer screens are some of the literacy practices that are seamlessly part of the work.

I chose to shadow the people who ran machinery because they were front-line production workers who dealt with a lot of documents. "Twenty years ago there was no paperwork. Now there's lots," one pro-duction worker told me. This is exactly what all the literature says about workplace change as discussed in the Introduction and elsewhere in this book. But I wanted to know in living detail how production workers in this high-tech manufacturing plant used their literacies. What mean-ings did all the documents hold? How did they see themselves, their "literacies-in-use" and the documentation system?

Because I was tracing the documentation system, I could see that many forms, charts and checklists, points of data collection for the overall information system of the company, passed through their hands. Most of the critical information about their work seemed to be conveyed through print, even when it was also expressed orally through interaction with a lead hand, or when it was well known to them through experience and routine. Feedback on production tar-gets, on-time delivery and warranty returns came to these workers through charted data, usually explained in person and then hung on a bulletin board for reference. Through these charted data, managers believe they are communicating vital information about production and quality. Both the workers themselves and managers told me that the literacy and communication demands of these production jobs were increasing, not just through production documentation, but also through team meetings and problem-solving groups. This is also a well-recognized feature of what writers like Gee, Hull and Lankshear (1996) term "the new work order."

Machine Operators are people who run a computer-controlled machining center, but who do not program the machine for new set-ups or unusual occurrences. This is not an entry-level position, but it is not considered very difficult. Some people become operators after only a few months on the job. The machining centers are all a bit different, with different equipment. Most of the time the individual worker (or someone before him) has had a hand in placing and spacing the machine: the little tables, benches and stands and the secondary equipment for cleaning up and polishing the parts.

For example, a medium-sized machining center dominates Albert's station. It is about the size of a family van. Long cylinders of aluminum sit on an inclined feeder at the back. The computer controls are over the double doors in the center section, which open to reveal the cutting tools, fixtures and the other bits that actually shape the metal, and the finished parts drop gently on to a conveyer belt that runs along the front. Should Albert not pick up the parts right away, they drop into a bucket of water at the end of the belt. The water is clouded with lubricant and metal filings. This machine takes about 4 minutes to make each part. During that 4-minute cycle, Albert cleans the part of any bits of metal, tests the dimensions for size, and charts the size of every fifth one on his SPC chart before adding it to the rack. Figure 4.1 is an example chart. The charting is seamless with the measurement, done in the few seconds available in the rhythm of the job process.

Another rack of work-in-progress sits beside a machine at Albert's secondary station, where he performs a side job on each part. He can perform this secondary job on two or three parts in a minute. The next step is to hone or polish the part, and clean it up for an anodized coating process. All of this seems to me to be noisy and tiring work. Albert stands up for his whole shift, and so do I. The machines make loud noises as the metal is shaped, and the pressurized air used to clean off the parts is even louder. I strain to listen to Albert through my protective earplugs. I soon make a note to myself that there is some irony in identifying communication as a concern here. It is very hard to talk near the machines, and even harder to listen. In my notes I write that a chatty person (like me) might learn to be quiet in this kind of job.

There are a few racks of completed work on the floor, waiting for the materials handler to take to shipping at the end of the shift. Albert told me he sometimes gets the handcart and takes them over, but most of the time they are picked up. He can do this job alone, but he talks to people at intervals through his shift to see if anyone needs help and to check what is happening in his area. His job is to supply parts to an as-

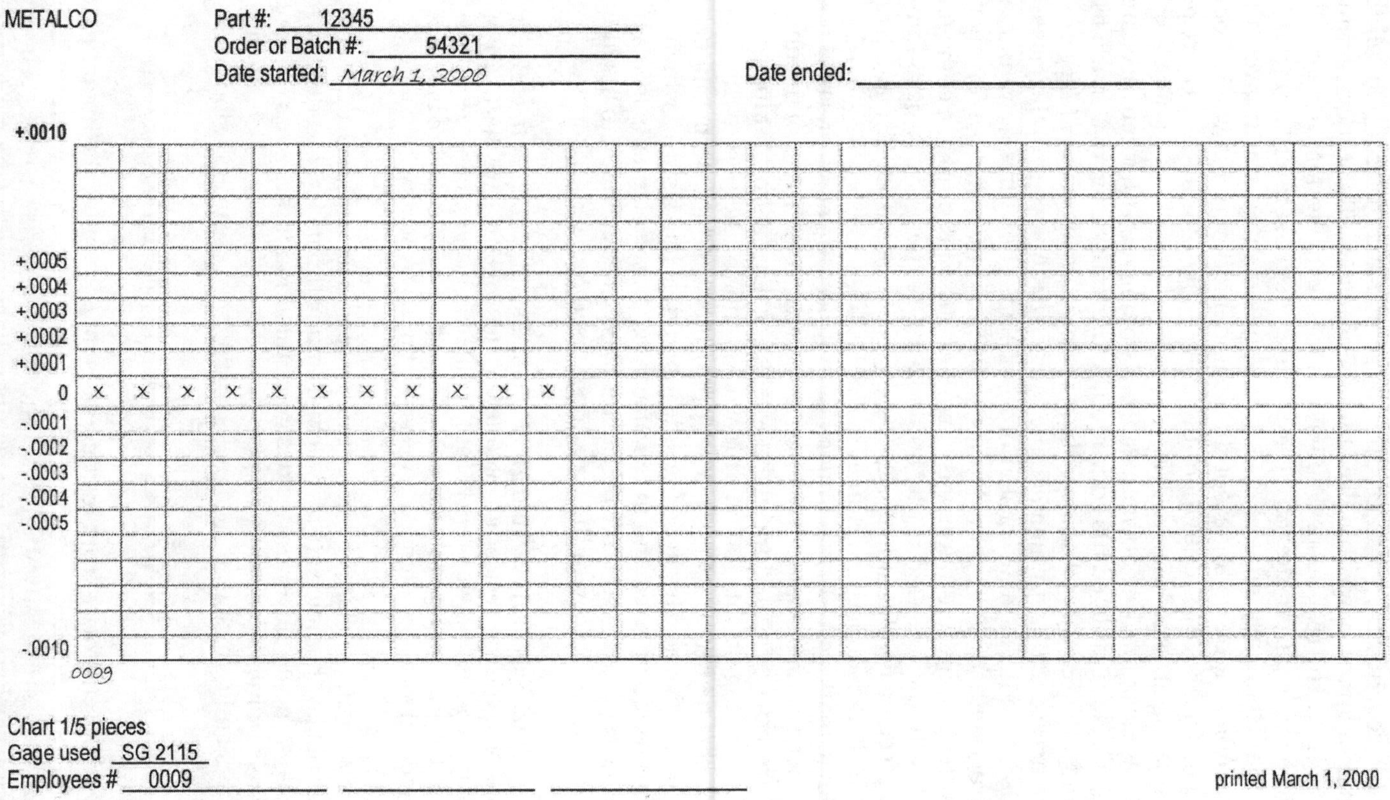
METALCO
Part #: 12345
Order or Batch #: 54321
Date started: March 1, 2000
Date ended:
+.0010
+.0005
+.0004
+.0003
+.0002
+.0001
0
-.0001
-.0002
-.0003
-.0004
-.0005
-.0010
x x x x x x x x x x x
0009
Chart 1/5 pieces
Gage used SG 2115
Employees # 0009
printed March 1, 2000

FIG. 4.1. SPC run chart. This figure is a composite from similar original documents adapted by the authors to preserve anonymity.

sembly cell, and his work group is large. I asked Albert about all the forms and paperwork that I see him using, especially at the beginning of his shift. His response: "You have to follow the system for a quality company. It's part of the job." It looks like the most interesting part of the job. His machine works with no adjustments from him on this shift. Albert appears to accept the documentation of his work. Soon, though, I hear of Machine Operators in the other building who were not completing all their paperwork.

Albert is in his 50s; born in Asia, he is bilingual with fluent accented English. He completed his education before emigrating to Canada as a young lathe operator. I know Albert from years ago when Mary and I were here teaching, though I am not sure if he took part in the classes. He is active in the new version of workplace education now, and encourages others. Albert invited me to spend time with him for my research. "If you want to know the truth about this company, come and work with me," he said. I was hoping for an exposé, but what I found was a senior production worker who feels he has seen things change for the better under new managers' ideas.

Participation at work is important to Albert. He characterized himself to me as an outspoken worker, and an active member of the union. One experience he told me about was the real decision-making role he had in setting up this job and his workstation. "I helped to make this process. I helped to make this set-up," Albert told me with a flicker of pride in his voice. He chose the side job and he had a say in which machines would be used and in the placement of the elements in his machining cell. He showed me the customized fixtures made to his liking. He contrasted this with the way things used to be:

> Before they decided everything and you had to do it whether it works or not. Now you can decide and make it work for you. You have the luxury of that. It comes from different bosses or different management ideas. This kind of involvement or participation is good for people. Before they pretended that you could make a decision, but now you can.

This is what managers told me they were trying to do, and again, this is in keeping with management system thinking (Imai, 1997). I did not see many examples of workspace design of this kind in progress, although workers in many cells were helping to tinker with their space, changing fixtures and reducing storage racks during the research period.

THE MEANINGS OF DOCUMENTS AND LITERACIES

I have chosen stories from my time at Metalco to show the meanings of documents and literacies in use as I observed them and was told about them. They are mostly about Machine Operators; as we have seen, production workers who run the machines that shape the metal parts that are later assembled into Metalco products. These men give similar meanings to the reading and writing they do. The stories move along a technology curve, from Albert, an operator working alone in an old-fashioned process, to workers in a new production system machining cell where they work in flexible groups, to workers in the most high-tech machining cell in the company, where many different parts are made to order. To understand these stories, we will stop in the Quality Assurance work group, which originates and collects the process documents and charts. The understandings people have depend upon where, how and with whom they work closely.

Albert and the Old-fashioned Process

Machine Operators work with a surprising number of forms. The document practices required of them have at least two meanings for them. The information is required to show what happened in production and for warranty; and keeping careful track of work processes through documents also reassures operators that the parts and the process are good. Some of the paperwork Albert showed me is common to all machining jobs at Metalco. Every machine has a daily maintenance checklist. This is a standard form with a list of functions and fluids to check off every day. There are about a dozen things to check: lubricant and coolant levels, electrical connections and the like. The check is usually done at the start of the first shift.

Every machine also has a small white board marked with a grid table somewhere nearby, usually facing the green-lined walkway. The grid on the white board shows which jobs and parts are running on the machine, and which ones are coming up. All the shifts are represented with projected numbers for the parts or products to be made, the actual numbers and a comment area to explain any difference. These boards are part of a "visual display system" that is another textbook feature of high-performance manufacturing (Imai, 1997). Anyone walking past can see at a glance what is going on with any machine. Across the top of the board, on little colored cards the size of business cards, are job order cards. These represent the production priority of the present and upcoming jobs. There is a weekly list of parts shortages printed out from the materials management system. A parts shortage could change the priority of jobs to be run.

In this example at Albert's station, as throughout the production floor, getting meaning from the visual display means interpreting representative numbers, colors and shapes, a sophisticated literacy that requires detailed understandings of the job. To read these displays is to read the entire work of a production cell in a few key numbers and words. To me it seems like explicating poetry, where relationships and layers of significance reveal themselves only to the most knowledgeable readers. And like poetry, the readers may draw meanings not apparent to the writers. These are meaningful communications only to those who understand the job, the products and the circumstances.

As he works and explains his job to me, Albert moves among checking the machine and the newly made parts, the side job and the cleanup, and the documents that he uses to guide and record what he is doing. It takes almost an hour for Albert to show me all the charts, drawings and print information involved in his job. He talks to me between the machine cycles, and as he does so, the side job and the honing and polishing fall behind. He interrupts his explanations to measure many more parts than the minimum required by the charting. He explains that he does this for his own peace of mind. He also explains that he views the work process documentation that he uses intermittently as part of the job, part of how things work in a quality company:

> No matter what kind of parts you are making, it is important to do the check [of the part dimensions]. It makes us feel more comfortable to run the job. For us [Machine Operators], checking the gage and checking the parts is more important than the writing down. Writing it down [on the charts and inspection forms] is for the records. In case maybe assembly has a problem and they need to know, then we can look.

Albert was not the only Machine Operator to talk to me about his feelings of comfort and confidence in his job. The margin of error is very small. For most parts it is one tenth of a thousandth of an inch, 0.0001 inches. This is a tolerance too small to see. Digital read-out gauges are essential. Knowing that the parts are just the right size makes the operator comfortable. If he is not sure or not confident, I learned, he is supposed to stop and get help solving the problem.

There are other documents that are filled out for particular parts made and job orders being done. During the time I was with Albert, these documents came to him in a blue folder. In other parts of the plant further along in MPS/TPS implementation, the job order comes directly from a list of customer orders. These parallel systems, one being phased out and the other gaining prominence, are another example of change in this workplace. Although Metalco is striving for world class manufacturing practices, there are many instances of uneven implementation; the parallel order system is one of the obvious ones. Albert is working on the old system, but his job, and in fact, Albert is making the transition to TPS/MPS manufacturing.

Albert's jobs come to him in documents tucked into folders. For each job the folder contains the job order form or routing sheet (a computer printout of the details of the quantity and part order with a bar code on the page for tracking labor costs), the most up-to-date engineering drawing of the part and the Inspection Form for intensive verification that the first part run is within all specs. SPC charts for tracking part size through Statistical Process Control are also in the folder, ready for use. With the raw material or the in-process parts comes an official tag called a Materials Movement Ticket, which is used to indicate the status and process of the parts as they are made and moved around. Albert showed me how he entered his employee number and tracked his work and the parts' status. I watched as he measured two interior dimensions and saw that the parts were near perfect to the center of the measurements, what they would call "near zero." Figure 4.1 is an example of this kind of chart.

Albert works on a stable process that he says is "set up with confidence." Feeling confident is important and meaningful to him. He shows me the Statistical Process Control sheets for that week and for the previous month and how they document the parts' size right down the middle—near perfect and well within the tiny tolerance margin. He seems proud of his work. Although he said earlier these charts were for the record, his actions indicate that the charts have a second meaning. They show him that the machine is running well and requires no adjustment. It is clear to me that his understandings of how the charts track the process lead him to faithfully use print. He does this to satisfy himself as much as to fulfill his formal job requirements.

These two meanings are the ones I heard repeatedly on the shop. For example, another day on another shift over in the other building, I saw Frank, a new Machine Operator learning about the same kind of process tracking SPC-run charts that Albert used. He works across the parking lot from Albert, in the New Building, where the production floor space is easily identified by cell. Here they never did mass production or old-fashioned manufacturing. The distinctive U-shaped assembly area cells are well labeled with hanging signs naming the part families made there. The machining centers that supply the assembly cells are nearby. Here there are only new machines, some as small as household refrigerators, but most larger than family vans. Again, the colors, the oily metallic smell and the range of sounds are surprising. The New Building production floor has three stories of orange shelving, floor to ceiling, for racking parts, and some colorful machinery. The area is very clean and the high ceiling and natural light make for a pleasant space. In summer, though, the windows that let in the natural light have a greenhouse effect, and the New Building production floor is hot.

It was a very warm summer afternoon when I shadowed Frank, a worker in his early 20s. He had been in his job only 2 weeks and I did not know him. I was shadowing other people in his work neighborhood, and eventually he asked me what I was doing. I got his consent to hang around and research his experiences. His work group was using the newer system where more communication is printed from the computer and presented only as numbers in columns. He was running parts and building products to customer orders, based on a single order summary sheet from the computer data system. The other forms in use were standard, the same as the ones Albert used. The engineering drawing for the part was held onto the machining center with magnets. The maintenance checklist hung on a clipboard and the Statistical Process Control charts were on the top of a red tool crib at table height.

About an hour into the shift, Frank is checking parts when the group's lead hand, George, stops by to recalibrate tools with him. I know George very well. He was one of the first production workers I followed, and he is an enthusiastic learner in the workplace education program. Adjusting the gauges, or checking that they are adjusted correctly, is a little tricky and Frank has been waiting for George before trying it. George is in his 30s and has been with the company for about two years. By Machine Operators' standards, they are both "new guys." While the machines grind around us, I remove an earplug to try to listen in on their conversation, writing their words as quickly as I can. The leader shows Frank how to check that the gauge is adjusted correctly, and then together they put an "X" on the SPC chart. "If we get out, even by say a thou, then the parts could go off spec over a long time." George tells Frank the charts show that everything is okay, but George can see that the chart is almost full, with little room to record part sizes in the afternoon's run, which means they will soon be ready to send off to the Quality Assurance Department. So George says: "We can finish this job tonight, then the chart will go to Dan [in Quality Assurance]. He will see where it is off from the zero, and he'll come back and tell us, but we already know. That's our job to keep the measures near zero."

In George and Frank's conversation, we can hear the special meanings the recorded numbers and the relationships between the numbers have for them. As outsiders, how could our numeracy or literacy transfer to this particular way of reading work if we did not know that the "zero" in their conversation has two referents, just as they had for Albert? The first is physical. The inside diameter of these round parts is measured on a calibrated gage set to the ideal exact size. A reading of +.001 is a bit too big; −.001 is too small. Zero is just right. In the conversation between Frank and George, the second referent is on the SPC chart. The mid-line is zero and sizes plus or minus are charted either side of the zero, trending small or large in .0001 increments.

Another Machine Operator stops by and joins the conversation. I later learn he is one of the people who taught George. He tells them, "The charts are basically for us so we can see how the machine is doing. If it suddenly changes, then we will know. Also, Quality picks them up. They need to keep track too." Some charts, he says, are more complicated than others: "The main thing is to be consistent. Some people they see the same chart month after month, and they wonder why. But we have to do this for warranty and for if anything happens in the field."

For these workers, who were farther into the implementation of TPS/MPS and data-driven work, the two meanings are the same as they were for Albert in his more old-fashioned machining cell: Charts are for keeping track of the process and keeping a record of product quality for warranty. And here, in a work group of "new guys," I saw how workers learn together how to work with these data-intensive documents. I saw them learning what the documents are for, how their work touches the work of other departments, and how charting matters to the customer in the field. The workers' knowledge is passed along; their meanings are shared. The new worker is brought into the group of Machine Operators. Their literacy practices are socially constructed through these kinds of interactions. Here at Metalco, their participation is infused with understandings that make their work and their literacies meaningful.

Quality Assurance: A Documentation Hub

Leaving the shop floor, toward the offices at the front of the Old Building, takes us past the Quality Assurance work areas. These two rooms on either side of the passageway are a transitional area between the industrial production area and the office. There are desks, workstations and cubicles, and also simulators and elaborate measurement equipment. The people who work in this area wear white lab coats, with their names over their hearts. They greet us with a big smile and we stop to talk for a few minutes.

I found the people in this department to be keen learners. They were studying through the workplace education program and one was a volunteer mentor. They were quick to seek help and to offer it. Quality Assurance work puts these half-dozen people at a hub of the evolution of technology advancement and the changing documentation of manufacturing processes. They are among the people who suggest changes to the ways products are measured and the ways records are kept.

All of the half-dozen people here are "old guys" who have social ties throughout the company. They came out of production to invent and fulfill the jobs of assuring quality for Metalco. They have done this job since before the laser-measuring devices and databases they use every day were part of the tools available. They have a range of job duties and frequently interact with people over production, design and marketing. They also interact with customers and suppliers. Among their responsibilities, they program and run technical equipment to measure and simulate processes. They initiate, maintain and file the records that document process controls and production equipment calibration. They are included in problem-solving teams. One of the Quality Assurance workers is responsible for setting up all of the run charts and graphs for collecting the piece-by-piece data for Statistical Process Control. Another figures out how parts will be measured and how the measuring tools will be calibrated, and keeps all the information about measuring tools throughout the company. Quality Assurance workers also do, and track, the more difficult product measurements, like flatness, concentricity and perpendicularity, using specialized programmable equipment. Their work area and white lab coats signal that they are not production workers, but not office workers either.

Joe Lang works in Quality Assurance. He is in his late 40s, and quick to smile. He is an example of a worker with high participation in the print communication systems of the company and a high level of knowledge of the quality documentation systems. He shows me a sample of the documentation that originates here, circles through the production areas of the plant, and ends up back in Quality Assurance. Joe pulls out an engineering drawing of a small part, a component in one of the company's main products. For the feature of the part described on the drawing as critical to functioning, in this case the diameter, two forms are started for the product run initiated by a customer order. The first form is used to check that the machines are set up and running correctly and that the parts are the right size. It is called an Inspection Form, and has places for the exact values of several dimensions of the part to be entered, and places for signatures and dates to verify when the parts were made and by whom. The second form is for collecting size data over a production run of parts. This Run Chart is the data collection instrument of the Statistical Process Control program.

There are other forms, too. A Scrap Log to keep track of the numbers of and reasons for rejected parts, for instance, is started and checked by Quality Assurance. Joe shows me more of the system of databases and intersecting bits of information that are invisible from the shop floor and from the educator's desk. Each kind of form is part of a series; cumulative data are kept so that changes over time can be charted. Every one of these documents is like a data point in the overall system. Few production workers would see them all the way Joe does.

Joe knows the reasons for all the measurements and he knows where the forms come from, whom they come from and how they work in the system. His overview is close to that of the engineers and the managers with whom he works closely. One of the things he tells me is that the system depends on Machine Operators and lead hands collecting accurate data. The little X marks and dots they put on graphs and the reasons they note down are transcribed into numerical data that are again presented in charts, extrapolated and used to make decisions. Poor data will give a false picture when it is accumulated, and a badly distorted one when it is statistically projected. For Joe and the other people in Quality Assurance, the production data collection forms are very meaningful, and those forms feed the even more important systems data on the quality of products.

The Quality Assurance people see the layers of meaning and layers of priority in Metalco's documentation. For instance, Joe told me that a trend, even one distorted by a projection, might trigger an expensive action such as purchasing new equipment or redesigning a process if a high-priority part critical to product function is shown to be in jeopardy in an analysis of SPC charts or other data collected by production workers. Those same forms in use in the production shop are less connected to the system. It is harder for workers, and for me as a researcher, to generalize about the overall system from the floor, where each form is identified with a customer order or a product run. In other words, from the information hub of the Quality Assurance Department, it's easier to understand how all the forms fit together into a system and what they mean when they are put together. For any individual Machine Operator, dealing with only a few parts and the documents for those parts, it's harder to see or understand the many layers of meaning of how everything works together.

SPC Compliance: Meanings Behind a Skills Paradox

The following is a different SPC chart story. It is still about workers' literacies in relation to quality documents, and their encouragement to write and chart numbers as part of the culture of documentation of this workplace, and as part of the system that tracks the reliability and quality of the production process. The story explains a workplace documentation puzzle: Why do older "low-literacy" workers keep accurate work process charts while young workers with complete educations do not? The answer isn't a skills contradiction. The answer is in the local meanings the documents have for the workers.

One day I was told by several different sources that workers in one of the New Building production cells organized on a job rotation system were not keeping their charts correctly. These were the same SPC production process tracking charts that Albert in his old-fashioned batch set-up, and Frank and George in their fully implemented MPS/TPS machining cell, were keeping just right. On the surface this might look like a classic issue for workplace training. Compliance with quality program documentation is basic to doing the job. Albert told me that; Frank and George showed it, too. Other workers at Metalco, ones who might be characterized as the least flexible in that they have done the same work for many years, were keeping perfect charts. Here was a paradox. Older workers, some with minimal education, many with limited English, were doing a great job of following the documentation system. Younger, well-educated workers were not. They were measuring the parts and writing down the measurements over time, but not actually plotting the graph. There was an issue with their literacies-in-use here. But was it a literacy skills problem? I doubted it. The workers in the flexible cell were young, with a minimum grade 12 education. At least one of them had a machining ticket from a local technical college.

When I spent time in their machining area, what I saw was not very different from what I saw other Machine Operators doing. One difference was that most machines are mass-producing parts in runs of a thousand or more. A few machines are dedicated to one part. The machining center in this area is specially made for short runs. A hundred, or even a single pallet of, for example, 20 parts is a normal run. This is a responsive, "just-in-time," make-to-customer-order machine for the parts in less demand.

Every machine that is shaping metal in this area is running a specific program. The program has a cycle time, the time it takes from loading the pallet with raw or partially machined parts to the finish. The cycle time can be anything from a few minutes to 20 or even 40 minutes, depending on the complexity of the part. The machining center that this three-person crew works with is the most complex in the place. It has an incredibly short set-up time, and a very large number of cutting tools and pallets.

Because the parts run changes frequently, the job does not have the cycle rhythm of the other machining jobs I observed. Where other operators get into a rhythm and an automatic sense of when the cycle would stop, these guys react to the machine, keeping an eye on the digital time readout, rather than becoming accustomed to the time between loads. They read engineering drawings for exact part measurements, measure and record the dimensions of the parts they made, do the intermittent measurements of critical features of the parts, and fill out the SPC process tracking charts. Like all the Machine Operators, they also have side jobs to smooth and polish the parts that come out of their machining centers. By the time I got over to see them, they were measuring, charting and plotting their parts, and there was a new gung-ho leader assigned to the cell. "So what happened?" I asked. It seemed as though these workers shared the meaning that we heard from Albert, Frank and George, that keeping charts was for warranty, but they did not share the meaning that keeping the charts made them feel confident that things were running right.

I heard the story of what happened in this cell from several sources. Managers and people from the Quality Assurance Department told me they traced a couple of contradictory messages from different sources in the division. One was from the Manufacturing Engineer (ME), who confirmed in conversation with me that it was his opinion that keeping SPC charts on small lots wasn't statistically useful for collecting data for tracking trends: "Because you don't do a whole bunch. A run of a part for that machine might just be 20. And then you run 40, and then in two weeks you run 20 again. You just don't get useful data." But a little later this ME said, "I don't want to be quoted saying that SPC is not important. It is."

This is a key message to the Machine Operators who would have daily contact with their Manufacturing Engineer. SPC is important in lots of ways to production, but maybe not here, in the case of these short runs. Another contradictory message this crew had been receiving was from their Production Manager, who was not placing any stress on these charts. He was oriented solely to the production numbers. If the product was good, and shipped on time, then he was happy. Not long after this, his responsibilities were shifted and this crew reported to another Production Manager. Joe Lang in the Quality Assurance Department was clear on the root cause of the failure to chart:

> It's up to the leadership. At first [that cell] didn't keep their forms [charts], but now, with the new leader in there, they do.... A person will give thousands of reasons not to do the charts. "Too busy," "I forgot." If they don't do it, it's attitude. It's simple stuff, not complicated. ... I think the old ones understand. But new people, maybe not. If you do the charts, the reports make sense.

The reports referred to here are the quality reports on long-term trends, the statistical spread of part sizes within the allowed specification. These are meaningful reports to the Quality Assurance people in both a mathematical and practical sense. What was most interesting to me about this story is that no-one blamed the workers. No-one suggested they were unskilled, or that they needed further training on how to keep control charts.

When I spoke to the leader, I asked for his perspective. What did he do when he joined the cell? His answer? "Complain, complain, complain." From his point of view there were a lot of barriers to keeping the paperwork straight in that machining cell, and he needed help from several departments to set things back on track:

> I know the stats are important, so I just went to the different managers and said we need better gauges, and we need all the right stuff for all our parts. And then, with the crew, I went and got all the charts (they weren't there), and just started in. We took a new start, and retrained on it together. It wasn't hard once I had everyone together.

I understood better how this came to reflect on the manager. If they did not have the charts and gauges, then it was at least partly a management responsibility. Of course, the workers told me that they all knew they were expected by the ISO registration to complete all procedures in the standard way. And they all knew that, ISO or not, they are required to measure and record exact sizes during production. They just came to think that it wouldn't really matter if they didn't fully complete their SPC charts. So they didn't.

As I worked through these points of view on a seemingly simple story about some people not completing their process documents, I saw contradictions in the quality system, too. These workers are now keeping complete forms for the sake of being in complete compliance with the system. If the engineer is right, the data is useful only for warranty and not for process control. I realized that the Machine Operators must have very high confidence in their programs and cutting tools, or they would need to chart the measurements if only to know when a cutting edge was getting dull and needed replacing.

A Production Manager from a different department than the ones these Machine Operators worked in offered the opinion that completing documents was about following through and doing the job the way it is supposed to be done. He was quick to take on responsibility, saying: "Following through, you know. It's a lot of time; it's created by us (mangers) because we are so busy. A lot of times they would do certain things and they meant to come back and fill it out afterwards ... and they forget."

I asked this manager, who is one of the younger ones, if he has ever disciplined a worker for something like that. He said he never had: "No, what we try to do is encourage people to explain to them what it means." This is one of many instances where managers at Metalco focused on meanings, and on communicating their meanings to workers as one of their responsibilities and sometimes one of their failings. My experience supports what this manager says. I never heard a story or saw an instance of a worker being disciplined or yelled at for not "following through."

Joe, the long-term employee from Quality Assurance, told me a lot about the original teaching of Statistical Process Control (SPC) and about how it works today. "In the beginning, nobody could see the benefit. We tried to show and we tried to teach it [SPC]. If you do this, you will have a good process and less chance to make errors and feel bad. If you do this, you'll feel good about yourself. You'll feel confidence."

Here Joe is telling us how they constructed the usefulness of SPC as a way to understand the processes. Benefits hold meanings for people. He is also expressing the same need for comfort with the job, to know that errors are not happening and bad parts aren't being produced. Joe said that workers who stay in one job for a time have the chance to see improvements made to the process using MPS/TPS (flexible manufacturing) and the SPC charts, both while the process is running and through the reports his departments sends back when the charts are analyzed. In the New Building, according to Joe, with people moving around, they weren't seeing the benefit: "Put yourself in their place," he urged. "You're sitting there all day doing de-burring. All day long. How do you feel? It feels unimportant. All day long, so you are just not motivated to do the charts."

To read your work, to engage in literacies at work, a person has to be motivated. This seems to be a characteristic Metalco understanding not shared at our other research sites. Joe went on to suggest that workers who are not keeping charts should be part of a project so they can see the benefits of keeping data. Again, benefits stress purpose and meanings. Then he said, "Take another step back. How much training do they get? Not much." Here is one of those instances at Metalco where people talked about work, feelings and training in the same breath.

Joe seemed to say that training is important and people working in production need to know how to complete the forms, but also they need to see the benefits of these SPC practices that are on the surface conceptually disconnected from parts production. And finally, people need to be encouraged and supported to feel good about what they are asked to do.

Joe has managed to tie together much of what we were seeking to explore through our project. Literacies-in-use at work are social practices, not neutral, depersonalized skills. Even the simplest of all possible acts of writing, the archetypal act of illiterates—marking an X—is an act of social interaction and engagement in meaningful literacy. And whether you participate in documenting your work depends on the particular local meanings of those acts and those documents.

LAYERS OF MEANING

As a workplace educator, I have a lot of experience in helping to identify issues and solve problems, and also in figuring out if there is an educational aspect to a workplace issue. When I first heard that the men in this high-tech machining cell were not completing charts, I asked if they were ticked off about anything. I suspected that it was an act of resistance or an exercise of power on the part of the workers—the power to not comply or cooperate. I did not think they lacked document literacy skills or that they needed retraining in how to complete the charts. No one in Metalco suggested retraining workers, although in some of our other sites that might have been the first solution offered. Interestingly, though, the leader eventually described what he did as "retraining together," and he included himself, I think, in those who started over in the dimensions of those particular jobs. I might have also said when first hearing of this situation that people are always learning at work, and sometimes what they are learning is that in some cases it is okay to not complete the chart. That is what the "mixed messages" from managers and engineers taught them.

But as a researcher, I was looking for a little more—more complex or multidimensional explanations consistent with our overall research study experience. Only by paying attention to those specific local meanings workers attached to the document literacy practices of the cell did the paradox make deeper sense to me. Learning the culture of Metalco includes learning to accept and enmesh documenting your work process and your products as part of your job. The Machine Operators' job is to make the parts, but even in this very physical task there are many reading and writing practices that cannot be separated from making the parts, or you are not doing your job. The documentation system is part of the quality system: to check the part and write down (or type) that you have checked. Literacies in work cultures are caught up in the social dynamics of power, and in these new work-places, in social practices in the name of quality.

The Internal Audit, Part I: "Not a Witch Hunt"

About halfway into my 9-month data collection period, I followed a six-person internal International Standards Organization (ISO) Audit Team, from the planning session through the 2-day audit to the oral and written reports delivered to managers. The auditors' task, from their point of view, was to focus on a few aspects of the overall standards system and look for evidence that practice matched promises. From my perspective as a researcher of literacy practices, I saw that the ISO audit process played out in many respects as a careful monitoring of local work practices, including literacies-in-use and documentation practices. The story of one particular homemade checklist and the little crisis it caused in the audit illustrates how the ISO standards leave workers with little scope for individual autonomy or initiative in documenting their work. More than that, this story casts further light on the relationship between managers and production workers at Metalco. The outcome shows the social practices of Metalco in contrast to those of the other sites we researched.

The Audit Team was made up of managers, engineers, coordinators and quality specialists. One auditor was from a supplier company. She was invited along as a pair of fresh eyes, and to help develop a closer working relationship between the company and its suppliers. Following the audit gave me a chance to see the whole quality documentation system through the ISO filter, and let me see which paperwork and data collection tasks were driven by production needs and which were in place as standard ways to document procedures for the International Standards Organization registration. People had tried to explain this to me by saying that a practice or a form was important for a customer, or for a certain design need, but I didn't understand that not every form in the place was for ISO until I followed the internal audit. The distinction is that the forms and the data collection are needed for production. ISO makes the standard practice a controlled practice, and the documentation system a network of controlled documents. In following the audit and in beginning to understand some of the meanings ISO gave to documentation practices, I started to think of Metalco as having a "culture of documentation."

Remember that Metalco is aiming to be a "world-class" manufacturer. Everything is documented, and through the audit I started to see that all the documents and the processes are standardized. Anyone who visited the shop floor would notice the documents. Papers are held to the side of machines with magnets, fastened to clipboards neatly hung up in production cells. Loose papers covered in X's, dots and numbers are pored over by pairs of workers dressed in blue overalls. Outside the production floor, all of the departments have their own Quality Procedures. These are the written formalizations of how things will be done in Accounting, in Human Resources and even in the President's office. The auditors checked to see that the actual procedures—including the record-keeping—followed in the departments were the same as the documented procedures.

One of the important procedures is control of materials in the production areas, which means that all material must be identified and labeled. When a workplace is registered with ISO, the company has to demonstrate that they have control of materials. Production materials are labeled, contained and controlled. Production documentation is standardized and controlled. At Metalco, this means that production forms can be photocopied by anyone, but only printed from a controlled source, the original file on the Metalco Intranet. It also means that the same form is used to collect production information across many areas. No product or machine has a unique form. No production group or cell keeps records on a form they make up themselves.

Controlled documents also mean that the written processes for reference are the official record of how a particular job is performed. All of the forms, the production drawings and the maintenance checklists are Controlled Documents, and are clearly labeled with the abbreviation CD and a number, like "CD 12." Even labels and tags are controlled documents. Outside the shop floor, it's okay to put a sticky note reminder on a pile of papers; in the shop where the company's products are made, an authorized label, completely filled out, is required. Managers say that customers demand this kind of system. The quality department says that ISO requires it. The engineers say it has helped them standardize and streamline processes. Employees told me that this is just the way it is in an ISO 9001 plant. It's a characteristic that means "this place makes good products." It's "world class."

What are the production literacies practiced in a culture of tight controls? Does the act of writing make a worker subject to audit? I wondered about the power relations embedded in the close monitoring when I saw that all of the internal auditors were from the office staff. I asked the Quality Manager if there were any auditors from the shop. He said he wished there were "because sometimes people sort of worry that we are trying to catch them doing something wrong. Like we come from the office to do something scary."

The ISO system was presented as a neutral standard that everyone takes part in maintaining, but I found there is not much opportunity for participation, either in writing the standards or in auditing them. Later, as I wrapped up my research, auditors from the shop were being trained. At the time, though, because workers feared getting caught doing something wrong, I wondered whether there was blame.

During the internal audit planning session, the auditors and the Quality Manager reviewed sections of the Quality Procedures Manual and made an audit plan. They also reviewed the purpose of the audit, which was to make sure the Quality Procedures were being followed as written. The plan included time for the audit team to (in their words) "argue about whether something is a 'finding' [a problem] and about whether it's the question or the evidence that is the problem." The questions came directly from the standards. The auditors had the chance to suggest revising the standards through their audit report. One of the auditors' comments made me wonder about the work climate at Metalco, especially during the audit.

As the auditors returned to their planning after a short break, one of the engineers told a story from a past audit about one of the manual sections they were planning to audit the next day: "One time I did that one [element]—Inspections—and I went in right to something I knew Joe Lang was hiding (in the Quality Lab). And he just looked at me. He was almost crying and he said, 'Why are you doing this?'"

Some people laughed at this story. The Quality Manager expressed quick disapproval: "You're not supposed to know. The trick [of doing a good audit] is to separate what you find [using the audit procedures] from what you 'know is there.'" The laughter died out.

The next day, as the auditors assembled before splitting into two three-person teams, the Quality Manager warned them that the audit was not "a witch hunt." Again, in a company that is trying to run a no-blame management style, I wondered about the potential for finding fault, for embarrassing people. I did not know what to expect.

I shadowed one pair of auditors as they went through the buildings asking to see documents and questioning people about how they did their job, as they traced the Quality Procedures according to the manual. Even though I had spent many days in the plant and on the shop floor before the audit, I learned a lot that day about how the paperwork flowed, and why. Production itself was secondary to the audit. Auditors only looked at parts in crates to see if they were labeled. They checked clipboards and engineering drawings and work orders everywhere. They checked that people were recording their employee numbers and signing documents in all the right places. Paperwork was everything to the audit. It was rich and meaningful. There seemed to be a sort of sacred trust between the standards manual and the documented practices in the company, and auditors took every breach of that trust seriously.

The Internal Audit, Part 2: The Homemade Chart Crisis

On the second day of the audit, an "Uncontrolled Document" was discovered in use in a production area, and it caused quite a stir. The document in question (Fig. 4.2) was a single-page table made and printed by a Machine Operator. He was using it to track detailed measurements to one-tenth of a thousandth of an inch, of five dimensions of the

M/C 3942 Checklist

Name: Housing, Gear, E33   DWG. D. 1889   PID. 214056
Name: Gear Pressure Plate   DWG. D. 1910   PID. 214157

Date	3/29	3/29	3/29										
CHARACTER													
HOUSING, GEAR, E33													
BORE DIA. 2 X .5626-.5630	✓	✓	✓										
10-24 UNC-2B X .5 DP MIN.	✓	✓	✓										
DEPTH .3273-.3277	✓	✓	✓										
BORE DIA. 2 X .2498-.2502	✓	✓	✓										
THICKNESS .690-.695	✓	✓	✓										
GEAR PRESSURE PLATE													
BORE DIA. .2498-.2502	✓	✓	✓										
THICKNESS .335-.345	✓	✓	✓										
OPERATOR	949	949	949										

FIG. 4.2. A homemade checklist. This figure is a composite from similar original documents adapted by the authors to preserve anonymity.

part his computer-controlled metal machining center was making. Jonathon was the lead hand in his work group, and he was teaching others to run machining centers. He kept a binder of his own notes, mostly word processed, but some in his neat printing. The Quality Assurance system required Jonathon to sign off on a First Article (Fig. 4.3) form when the first part following a new set-up is made, and then track six dimensions of the part through its production run on a Statistical Process Control (SPC) record chart. He was completing this official document, but also using his "homemade" chart to keep more detailed information. This homemade document drew the attention of the audit team because he had not stamped it "For Reference Only" with the required red-ink stamp. This made it an Uncontrolled Document in use in the Controlled Materials area, which is a violation of ISO rules for document control.

The Auditors were initially excited by this find and hurried back to the meeting room talking animatedly. I learned that this kind of finding

METALCO   CD01

Part name #: __2112__   PID #:   __214056__   Freq. of issue: Each order
Drawing #: _300-2312_   Drawing rev.: _D_   Type: batch, in-process
ES #:   None   ES rev.:

Incoming, In-Process or Final Inspection
Inspection to be in accordance with applicable training standards except as detailed below.

Specification	Type	Gauge	Size / Freq.	Chart Type
Thickness 0.693 Nom.		OM 0074	1 / 10 Pcs.	histrogram
Pin Hole Position to Datum A		DI 0095	1 / 10 Pcs.	histrogram
O.D. 0.250 Nom.	significant	SN0012	1 / 10 Pcs.	histogram

Date printed Thursday, March 24, 2000   Page 1

File: InspectionSheetApp.mdb   *Controlled Locations*   Reviewed & Approved by:
Revision: Sept. 24, 1998   Sources: Inspection database   Manufacturing Engineer
                                  Records: QA Department

FIG. 4.3.   Inspection sheet. This figure is a composite from similar original documents adapted by the authors to preserve anonymity.

could be treated as a major breach of documentation practice if found by "external auditors." Too many such breaches could threaten the company's ISO certification. It was a dramatic moment in the audit.

The mood of the group shifted quickly as they considered the risk and the source of this breach. The auditors talked through their concerns as the guest, the Quality Manager and I sat silently. One of the auditors started in almost immediately. "I don't want to discourage initiative or say that people from the shop can't add things to their work. So what can we do, can we let this happen?"

No-one suggested this worker was doing a poor job, or that his homemade checklist form was not helping him in his work. All the right forms, the Controlled Documents were being used correctly in this instance. This Uncontrolled Document was extra. Jonathon was running a new product on a new machine. He was double-checking, using a form of his own making. Two other auditors chimed in. Jonathon's checklist would have been okay if it were handwritten. It would have been okay if it were stamped "For Reference Only."

In a little over 10 minutes, the auditors decided to write the document up as an "isolated incident of an Uncontrolled Document in use in production." It was not part of a pattern, just a single case that was not a threat to product quality. With this resolution, there was no requirement for official Corrective Action. Someone would speak to

Jonathon about the "For Reference Only" stamp, but there would be no confrontations, no retraining or corrective action.

Later that day I asked the guest auditor from the supplier company about this. She felt that the auditors had reached a good decision and had not been swayed by the "classic feelings of superiority of office people over shop people." But she had more to say about the form:

> That should tell you that the inspection sheet isn't working for him [the operator]. [Jonathon's] form was better. It was clearer. I understood it right away. That didn't seem to be on [the auditor's] radar, that this was better or maybe that the system [and the controlled generic form] wasn't working for people.

So I asked the auditors if Jonathon's form was better. They said: "It's not that simple. The Controlled Document is generic for all parts and products in the company. If we put exact dimensions of any one part there [as Jonathon did], then we tie ourselves into maintaining it."

One of the reasons Jonathon's checklist of part dimensions was so easy to understand is that he had copied the exact dimensions of each size from the engineering drawing, and presented the dimensions in a table, with spaces to check off when he got them right every day. The Controlled Document is generic. It has spaces for the important measurements, but you read them from the latest revision of the appropriate engineering drawing. The drawing is controlled and the form is controlled, but the one does not update the other. Transferring the numbers risks an error. The system controls for that error by not copying the exact dimensions, since they may change with each new drawing revision. So here, in the perspectives of the outside guest auditor and the internal auditors, we see very different interpretations of the local meanings of the homemade form and the official Controlled Documents. The guest places value in the functionality of the checklist in production. The engineers place higher value in the overall system and how the documents work together for everyone, not just for one machine or one part.

This whole incident brings to light the opportunities, the constraints and the potential perils of literacy practices at Metalco. In particular it shows that much more is at stake than relations between co-workers in production who learn together and negotiate the meanings of their charting and writing and reading in the course of doing their work. Literacy practices at Metalco were about more than making parts. I was impressed with the constraints of the audit and the jeopardy of the unexpected homemade checklist. The different meanings that different people had for Jonathon's act of making the checklist and using it were clear to me. I followed this up and asked individuals for more of their thinking about the homemade checklist until I felt I had an understanding of all of its meanings. Here is a summary from a taped interview with one of the auditors six weeks later:

You don't want to come down heavily on the lay person who was doing
something outside the defined system ... not holding it up as a wonderful
example, but at least to say "He's taking good initiative," but then explain
to him that if you need to do this kind of stuff, there are channels through
which you really should move to get it done.

"Do I subvert the system?" answered another one of the auditors
when I asked him to explain why they decided not to take official corrective action over the incident of the Uncontrolled Document, "Sure, I
do." He elaborated, saying that sometimes you need to get things done
and follow up later with the papers. He explained that with experience,
he learned to take responsibility and to recognize what can be a problem: "Maybe two cases in a hundred is there a problem that will really
be a problem with the product. For ISO, every problem is the same. It
tries to make it black and white, but it isn't. Manufacturing is more of
an art."

For this auditor, who is an engineer, making a big deal out of the
homemade form might have risked the confidence the shop workers
have in Engineering. He recognizes that there is a relationship between
the way he treats people and the way they will treat him, and, by extension, engineers and the company. "An experienced [worker] like
Jonathon, he knows. Machinists are about perfection. What we give
them should be as perfect as what they give us." His implication is that
he trusts Jonathon, so he did not want to give Jonathon, and by extension shop workers, unnecessary trouble over a systems breach that he
judged did not put any product at risk.

What did Jonathon say later? I shadowed him for hours with his
permission before I brought it up, in case it was a sensitive subject. It
wasn't. He said he never felt personally at risk because of the form. The
crisis happened away from his hearing. His Production Manager, who
was not part of the audit and was only passing on a message, reminded
Jonathon about the "For Reference Only" stamp. Jonathon knew that
his form was reported as an "Uncontrolled Document in use in production," but he did not see that as him getting into trouble personally.
He explained that he had not easily found the stamp, and that he
should have written "For Reference Only" on the form himself, but he
didn't. It was a busy time, the new program for the new product was not
stable, and he was working a lot of overtime. He showed me that he has
preserved his checklist along with his other personal notes in a binder.
"For Reference Only" was stamped neatly in red at the top right margin
of the page.

This incident showed me a controlling, judgmental side to the culture of documentation that I did not experience on the production floor
outside the audit. The tension and animated discussion generated by
the homemade document also showed me that there was a risk involved in writing things down, and not just a risk of error or a risk of

disclosure, but a risk to the quality designation of the company, which they needed to stay in business. And as the auditors decided in their response, there was also a risk to social equilibrium, to trust, to respect and to participation.

The standardization and the control of documents met an external need, the need for ISO registration to show that there was a system and that the system was in use—exactly as written down. The Quality Procedures Manual and the audit gave external meanings to both the documents themselves and to the act of using them. This was literacy practice as an international movement for reliability and control.

More than that, the auditors who were managers, coordinators and engineers found the system meaningful. They saw value in having not just the registration, but also the standardized forms. One of the senior managers described the Inspection Form to me as the "gold standard" for them. They had managed to combine five old forms into one that was used and signed off each time a part was inspected, as the first part in a run, at a change of tool, or at other inspection points in the manufacturing process. He explained that no new record-keeping or production tasks were added to inspections through the ISO documentation, but there was now one standard form, no matter what the part was, no matter what the machine. As a different senior manager put it, "ISO hasn't really added work for us, but we have had to standardize things. There is more written material and it's more important than it used to be."

More important indeed, if so many levels of relationship between the company and customers, between co-workers and departments can be put at risk through a homemade checklist. This manager recognized that the written material is much more important for initiating work, for processing materials and even for ordering supplies, as well as all the quality and documentation meanings of those same writings.

The people who took part in the internal audit, and the senior managers who received the results and committed resources to address the problems identified, felt the system helped them focus on problems. This was another meaning of the documentation system. It was a route to understanding problems and ultimately through the Corrective Action Reports, a way of getting problems solved. The written procedures and the structured audit process had this meaning of focusing on problems that could be resolved to improve quality.

Among the managers and the senior engineers I found the actual authors of most of these forms and procedures. They worked with a consultant setting up the Metalco quality system to ISO, and much of what they adopted was based on the consultant's templates from other companies. They could see the whole system level of meaning expressed to the whole controlled document network. Like the Quality Assurance worker, Joe Lang, these managers and engineers could see the intersection of all the bits of data and all the collection points in the documentation of the work processes of the company. This perspective was not a local meaning on the shop floor. I didn't see it until I followed the audit and spent time with the people who had that perspective.

"It's a Management Thing"

Matt is an engineer and a manager. He has been part of this research all along, and he was interested in the idea of "a systems study of print communication," his terms for what I was studying. His office was in the engineering section in the Old Building, where there are two floors of offices divided into several rooms. Most people work cubicle style, divided from co-workers by partitions, but Matt has an office with wall and a door. In an audio-taped interview in his office, I told Matt that I was interested in the internal ISO audit and in the findings. He is part of the management group that receives the audit report and agrees to the Corrective Actions. I also asked about the seeming contradiction of which workers were found to be keeping all their documents, and which were not. He offered the interpretation that the workers' literacies and their competencies, whatever they are, are not at the heart of the issue. He looked for an explanation among his own group:

> I guess what seems to have happened with our quality system in general is that we have written down a lot of rules and we've tried to make them simple, and we're simply not explaining them to people and getting everybody to follow up. Generally, people in this [Old] Building have been with [Metalco] longer. Probably a lot of [the production workers in the Old Building], their education is lower. So it doesn't quite tie into that. It's just that they have had somebody explain to them, "Okay, this is what you need to do." In the other building [the New Building] we're being sloppy for some reason ... we're just not doing it. And it's not an education thing or a literacy thing. It's a failing on [Metalco's] part to provide the training, then support it and follow it up. And so I guess it really comes down as a management thing.

I learned that Matt and his management colleagues see themselves as part of the social system and part of the problems at Metalco. This seems to be another degree of difference from our other research sites. Where some people would be quick to retrain or to blame the low skills of their workforce for problems, these managers have settled on a way to frame that problem that gives them a place to act without blaming the skills and attitudes of production workers for every problem. Metalco's workplace educators would say that there is a "continuum of ease" with reading, writing and math tasks among the production workers, some of them facing challenges in regards to their "essential skills." That turns out to be only one view of the puzzle here. Matt goes on to say that the company and the mangers are "not getting everyone on the same page ... even though these things are documented." He doesn't actually say that workers who were not completing their charts fully don't see what the charts mean to the overall system and to the company. But I took him to mean that the focus wasn't so much just on simply reading the page of procedures, but understanding it and reading it together so that its meaning is shared.

When I first started to learn about the quality system and the ISO documents, I thought that some people believed that because it was documented it was real. This seemed endearingly clueless, like the Dilbert cartoons by Scott Adams that chronicle the absurdities and contradictions of working life. Writing procedures down does not make people follow them. The lived activities are more real than the ISO procedures for workers, even when the two match. In listening and asking more, I learned that maybe most people in the company saw the contradictions between the contested reality of documented procedures and their lived experience, and despite any contradictions, they focused on getting better at what they did within the constraints of working life at Metalco.

CONCLUSION

What did I learn from all those months researching literacy and literacy learning at Metalco? I learned a lot about how completely enmeshed literacy practices are in the working activities of production workers and others at this high-tech company. Until I stopped to watch, I had never seen the reading and writing that goes on in the moments of a machining cycle. I had never really thought about the group learning and the negotiation of meaning that goes on in work groups surrounded by a noisy production floor. I also learned about the overall system to document work and communicate important information through the shorthand of data, of graphs and of drawings. I saw literacies in use that depended on a deep understanding of work gained through experience and interactions with experienced workers. As I have recounted, I learned about the International Standards Organization, and the constraints it places on literacy practices. Who would have thought that making a checklist on your home computer, as Jonathon did, could matter to so many people in so many ways? I also learned about Metalco Production System/Toyota Production System and the procedural controls it demands from a workplace. I learned that machined metal parts are defined and created on three axes (x, y, and z) and that you need all three coordinates to define a point in space so the machining center can mill it from a piece of metal.

I think that a social practice view of literacy and learning aims to be just that kind of three-dimensional view that allows for different perspectives. Reading work at Metalco is not easy. The fast interpretation of situations can lead to misinterpretation, as we saw in the story of the workers not completing their charts, which at first seemed paradoxi-

cal. This is surely a cautionary tale for those of us who try to understand work, workers and their literacies. It is easy to jump to conclusions about someone's skills in use, and it is difficult to listen for all the
rich local meanings that give a situation logic and depth.

We have said that Metalco has a "culture of documentation." And in
that culture of documentation, work itself is a literacy practice. I have
tried to cast some light on that work, and on the complexity of issues interwoven with print literacies in the evolving work culture of Metalco.
Literacies at Metalco are also inseparable from participation, training
and change. Metalco is evolving so rapidly that by the time I wrote this
research up, much of what I described physically had changed there.
Metalco's managers are responding to global business forces and the ac-
cumulating constraints of a world culture of quality programs. At the
same time, those managers are trying to set a course for planned change
and Continuous Improvement that depends on shared meanings.

The managers at Metalco gave us pause, and they gave us hope. They
spoke a lot about the need for understanding, for seeing the benefit, for
seeing participation and compliance as "a management thing." They
also set themselves a unique task among our sites: to try to create a
no-blame culture where improvements could be made by focusing on
the system rather than scapegoating the people. More than that,
Metalco's managers and other workers recognized learning as a human activity and not a neutral transfer of knowledge.

Metalco is farther down the road on the Quality Journey. That road
is not just the road to manufacturing excellence and MPS/TPS implementation. Metalco is farther down the road to understanding that
learning and participating in work depends not only on individuals,
but also on the way their work is organized, on the climate they work
in, and on how they are managed. Literacies at work at Metalco are
literacies recognized as embedded in the social practices of the people
who work together there.

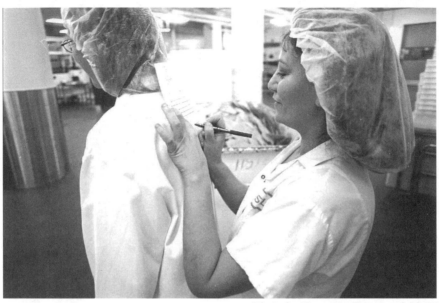

Photo by Vincenzo Pietropaolo/CAW

Photo by Ruth Farrell

Part II

Reflections on Learning

In the remaining four chapters, we reflect in different ways on what can be learned from the stories and the research settings described in Part I. Chapter 5 explores key moments of teaching and learning that illustrate barriers to both learning and *using* literacies in the classroom and on the job. Chapter 6 explores how a social practice view of literacies can pose new challenges, as well as offer new horizons, in the practice of workplace education. Chapter 7 offers a more in-depth discussion of social practice theories, illustrating how they shape our research stories. It also invites readers to think about ways that these theories relate to their own everyday practice as educators. Chapter 8 offers a brief conversation among the five of us on the joys and pitfalls of collaborative research.

5

Workplace Learning and Literacies in Practice

Mary Ellen Belfiore and Sue Folinsbee

This chapter addresses workplace learning by examining a job training session and an orientation session at two of our sites, Triple Z and Texco.[1] Although our stories take place in formal sessions, the lessons we want to emphasize can be applied to any type of workplace learning: formal or informal, in the classroom, on the job or in meetings. By bringing a social perspective on literacy to this training and learning, we hope to show that many aspects of learning are missed when the focus is primarily on transmitting knowledge and skills without considering intervening social factors.

In previous chapters, we have looked at the social practices of work and literacy by asking what, why and how people participate in literacy practices as part of their jobs. We explored how social relations, power dynamics and accepted ways of working structure how people deal with print. Similarly, in this chapter, we want to examine literacies, and learning within the fabric of working life, because it is there that people find opportunities, meanings and thus reasons to participate in learn-

---

[1]The names of the companies and the names of people in this chapter are pseudonyms.

ing or not. How well people can apply their skills on the job depends on the social practices within which they learn and use them.

Our treatment of literacies in job training and in other forms of workplace learning necessarily includes work practices where people use what they have learned. This issue of use[2] is not separate from literacy practices or training practices. In people's experience, literacies, training and use are interwoven, and we want to examine that weave, not single, separate threads. Job trainers are more likely to focus on how well people use their training on the floor, but workplace educators often stop at the classroom door and miss how people use or don't use their literacy learning to get things done at work.

Educators might say that what happens with literacies on the floor is not their business or their responsibility; issues of the social and power relations that structure work practices might appear to be about organizational development, not literacies and learning. In this research, we see them as inseparable. In taking a social perspective on literacy, we follow the thread of literacy throughout training and onto the plant floor. We want to see literacies as they are enacted, as people use them to participate. This notion of use is important because meanings reside in the uses we make of language and literacies, not in abstract words and letters taken out of context. The meanings-in-use of literacy practices determine, for instance, if and how operators will fill out their production forms, safety reports or quality documentation no matter what training they have received.

We direct this chapter, then, not just to company trainers, human resource developers and workplace educators, but also to production managers, quality assurance directors and supervisors, who have their share in creating the social practices of literacy on the plant floor. To explore these practices within the social fabric of work, we present stories from formal training sessions for quality and food safety. Because we come at these stories from nontraditional ways of viewing training, the stories sometimes take unexpected turns as deeper layers of meaning are uncovered. The stories trace the thread of literacy through training and onto the plant floor. We begin by covering some familiar territory in addressing the language and literacy barriers that discourage involvement, interest and engagement with the training in the classroom, but then we push further by examining the social practices of literacy outside the classroom that present quite a different picture. The contradictions between literacy use promoted in idealized training sessions and literacy use on the floor are dramatic and offer convincing evidence for adopting a complex, socially situated view of literacy.

Giselle Mawer (1999) in *Language and Literacy in Workplace Education* argues for this wider social practice view, and says educators

---

[2]Taylor (1997) uses the term "transfer of learning" to refer to the application or use of learning on the floor.

have to learn how to "navigate the multilayered discourses of the workplace." She comments further on what this view means for the roles of workplace educators: "With the scope of workplace education moving beyond the classroom, holding in tension the various paradoxes of the 'praxis' of individual and organizational learning involves a delicate balancing act" (p. 286).

With these stories, we hope to stretch our collective understanding through insights into workplace life, including training. We want to shine the light on issues and practices that trainers and educators don't usually have the opportunity to investigate in as much depth as researchers do. We want to show how deeply important these issues are to workers and how they influence what and how workers read, write, communicate and learn at work.

TRAINING IN PRACTICE

Across all our research sites, various kinds of training are mandated by Standard Operating Procedures and/or by international certification systems for quality and safety. In these cases, the procedures usually require workers and staff to sign off on their training to show they completed it, and sometimes that they understood it. This training is aimed at bringing people in line with standardized quality or safety practices, as well as shaping their attitudes and behavior to fit the goals of the organization. So, in theory, as people become more engaged with the quality practices, they become more the type of employee the company wants. But in real life, in that crowded intersection of practices, people, learning and identities, we often find a complex set of relationships that is not as predictable. The growth and transformation of identities takes place within that complex fabric, in the relationships between work, people, learning and literacies. There we find multiple and sometimes conflicting reasons for accepting, resisting, modifying and making sense of training that is offered and learning that is intended.

We observed some similar training practices across all our sites where a gap between intentions and achievements in learning was evident:

- Sign-off procedures for mandatory quality training. This system ensures quantity (numbers of training sessions), but may not reflect effective participation and understanding.
- Lecture-style teaching, with the trainer's talk time far outweighing workers' participation.
- Print materials with dense text, sophisticated vocabulary and jargon beyond the reach of many workers; in oral presentations we often saw the same use of inaccessible language.
- Long stretches of reading aloud by the trainer and sometimes by the workers.

- Different types of written tests, quizzes and games to verify workers' attention and knowledge.

In the stories that follow, we begin by exploring the dilemmas associated with each of these common training practices. They are characteristic of transmission-based training methods that present information as passed on unchanged from trainer to worker, regardless of environment, social relations, status and other social dynamics. These practices are also familiar in how they maintain a hierarchy of teacher as superior to students, or, in this case, of trainers as superior to workers. We found it ironic that these practices persisted in our research sites despite their contrast with these organizations' stated visions, goals and commitments to empowerment. Even more surprising, these training practices persisted despite the workers' frequent and visible lack of engagement during the training itself and the often much-lamented failure of such training to lead to changes on the job.

These training events were often conceived and mounted as the company's best efforts to support learning. As such, they reveal as much about the culture of the organization as they do about the content and method of training. But here we have the added dimension and irony of a conscious learning activity aimed at changing practices through increased knowledge, awareness or skills, yet still reproducing the same barriers, gaps and shortcomings. These contradictions persist because learning is a social process. The fundamental goal of training may be to harmonize meanings and align workers through standard work practices and shared goals. But individuals give different meanings to training and print materials as surely as they do to quality regulations and to all the work practices they engage in. As a result, these training stories are full of the contradictions that characterize many activities connected with work practices, most clearly a contradiction between the theory espoused in training and the reality of using what was learned in practice. Until job training and workplace learning take these contradictory meanings into account, they will continue to be less than effective in achieving engagement and active participation from workers as well as staff and supervisors.

Most companies promise and hope that training will actually result in better quality, better safety and a more aligned workforce. Trainers share these hopes along with making the training relevant and interesting to their participants. The workers we talked to about training indicated they wanted their learning to be practical, useful and interesting—not "over their heads," with the trainers trying to display their own knowledge or "talking down" to workers. Our stories attempt to uncover some of the practices around work and learning that could account for whether people engage with literacy and with other goals of training.

We begin with Triple Z, the food processing plant, and its metal detector training, which is part of the company's food safety certification program. The trainer herself pushes literacy and documentation practices beyond the training room to get answers about the real practice on the floor. In contrast, at Texco, the textile manufacturer, the trainer confines her ISO orientation and documentation issues to the training room. The researcher is left to uncover the contradictions between the ideals promoted in the orientation session and the real use of documentation in work practices. Each story begins with a brief summary of the research site to remind readers of key issues described in previous chapters on Triple Z (chap. 1) and Texco (chap. 2).

TRIPLE Z AND HACCP TRAINING: MARY ELLEN'S STORY[3]

Triple Z, a food processing plant, is a multicultural and multilingual workplace with an older workforce. Immigrants form the large majority of workers, staff and managers. English is the second language of this majority, and the range of competence in both language and literacy varies from basic to near native speaker levels, with many older workers near the basic end of the scale. At the time of my data collection, Triple Z was preparing for certification with an international food safety program called Hazard Analysis and Critical Control Point or HACCP.

HACCP is an all-encompassing system regulating many aspects of the company's operation: the physical plant, finance, sales, production and training, as well as values, beliefs, behaviors, language and literacy. Through its standardization and conformance policies, it creates new forms of social practice within the communities in the company, such as completing paperwork in an acceptable and timely manner. Training is mandated in this system as one way to initiate people into these practices and then to maintain their compliance. Gradually, through voluntary compliance or through discipline if necessary, managers aim to align all of the workforce with the standards and identities required by HACCP.

I attended a variety of formal training sessions that took place both on the plant floor and in the small company boardroom. In addition, there were innumerable opportunities for managers to promote the HACCP vision: the safe, standardized, documented operations of a company that has seen the light about the importance of quality and safety. Managers talked about HACCP in meetings and regularly introduced newly designed forms for supervisors and for workers in production. Managers used HACCP certification as a motivator, a threat, a sales pitch or the driver for tougher discipline. Without this certification, they would lose their most lucrative accounts, a big box retailer and an international fast food chain; both customers required certification by a speci-

---

[3]An adapted version of this story was published by TESL Ontario in Belfiore and Folinsbee (2002). Quotations in the text are from verbatim notes taken during the training sessions.

fied date. For Triple Z managers, the literacy practices required by HACCP moved from being an extra responsibility to being part of the core work of the plant. They treated training seriously and had high expectations for what it could accomplish in changing people's sense of themselves, their roles, responsibilities and behaviors at work.

On-the-Job Training Sessions

First there was a series of on-the-job training sessions to help workers check their product coding for quality and safety, and to complete their checklists accurately and fully (see chap. 1, Literacies, Compliance and Certification). These sessions came just before a preliminary HACCP audit by external examiners. The HACCP Coordinator, seeing these sessions as just reminders of good practice, decided that a quick review on the floor of correct documentation procedures with the quality trainer would be sufficient.

But even after the training on the floor, inaccurate reporting continued, raising the potential for wasted product, loss of revenue and low grades on the official audit. As the story of the meeting in the Triple Z chapter shows, these sessions failed to produce the managers' desired results: understanding, accuracy and willingness. The message they wanted to get through to workers was that their documentation counts; in fact, it's all they can count on when there are recalls or returns of product. The company had to depend now on accurate, fully descriptive documentation to prove that it had conformed to HACCP standards. From my observations and interactions, I think workers realized that the company was at risk of losing important customers, but never fully understood the connection with HACCP.

After these on-the-job training sessions, I spoke with Bozena, an Eastern European with English as her second language, who was the Coordinator for HACCP and for Quality Assurance. She said she had specifically used a trusted and skilled lab technician as the trainer to ensure that operators would get the best training. In her eyes, the training failed because workers didn't pay attention; this was, after all, only a review of documentation practices that they should have already been following.

From an educator's viewpoint, I saw the problem quite differently. I saw the training process itself as partly responsible for discouraging involvement, attentiveness and understanding. The training for machine operators to improve their documentation was delivered while the lines were running, with noise loud enough to miss 50% of what was said. I watched this training process closely and saw workers' eyes and ears tuned to their responsibilities in production, not to the fine points of documentation. Most educators would recognize the importance of these environmental conditions that affect training. But in fact, those conditions were just one strand of the story revealing why there were problems with documentation at Triple Z (see chap. 1).

Training for Critical Control Points

After this on-the-job training, Bozena began a series of more formal training sessions for all workers responsible for the five Critical Control Points (CCPs). These small group sessions were held in the boardroom and featured overheads, handouts, group discussion and "signing off" procedures to satisfy HACCP training documentation. These sessions provided sharply contrasting examples of training practices that seemed either highly successful or highly problematic.

The Presentation

For the group sessions, Bozena focused on the procedures necessary for routine work and for corrective action in that job position. She only briefly reviewed the paperwork to reinforce key points in the correct completion of documentation for each CCP, because that paperwork had already been the focus of the on-the-job training described above and of the follow-up meeting. She was trying to bring the big picture of HACCP to the operators and to show how their jobs fit into the overall safety system.

Bozena began each session with a review of the steps in the target job, directing the group to the overheads that she read and commented on. I saw trainers use this style with stronger or softer delivery in most of the sessions I attended. Everyone had copies of the overheads as handouts, although few people actually looked at them. I noted the use of HACCP jargon as well as quite sophisticated vocabulary and dense text on handouts and overheads. For instance, the term "non-conforming material" was used in HACCP documents, but I never heard workers use it in conversation. Yet for the training sessions, Bozena used this term and others like it on the overheads and handouts, apparently without considering the trainees' actual capacity to understand. Another example appears below.

Metal Contamination

Any sample that is rejected into the rejection area of the detector must be passed through the detector again to confirm that there may be metal contamination

This overly scientific and sophisticated language was used in many of the training sessions I attended with both in-house and external trainers. In Bozena's training group, the participants were quiet during this presentation and didn't ask questions even when she asked if everything was clear. She was reviewing the jobs they did every day, although with language they may not have recognized. I could see that the company was following its 4-year-old policy of using only English as the language of communication. But knowing how many workers had a limited range in both oral and written English, I expected to see the use of plain or clear English, particularly with safety and quality procedures. Unfortunately, that style seemed to be the exception rather than the rule in the printed documents, overheads and handouts used in these training sessions.

Similarly, I was uncomfortable with the familiar practice of reading aloud, either from overheads or written texts, to get around the problem of limited reading abilities. This strategy fits with a "transmission" theory of learning, in which knowledge is seen like a package passing from one person to the next, out of context and transferable to a range of settings. But recent thinking suggests that this theory simplifies the complex interrelationships between knowledge, people and work practices. Lave (1996) argues that this idea of "learning transfer" "is an extraordinarily narrow and barren account of how knowledgeable persons make their way among multiply interrelated settings" (p. 151). In its place she proposes a more social view of learning that shows how many environmental and social circumstances change what people come to know and how they participate in learning. Why did Bozena design her training according to the "transmission" theory, in a way that overlooked familiar problems?

I thought about the fact that Bozena herself was a second-language speaker, and she operated totally in English on the job. She rarely lost a beat in conversations, and only occasionally did she throw a listener off-track with incorrect grammar, unfamiliar pronunciation or an inappropriate word choice. She had mastered HACCP jargon for her own use, but perhaps she hadn't considered translating it into clear English. She had also invested her career at Triple Z in this certification and was totally immersed in the fine points of this highly detailed, legal-like documentation. Had she lost perspective and now assumed that the terminology and concepts that informed her thinking and actions were simple and understandable to others outside the system? True, she wasn't hired as a trainer or educator, but the stories that follow show that in other instances, she set up exemplary learning situations.

To understand this on another level, we can refer to Gee's (1990) explanation of Discourses: "ways of being in the world" that integrate language, values, behaviors, identities and how we present ourselves. In her analysis of language and ideology in a study of a small manufacturer in the communications industry, Katz (2000) further explains that "our engagement in them [discourses] entails displays of membership in social groups and communities to which we belong" (p. 146). Bozena's use of unfamiliar corporate jargon, her lecture-style presentation, and her position of authority establish her as a member of the HACCP community. They set her apart from her audience even though her role as a trainer is to bring them into the HACCP discourse. Her membership confers power and she can use any aspect of its discourse, including language, identity and her behavior, to display this power and to try to enforce compliance to regulations.

Katz (2000) says that participation in a discourse "naturaliz[es] certain modes of thought, distributing roles and sanctioning unequal relations of power" (p. 147).[4] By looking even briefly at Bozena's language, we can begin to see how it is embedded in the world she inhabits, in the concepts that guide her work as well as her relations with staff and workers. Her language registers her status and her power to direct others. It seems natural that trainers will speak and act from within their own discourse or their own community of practice (even when it defeats their stated purposes) unless they become aware of how their language and their behavior work against them. It does not invite or encourage people to enter into that world; in fact, it reaffirms the hierarchies of power.

Reality Check

In these same sessions I also saw Bozena using strategies that had profoundly different effects. She demonstrated that she also knew how to teach from an "inquiry mode," in which she became the listener, the one seeking knowledge. As an educator, I felt the most successful part of the 60- to 90-minute sessions was here, with questions and comments from workers on the success of the procedures to date. Bozena's questioning stance allowed her to listen to the world inhabited by her workers. In response, front-line workers, staff and supervisors laid bare the intricate patterns of their work practices, that intersection we spoke of earlier where work, people, communication and documentation all intertwine. Only then could Bozena see what needed to be taught in order to draw others into the company vision or discourse that she participated in.

In one of the early sessions of "speaking their truths," an operator said she was actually berated by a co-worker for following the HACCP standards. I could see that Bozena knew she had to understand this social world, the actual details of life on the floor, if she was going to effect change, get people to buy into HACCP and to comply with its demands. Her job was to get the company certified. But she knew and demonstrated, I believe, that certification would succeed not through training events alone, but through constant attention to how people worked or why they didn't, and through vigilant efforts to align those realities with the work practices she was trying to teach. Reminders

---

[4]Here Katz (2000) is explaining Foucault's suggestion, in her words, that "power is difficult to pin down since it operates invisibly through ideology (discourse)" (p. 147). She also draws on the work of Fairclough (1989, 1995), who she says takes "an explicitly more critical stance on discourse than Gee" (p. 147).

alone about what was now required would never change a reality in which non-compliance made the most sense to workers.

In these sessions, if workers didn't speak up about problems and contradictions in the system, Bozena provoked them by referring to the story of the operator being berated for following standards. She opened up the possibility for real talk, and the groups, taking the leap of trust, revealed their dilemmas and sometimes argued over the solutions. Bozena used the sessions not only to get information for improving the system, but also to build alliances with the workers. She tried to bridge her quality community with the worker's front-line community, to bring the workers into the practices of quality not just in deeds, but with their minds, trust and a shared goal.

In one session on the use of the metal detector, workers needed no help in taking the opportunity to give Bozena a clear idea about what was really happening on the floor. In the dialogue that follows, Ivan, a Russian-born mechanic, takes the lead in pointing out where contradictions hobble the safety system. Mechanics are responsible for calibrating or setting the metal detector first thing each morning and each time a new line is set up. They document all their procedures. It is important that the metal detector be set before any product is run; otherwise, product could be packed without being checked for metal pieces, obviously posing a safety risk.

Here is the overhead that Bozena presented earlier in this session on these essential points:

REMEMBER:

Line <u>CAN NOT</u> run without the metal detector!

Line <u>CAN NOT</u> run without proper calibration in the morning and later during the day when necessary adjustment is needed!

Direct impact if metal detector is not in function but line is running:

Product is Garbage!!!

The mechanics who calibrated the metal detector and the workers who checked it every hour were required to document the date, time and threshold levels, among other items on their checklists. If lab technicians were tracing a problem with a run of product, they could use this documentation as evidence in finding the source of the safety or quality error that resulted in the product being "garbage." But frequently, workers noticed errors themselves as they operated the line, and not by referring to documentation.

Ivan the mechanic, drawing on his experience from morning calibrations, offered this perspective:

Ivan: Sometimes the line starts without calibration.
Bozena: That can't be.

Ivan: But it is [happening]. People start the line. One hundred
           and fifty jars [of relish] already gone to the pasteurizer [be-
           fore he does the calibration].
Bozena: It's something [proper procedure] people know already.
Ivan: But they don't do it.
Worker: You have the opportunity to tell people not to start the line
           until you've come.
Ivan: Do not start the line until I say OK? [He shakes his head as if
           impossible.] The supervisor has to know [that the line can't
           start until we have done our calibration]. There are three
           metal detectors. We need time. We need two minutes for a
           full calibration on an empty tank. I told them many times in
           the kettle room to wait to fill the tank, but they don't.

Bozena was alarmed to hear that every day some relish got processed, packed and shipped without being safety checked for metal
pieces. For her, this was a very dangerous reality, in which the reputation of the firm was stake. But she knew as well, as these workers did,
that most supervisors and many workers were still focused on quantity, getting out as much product as possible. Supervisors and workers
sometimes made demands on each other to keep production moving,
not to stop the lines even for quality or safety reasons, despite the official guidelines. In this case, kettle-room workers and supervisors were
ready to run the relish before the mechanic's startup time; they often
filled the tank so the operators would have relish available when their
shift began. This procedure made for smooth transitions in the morning, but didn't account for safety measures. The mechanic's documentation would show that the metal detectors had been calibrated with
date, time and results. In this case, the documentation apparently fulfilled the requirements of HACCP. But, in fact, work practices and different understandings about priorities and requirements resulted in
the opposite, a potentially unsafe product.

An operator in the group who saw how dangerous this could be wondered how they could recheck the relish that had missed the safety
checks:

Operator: Going to take a lot of time to put all that relish back
           through the line ...
Bozena: Do you have any ideas how to do it?
Ivan: That's your job, to find a better way.

Bozena did in fact find a better way when she brought this problem
up at a staff meeting. She acted on these reality checks by workers, reported what was really happening, and enlisted managers, supervisors
and staff to find resolutions to problems. In these instances, I felt she

was making an impact on both managers and supervisors by supporting the knowledge and experience of workers on the floor. She knew it
was difficult for workers to take action because she told me supervisors still kept hammering away at production numbers:

> They [supervisors] are judged by production numbers and I'm judged by
> quality and customer complaints.... It's all about trust. They [workers on
> the line] know they can trust us [lab staff] now. It was always there, but re-
> ally it was only on paper. Now they can see it.

During the sessions, Bozena also stressed the importance of a
worker's right to stop the line if quality or safety was in any way compromised. But stopping the line carried different meanings in practice
for Bozena and for the workers. Bozena told the group: "It's your right,
your full right, to stop the line. The wrong way is to keep the line running." In one too silent group she provoked them by repeating the story
of the operator harassed by a fellow worker. Then she urged them: "I
promise you. Come and talk to me. Maybe that person really doesn't
understand. The CFIA [Canadian Food Inspection Agency which certi-
fies HACCP] will come four times a year and ask questions.... So everyone has to understand."

How much did people "understand"? That is, how much did they
connect their right to stop the line for safety or quality problems with
stringent HACCP requirements, with keeping their most valued customers, with the reputation of the company and finally with their jobs?
That was Bozena's big-picture story for them; but what many of them
saw instead was the immediate rebound that their actions instigated in
the realm of social and power relations. As we saw, Ivan was already
skeptical about telling the supervisor not to start the line until the calibration was done. He left that job up to Bozena, "to find a better way."
As for the operators, they knew that they might face censure from their
co-workers as well as from supervisors for slowing down production
and reducing their output. One operator, a South Asian woman, described this dilemma as the "power to speak." From my observations
at Triple Z, I would say that speaking up orally as well as in text required a certain power that many operators felt they didn't have.

> Operator: The power to speak. We need the power to speak.
> Bozena: The people in the lab are friendly. It's not because of you
>   that we are dumping product. It's because something is
>   wrong. It's your right to take the proper action.

Bozena tried to deflect fault from individuals and find the cause in
the system or the work practices. In each session there were mixed
opinions about this power to speak. Some workers felt assured that
they could stop the line without fear or intimidation from supervisors

and co-workers; others did not. Camilla, a young Italian Canadian worker in the preparation area, recounted another story of how she had found a part of a knife (from one of dicers) and stopped the line. A heavy labor worker yelled at her and started the line again (in fact, it was the same worker as in the operator's story). Camilla was confused then about this power to speak and to act. Linda, a Newfoundlander, and her co-worker urged her to take action.

> Linda: Remember what Marty [the previous plant manager] said—"whenever you see something, you stop the line." I always stop the line when I see something.
> Camilla: Only the lab has the power to do it.
> Bozena, Linda, Ivan (together loudly): No!

I don't know if Camilla was convinced, but at least she heard another side of this story and would probably consider what she had learned the next time safety was at stake. As for documentation, workers openly admitted to me that writing down errors could easily get them or their co-workers in trouble. Although they might have the power to speak in text, many would choose not to. Managers, staff and workers all confronted these contradictions every day. I think they did their best to resolve them, acting on what they believed, understood and experienced in the routine of their daily work. That is, they all acted from within their own communities of practice or their own discourses.

In another group session, Bozena was searching for more answers, and Armando, an Italian unionized lead hand, pointed to a well-known dilemma:

> Armando: Supervisors put a lot of pressure on people to keep production up.
> Bozena: If people tell you "we can't stop [the line]," then tell them why or come and get me. I'll be happy to explain. I'm a manager in this place as well, and I can talk to them.... We'll go higher and higher until we find the solution. We have to be 100% sure that we did whatever we could.... There's going to be a lot of pressure, especially in the summer—pushing, pushing, pushing. What happens? We have $15,000 in the garbage. I'll recall everything. I don't care about the numbers. I care about quality.

Ironically, this particular session was pressured to end by a supervisor who came looking for her workers. She complained that the session was supposed to be an hour and it was already an hour and a half. She had to stop the line because she had no more relish to put into production. Bozena responded coolly: "They had a lot of questions." Sara, her lab technician, added: "Training is important." The supervisor said she was short-staffed today and had asked for the training to be postponed. She left angry and frustrated. Bozena dismissed her worries with, "They knew for three days about it, why are they short?"

So it seems that getting the word out is difficult at many levels as we see the clash of different and often contradictory meanings about which aspects of work are important and required for a successful business. In the participatory sessions, Bozena could let the workers lead and, by doing so, open up those meanings, literacies and work practices, as well as the contradictions that she would otherwise have a difficult time uncovering. As an educator, I too would encourage learning and training that addresses those contradictions, that acknowledges the intersection where learning takes place and builds on what people know and do in their social practice at work.

In the next story about an ISO orientation session, the researcher does that uncovering while the trainer sticks to her prepared script.

TEXCO'S ORIENTATION TO ISO: SUE'S STORY

General Training at Texco

This story is about an ISO orientation session that took place at Texco. Remember that Texco is a small, privately owned factory that makes specialized fabrics for a niche market. It has 60 employees, about 17% of them with English as a second language. Senior managers fully support the concept of training, and there are a great many formal and informal training sessions offered at Texco on a regular basis. Managers told me that the purpose of training and education was to provide people with tools and skills to do what they need to do, make people feel better, and to prepare them to be more flexible and interchangeable. They talked about the social responsibility of the company to provide this education as well. I heard that although the "results can't be quantified, they know that it is working. It makes people happy and at the end of the day it has got to be good for business." One manager also told me, "I'm sure it is doing the right thing in the same sense that eating the right kind of diet is good for you. By doing the right thing you have to have faith that it is going to pay dividends for you."

During my 6 months at Texco, I attended WHMIS, SPC, forklift, and mechanical training sessions. I also saw team meetings and general meetings used as a forum to address learning points important to managers. I attended the ISO and safety orientation sessions mandated by the company. However, like Mary Ellen at Triple Z, I observed that much of Texco's in-house training and learning was heavily print-oriented, with trainer-directed presentations. I also observed that the way these sessions were run directly contradicted managers' open attitude about the benefits of training and the empowered workforce they said they desired.

As an educator myself, I saw these as troubling signs. I had a great urge to do something to improve these training sessions and felt frustrated that in my role as researcher, there was little I could do to provide immediate consultation. In several cases, those employees leading the training told me that their training was participant centered and participatory. When I observed these same training sessions, I saw that this was true in only the most superficial of ways.

ISO Orientation

I observed and participated in the ISO orientation that every Texco employee was mandated to attend early on during my time at Texco. The ISO orientation story is important in showing why the ideal message promoted in training (and in the quality policy and procedural manuals) may not always make it to use on the plant floor. In terms of the training itself, it shows how facilitation methods may impede learning, and how inaccessible language, large doses of print material and getting people to read aloud can inhibit learning. But at the level of workplace practices, it also illustrates how what is advocated in the ideal world of training or orientation may not reflect actual use within the complex social realm of work. I believe that this story has an important message for workplace trainers and educators, union representatives and managers. It reveals the many levels of complexities in training and the factors that determine the effectiveness of that training.

In the ISO orientation I attended, trainers did not acknowledge or attempt to discuss the circumstances that existed on the plant floor that would inhibit workers from following the paperwork that was part of standardized procedures under ISO (filling in forms, ensuring that there are proper tickets with each process during the making of the product the product). For example, there was no acknowledgment of production pressures and what a worker should do if asked by a supervisor to circumvent ISO documentation and paperwork procedures. The orientation assumed that people were operating independently of social factors and that if they only knew the importance of ISO, they would follow the rules. Never during my time at Texco did I observe an open discussion among managers and workers about some of the dilemmas and contradictions that workers face at times in engaging in the literacy expectations of ISO and how these dilemmas might be overcome. Most of the discussion was aimed at how and why workers should comply.

These aspects of the ISO orientation were typical of the many training and informal learning sessions I observed at Texco and counter to accepted principles of sound adult education that many of us would take for granted.

There are many similarities between the training sessions at Triple Z and Texco. Like Mary Ellen, I also thought that the training method, language and the discourse used inhibited rather than promoted an understanding of the purpose and principles of ISO in the workplace. In addition, the style of facilitation that reinforced hierarchies of power and focused on the transmission of knowledge from trainer to worker operated in a similar way to some of the training stories from Triple Z.

With an inherent belief in the value of training, managers attempted to impart knowledge about the kind of behaviors they expected from employees, the kind of people they wanted working at the factory and their attempts to motivate people to accept company values and engage in desired behaviors. Yet despite their conscious effort to promote training, they were often thwarted because of both the style of the communication or training and the contradictions workers faced on the plant floor.

The first part of the orientation story focuses on the delivery of the ISO orientation session by an in-house company trainer at Texco. This focuses mainly on the first layer, the more familiar terrain of training methodologies and how these can create barriers to learning. These are the familiar signposts that educators can easily recognize, the troublesome spots that can be readily addressed and improved upon through our expertise. But to understand that even with the most participatory, well-designed training practices, learning-in-use might be different from that taught in the training or orientation sessions, we have to look to a deeper layer of meaning in the social realm of work practices. The second part of this story examines ISO documentation practices in use where we see the dilemmas of ISO documentation on the floor. If we view literacies and learning as social practices, we then see the dilemmas that come up in work practices as part and parcel of our work as educators in two ways. First, we can examine and provide opportunity for critical discussion about the dilemmas inherent in the work practices in our training sessions. Second, we can identify, report on and problem-solve the issues of learning-in-use that are contributing to rough spots on the floor outside of training

The Goal of ISO Orientation: In-House Training

During my first month on the floor as a participant observer, I attended the ISO orientation with three other employees who had been working for Texco for several months. The session was delivered by Janet, the Quality Coordinator, a young woman just out of a textile management program who had been with the company less than a year. From conversations with her, I found that she had good intentions and wanted to deliver effective sessions that met company goals and were of interest to employees. In conversations after the orientation, it was also evident that Janet was aware of some of the flaws in the method of presentation she used, and aspired, at least in theory, to do it differently. However, there were also contradictions between what she said about how she ran the session and what she actually did.

In an interview with Janet after the session, she explained to me that her goal for the ISO orientation was to give people a basic understanding of where the company stood on quality. She said that even when she started, she didn't know what ISO 9001-registered meant, and that people should understand this. Janet's statements showed that she had bought into the company discourse and goals respecting quality. She said: "It's nice to have a little bit of background on where that [quality issues] stemmed from, why we do it, why we inspect things and continuously improve, and how that affects us as a company. You know, we get more customers or more profitable, everybody's profit-sharing goes up or something. You know, it's nice to tie it all in."

I asked Janet if people had to know everything that is outlined in the 30-page handout we received in orientation. She told me that they have to be able to fill in forms for their particular job, and follow the Standard Operating Procedures for the particular job they're doing. She explained: "If they're following the procedures and they're using those tools (because basically those forms are a tool of recording information and passing it on, communicating it to other people) ... if they're doing those correctly, if they're doing everything correctly and filling it in, they're following our quality system."

I observed that Janet did not acknowledge the social realm of work in her responses about how to correctly follow the ISO quality system. Her response made me think that she saw these elements of ISO operating independently of the constraints and realities of what actually happens on the plant floor. Ironically, though, in conversations with Janet, she told me about her own fear of completing some ISO forms when she first started at Texco. She also told me how supervisors did not sign off on training and orientation in a timely way, and how this led to a mad rush before the external auditor came. However, in my conversation with her, she did not connect these stories to the barriers and contradictions that workers on the floor experienced in doing the documentation and paperwork required by ISO.

Attending the Session

The bulk of the hour-and-a-half orientation was spent with Janet reading handouts aloud to us or explaining how things work related to quality at Texco. Throughout the orientation, people asked few questions.

We started off in the Quality Lab, four of us crowded in a semicircle of chairs around Janet's desk. All three workers had been working for Texco at least several months. There were two men, both Caucasian, one just out of high school. The third worker was a young woman from South America who spoke English as a second language. The way we

were physically situated around the trainer was symbolic of training
where the trainer is the authority figure who imparts knowledge to students or learners. She handed each of us a folder with 30 pages about
ISO and the ISO 9000 series of standards. The first thing we did was
look at the company values, which Janet read off the company's business card. As Janet read them, she told us:

"The customer is number one."

"What we say is what we do."

"Our focus is being number one."

"We do a lot of training."

Then Janet turned to us and said, "Is everyone committed to reading aloud? Even you, Sue." I could feel my heart thudding. The silence
was so thick you could hear a pin drop. Only Todd answered with, "I'd
like to take it home and read it." As an educator myself, I was initially
stunned that reading aloud would be used as a learning strategy. However, during my time at Texco, I noted that it was common for supervisors and managers to read aloud to workers or get them to read aloud.
My first thought was that getting people to read aloud showed great in-
sensitivity to those workers who may have been uncomfortable reading in any way. It also had the potential to embarrass people and expose
their weaknesses and reinforce negative learning experiences that they
had in school. One of the production workers who was also a trainer
told me that having people read around is embarrassing for people and
that it was a way to have power over other people. I felt the same. I also
saw reading aloud as an example of how people might feel they were
treated as children (as some in fact told me) and in direct contradiction
to managers' visions for an empowered work force. I comment more
on reading aloud throughout the story.

The bulk of our time was spent going through the handouts in our
folder. The first handouts, "What is ISO?" and "What are Standards?,"
Janet read aloud to us. In doing so, she kept us close to the meaning
she wanted us to understand. I saw it as an attempt to draw us in to the
language and concepts of the ideal discourse on quality that the company wanted people to adhere to. But for me, the combination of unfamiliar language and hearing the text read aloud served to inhibit rather
than promote understanding of the ISO concept.

Janet told us that "standards help increase reliability" and that
"when we test fabrics [there are] certain specifications." She also explained that Texco was ISO 9001 registered, which meant Texco was
capable of measuring various processes. She commented, "There's a
lot of reading" and "Are there any questions?" Nobody asked anything.
She then showed us two huge red binders, which she explained were
the quality procedural and policy manuals. She showed us the chapters and the index and flipped through the manuals. The purpose of

this demonstration seemed not to be to engage us in the detailed information in these manuals, but to illustrate to us the importance and the seriousness of the ISO policies and procedures.

We then went to the area of the plant where non-conforming material and the binder of Non-Conformance Reports (NCRs) were held. At Texco a "non-conformance" means that something is wrong with a product or a procedure, and all employees are required to fill out an NCR when this happens. We examined the NCRs and Janet explained how to fill one out. This part of the orientation was quite interesting—it was real, visual and tactile. It appeared to me from their relaxed body language and conversation that people were much more comfortable with this part of the training than with reading from a sheaf of papers that used unfamiliar and complex language. We walked around, touched the materials and had a look at the NCRs in the binder. This part of the orientation came closest to the lived reality of ISO on the plant floor.

We then took our folders to the lunch room. We sat down at a table at the back and continued to go through the next section in our handouts, which focused on the "Evolution of the Quality Concept." Janet read this section aloud to us. She explained that "We don't use statistical techniques ... we use math, not hard math. Very simple. [It] helps us learn about processes. A chart can show where the problem is before the product is made. If we have good quality, more people will buy from us."

Once she finished the first page, she asked Reg to read the next section, "Internal Customer–Supplier Relationship" aloud. He read painfully and haltingly. I shuddered for him as I was transported back into elementary school. Asking him to read aloud was demeaning and childlike.

Janet continued to read parts of the handouts aloud to us and skimmed through other parts. It was interesting that one of our handouts stated that the only correct terms to describe results were "conforming" and "non-conforming" and that one must avoid terms such as "good" or "bad." To my mind, this attempted to remove the element of blame from the equation. I found this ironic because during my time at Texco, fear of being blamed for making a mistake affected whether people participated in completing the ISO documentation. Concern about making a mistake or being blamed was commonplace in workers' comments regardless of what was emphasized in the ISO orientation.

As we moved to the end of the session, Janet let us know that there was going to be an internal audit at two o'clock that would check out the procedural manual to see if it was the same as how people were doing their work in practice. Internal audits were done by designated people within Texco. Janet explained that internal auditors had to take a 3-day course, and that there was also an external audit every 6 months. An external audit was going to happen on Friday. I later reflected that this would have been a good opening to talk about the reasons why practice might not always be the same as what is outlined in the procedural manual, but it never came up.

Janet explained to us that during the external audit the auditor looks at the procedural manual and non-conformances. He or she checks out the system and tells them where they can improve. The auditor inspects how people do the job, usually focusing on 3 to 4 of the 21 quality elements to see, "Are they really doing this?" "Last time there was an external audit, there was only one minor non-conformance. Hopefully this time there will be none," Janet said.

Janet ended the session by telling us that we were good and patient and asked if there were any questions. She emphasized the importance of quality and that "training is a big focus for us ... if you need it, ask." Through this comment Janet revealed that she saw training as the answer to difficulties that workers might have with respect to quality in practice on the floor.

Post-ISO Orientation

I had the opportunity to talk to Janet a couple of weeks after the session. It was interesting to hear her reflect on when she had received her own ISO orientation. I wondered whether Janet obviously had learned from her own experience that this was an effective teaching strategy. She said, "I remember when I received the orientation. Garth, Jarrod and Alain and I, we sat around outside ... it was a nice day ... on one of the picnic tables, and we took turns reading. We had some questions and we answered them." This picture she described of her own orientation was much more participatory than the one she delivered. Her orientation appeared to be collegial, with everyone at the table being on an equal footing and contributing to the discussion. The kind of learning she enjoyed so much didn't seem to be replicated in the sessions she delivered.

I was interested in Janet's reasons behind about how she delivered the ISO orientation. She talked about reading out loud: "It's nice to have some people read out loud. It forces you to make sure that they're reading it and they're not just listening and wondering a little bit you know, *and* getting them to participate." She talks about being sensitive to whether people would be comfortable reading when she says:

> I said "Are you all comfortable reading?" I knew Dana wouldn't be comfortable reading. I get that from her. I don't want to force people to read something and maybe not understand what the words are. When there's a word and people are saying "Like what are you talking about?" so that's why I don't even like using that word.

The first thing I noticed was that although Janet had good intentions, she had little understanding of how asking people to read aloud might affect them or embarrass them. Moreover, she equated a person's ability to read with language ability rather than literacy. It also appeared that Janet's understanding of reading was that participants should get one meaning of the text: her meaning.

The reading of the text aloud follows the "transmission" theory of learning, that one can give the same information and message to everyone by imparting it to them in the same way. But meanings are multiple, localized in people's experience of events and relationships. If the meanings of texts are varied and contested, then an important part of "understanding" any reading material would be in people's interpretations of the text and what the text is telling them to do—the resulting actions on the floor. Janet's definition of participation seemed to be a narrow one: to be present and to be engaging in some way with the text. For me, participation and engaging with the text would be about making clear people's own meanings, and including a discussion of the dilemmas that occur.

I asked Janet how she planned and prepared for the ISO orientation She explained that she had delivered the session numerous times before. She said that this one was different because she had added a few sheets from a lecture she had prepared for the textile class, part of her textile management program. She said that you couldn't prepare specifically for different situations because you wouldn't know what people were going to ask you. She explained that she didn't really like to sit and talk all the time, but liked people to ask questions.

I asked Janet how she would instruct me to prepare to deliver this ISO session if I had never done it before. I was fascinated by the contradictions in what she said about delivering the session and how she actually delivered it in practice.

One of the things she emphasized to me was that I would need to "get through to them" about the mission, to make people feel part of something. Part of what she said reflected my previous comments about the need to transmit the official meaning of the company mission and ISO in the orientation rather than discussing the dilemmas of what actually happens on the plant floor. Janet told me I should also set examples specifically for the departments that people were coming from. She also instructed me to read over the material again and let people ask questions throughout rather than at the end.

As an educator, I found Janet's advice very much in line with what I would do to prepare an orientation or training session myself. Where we differed was in our interpretation of participation and the role of the facilitator as an authority figure. We also differed in our interpretation of why people did or did not complete ISO documentation in the official way intended. Janet seemed to believe it came down to individual knowledge and skills, whereas I tended to think it had more to do with the stresses and tensions in the social realm of work. Whether one participated in the quality system had more to do with the authority of others, relationships with co-workers, and workload. Perhaps the orientation session could have been more effective by designing participation in the way that Janet experienced it in her own orientation, and by having a real discussion of the dilemmas and contradictions around doing the paperwork required by ISO out on the floor.

Regarding the language used in training, Janet told me that she used words like "environment" instead of "milieu." Perhaps she was so immersed in the quality discourse that it was hard for her to see that the language of the quality discourse as a whole, especially as it was represented in print, created barriers in understanding for participants.

I asked Janet what was working well about the orientation and what she would like to change. She said she would like to have a plant tour and have other Texco employees talk about the part they play in the quality system. She suggested that more hands-on activities and visuals would have been better to pass on information. She reflected: "The package is nice as a reference, but I don't think it's always the most effective way to pass on information ... just to read through something, you know, or for me to read it to them."

I found that there was a sharp contrast between the ISO orientation and how people actually approached paperwork and documentation on the factory floor. The next story of ISO standards in use strongly exposes the silences that took place in the orientation session.

Contradictions Between Training and Learning-in-Use

The two scenarios that Jarrod told me comparing the ideal world of work practices and ISO documentation and what really happens on the floor were revealing. It illustrated the gap between the ideal practice promoted in training and orientation and the reality of what happened on the production floor. It was compelling proof of why we needed to go deep into the lived experience of workers on the floor to understand the trouble spots in training and orientation.

Scenario 1: The Ideal World According to Jarrod

A piece of fabric comes out of the Weave Room. A first quality check has to be done [to ensure the fabric is running according to a normal range of specifications]. A sample goes to the Lab to be approved. Then Stan takes the ticket that is with the roll of fabric and enters into the AS4000 system. He weighs it and puts the number of meters into the system. The next process is to heat-set it. Stan should receive a work order for heat setting. He should do the heat setting, complete the work order and enter it into the system. The next process is Coating. Tom should get the fabric and a work order from Elizabeth for Coating. He runs the fabric and enters the work order into the system. He prints up new tickets for it and then Ted takes it for Shipping. Ted then prints documents for Shipping.

Scenario 2: What Really Happens

The problem is that we are behind. A roll comes out of the Weave Room that should have been shipped yesterday. I ask Stan to heat-set it and give it to Tom. First thing is that there has been no sample. Stan didn't weigh the fabric and has no idea of the length. He heat-sets it without a work order. He passes it to Tom. Tom doesn't know the meters. No work order can be made. Larry doesn't know the meters and Ted can't ship it. The Weave Room says it is so many meters. This is imprecise and there is no traceability. It is run through the batches to get meters. Elizabeth makes work orders and tickets for work that has already been done.

We are trying to change. We only circumvent the system when we have something signed off by the Plant Manager. It's really hard to do paperwork because things take time and don't go smoothly.

As these contrasting vignettes illustrate, the reality of actually applying ISO standards on the factory floor is sometimes quite different from the "paper instructions" and what might be advocated in an ISO orientation session. This second vignette shows that even with orientation and training about the value and purpose of ISO and the necessity of documentation, the messy nature of everyday work life with its contradictions and different meanings intervenes.

In fact, over time I began to encounter several stories from every level of the organization, about every level of the organization, that showed people sometimes short-circuited the paperwork required by ISO. Although this practice may have served a need in the short term, in the long term people said there were negative consequences.

The first time I got an inkling of how quality procedures were short-circuited was when I spent time with Ted in Shipping and Receiving. When I talked to Ted, he told me he did not always follow quality standards to save time. For example, there was cloth in the Finishing Room that should have been QA stamped, but there was never usually a problem with it, so he shipped it without getting it QA stamped to save time. If he had had to go to the Quality Lab, he would have had to wait 10 or 15 minutes. So he did not get the cloth QA stamped to get the work done. He informed me that he had also shipped product without QA to an outside Finisher. He said that there was rarely trouble when he did this; people knew he did it, but there was hardly ever a problem. If there was a problem, the Lab (Sandy) would have asked for the ticket (Ted keeps them for a month) and said, "Why didn't you get it stamped?" Ted would have said he was busy and didn't have time. So then his supervisor would have gone over ISO requirements with him (although he knows them already), and he would have followed the ISO procedures correctly until he was busy again.

Ted also explained that he did not always follow the Standard Operating Procedure (SOP) for receiving goods. He said that he often signed for them and then looked at them (according to ISO, you are supposed to check the goods before receiving them). He told me that he had also received products that did not have a purchase order (PO) number. In the past, yarn came in without a PO because staff in Research and Development (R&D) had ordered their yarn without going through proper paperwork procedures. They ordered yarn on their own and did not give the order to Purchasing until several days later.

Later I talked to Camilia in Purchasing. She explained that there was a proper procedure involved in purchasing inventory items. A requisition had to be written out before inventory could be purchased and was entered into the system. Camilia told me that one particular supervisor in manufacturing or a manager in R&D had to sign it. Then the requisition got a PO number, which took it from Manufacturing to Purchasing. The items would then be ordered by Camilia. The vendor got a copy of the PO. Shipping and Receiving also got one so the inventory could be received into the building, and Camilia kept one.

Camilia explained that sometimes R&D did not follow proper channels:

> Sometimes in Research and Development it will happen. Someone, say Larry, is talking to someone at DuPont and he'll say, "I've got this project and I'm looking for a yarn. It doesn't matter what color it is, but I want to do some testing on it, and do you think you can send me a sample of four or five spools or something?" And another guy at the Research Department in DuPont will say, "Oh yeah I've got some of that hanging around. I'll send it out to you."

Camilia explained that then these items would arrive with no paperwork, so they were not officially in the system. Only documentation made them alive in the system. The items would arrive at Texco, but Ted didn't know whom they were supposed to go to because there was no supporting documentation.

She also said that without documentation, it wasn't possible to back up and track what various R&D projects were for. Sometimes if Larry got busy, he would have two or three projects with six spools that sat out somewhere on the floor. Then when he went to do the project three months later, he wouldn't be able to remember where the spools were, or what they were, or what they were for, because he didn't have any paperwork for backup. Then if he did the project and it turned out well, he wouldn't be able to repeat it because it had never been entered into the system. If it had been in the system, he would have been able follow it all the way back to the originating project and find out what he did, where he got the yarn and what came in. Camilia explained to me that she had to keep reminding R&D to do the proper paperwork. She admitted that it was a lot of paperwork for them to complete, and that sometimes they just found it easier to use little notes. She did say, though, that not following the paperwork could result in an NCR.

Mary, a worker in Finishing, related a similar story to me. She informed me that "they say that paperwork is more important than production, but when it comes to the crunch it isn't." She emphasized that when product had to go out the door, the rules were bent. She told me that Ted often took tickets and shipped product without it being QA'd. Then there would be a push to do it properly, everything would be QA'd and then people would slack off again. Supervisors would again get on the bandwagon about proper paperwork. But soon someone would need something right away and priorities would change. For example, a supervisor or someone in R&D would want to cut 500 meters without a Finishing Order—without the paperwork. Mary would get a call from the supervisor to do it for R&D without the paperwork, but then she would be asked "Why did you do it?" She remarked that supervisors were covered, but "we are damned if we do and damned if we don't. They do it without paperwork because they want to get it out the door."

Mary further explained that in team meetings they were told not to touch anything that didn't have paperwork. "For a month we are told we can't do anything for R and D without paperwork. Then Jarrod will say 'Just do this and I will back you.' Then Elizabeth will call down and say 'just do this and this.' Then they will get back on the bandwagon again because perhaps the Plant Manager gets after them."

When I asked why this happened, Mary said that "R and D has hot new items they want to get to the customer quickly. Maybe the sales man is going to see the customer. But it only takes a couple of seconds to do a work order."

These stories show that the message delivered in the ISO orientation was not always the one that was taken up on the floor. The stated message that the company tried to convey through its directives to employees, including the ISO orientation, was that paperwork was just as important if not more important than production. However, workers were often given contradictory messages about the importance of participating in the paperwork for ISO. Sometimes serving the production needs of the customer seemed more of a priority than the paperwork.

The ISO orientation story also showed that even at the level of methodology, there were several barriers to effective learning. An overreliance on print, sophisticated language, teacher-centered learning, and strategies like reading aloud obscured even the ideal message that the company was trying to relay about the importance of ISO and its accompanying documentation.

CONCLUSION

Our stories have shown how the literacy thread in job learning weaves its way through formal sessions and onto the plant floor. These experiences of trainers and workers reveal how deeply interwoven learning, literacies and use are in the fabric of working life. They are tangled in with the meanings, risks and opportunities that people create through their daily work practices.

As such, we see that our own practice as workplace educators will be grounded in literacy as it is lived when we examine, think and act within a framework of literacy as a social practice. Our experiences as researchers observing and analyzing job learning have shown us that different (and often contradictory) meanings of literacy in workplace learning determine how people will use their learning and their literacies. As workplace educators, we can direct our attention to uncovering those different meanings by providing space and safety for these discussions in our facilitation, initial planning, teaching and evaluation activities. In our collaboration with trainers, we can encourage them to get at the meanings-in-use of the learning and literacy on the floor, just as Bozena did in the participatory or inquiry sections of her training.

In our stories we examined facilitation and teaching methods commonly used in job training: reading aloud and trainer-directed presentations with dense, jargon-filled text for handouts and overheads. These methods impeded even the ideal messages that the companies were trying to convey to employees. Moreover, these methods assumed an ideal or unreal world of learning transfer that doesn't account for the complex realm of social practices at work. Nor do these methods account for the different discourses and communities of practice that people live in and within which they make sense of their words, their work and their worlds. Making sense of learning and making sense of literacy require that educators explore those other realms, those different discourses to find the meanings that compel others to words and action.

We close with a quote from Giselle Mawer (1999) on the integrative and challenging role of the workplace educator. We think her words not only capture the message that we have tried to convey about training and workplace learning, but also lead into our reflections on the practice of workplace education in Chapter 6:

> Educators' effectiveness then is greatly dependent on the extent to which they can work collaboratively and strategically with a number of different others in a role that facilitates learning, rather than delivers teaching. Such a role often involves challenging existing power structures and practices in workplaces, at the same time as working towards attitudinal shifts from key personnel, and inevitable dealing with passive—if not active!—resistance from others. (p. 66)

6

Implications
for Practice

Tracy Defoe, Sue Folinsbee, and Mary Ellen Belfiore

What implications for our practice as workplace educators do we take away from the experience of researching literacies in work culture through the In-Sites project? This chapter sets out our reflections on what we have learned and what it means for us as the three practitioners in our group. These kinds of reflections on an individual level are familiar ground. Improving practice is an ongoing process: reflecting on our actions, exploring new ideas, trying further actions, more reflections, more ideas, and so on. We each reach to improve our practice in this way.

Reflecting in a wider context, in ways for others to consider, is less familiar. It feels like walking away from the circle of chairs where we have spent several years swapping stories and discussing meanings. We're going back to our previous work, where the questions are not "What happened in your site and what did it mean?" but "What are we going to do now, and why?" We all feel now that the work world is a little grimmer than it was during the period we did this research. Political and economic factors have resulted in a less hopeful world, but workplace education is still optimistic work for us. We couldn't do it without the commitment to try new ideas. We couldn't take part in workplace education practice if we felt hopeless. So these implications for practice are written from a guardedly optimistic point of view.

Over the 3 years of our project together, we have all learned some-thing about workplaces, about literacies and learning, and about our-selves. We always planned on a bridge from theory to practice, but we have also realized that dialogue is two-way. If there is to be a bridge, it has to be built from both shores. In this chapter we are trying to build it from the side of practice, by writing about our experiences as practitio-ners doing research. We know there are others in the field who share our desire for and have contributed much to a broader, more social and critical practice of language and literacies education. We want to encourage them to join us in building our side of the bridge, by opening up our own practice to research.

With few exceptions, academics and practitioners are in different discourses; they work within different power structures with varying degrees of freedom to put forth certain ideas. As practitioners we are partly shaped by and often have to work within government policies that are mostly at odds with a more critical and complex way of think-ing about literacies at work. As practitioners, we have found that we have had to take small steps to implement some of the insights from our research. We are not yet ready to write a list of strategies about how to practice differently. We believe that it will take many years of back-and-forth on the research to build that bridge and test out our new awareness before we arrive at a substantial array of practical strategies that reflect literacies as social practice.

We have organized our reflections around issues and insights that we hope will resonate with readers. After many tries, we have settled on questions as the way to approach the issues, and we have decided that we relate to them best through examples from our own experiences. Taken as a group, these might be summarized as a caution to pay at-tention to ourselves, to our past, to resistance and practices in workplaces, to goals, and of course, to literacies. Some of the interest-ing issues in workplace literacy have always been power, politics, eq-uity and safety. Sometimes these have a lot to do with money and time. To this list, we would add risk and blame, and, of course, local mean-ings. We recognize the interdependent nature of these issues, but try to present them individually, in the manner of focusing on a thread in the weave and not, we hope, in pulling on the thread and taking it out of its complexity.

WHAT DO WE MEAN BY "PRACTICE"?

Before we discuss the implications for practice that we carry forward from our research, we want to try to describe what we mean by work-place education "practice." We know it is hard for people to imagine our work. Tell someone that you are a workplace educator, and they have almost no reference point, no idea of what you do. And practice is about doing. Being a workplace education practitioner often means being a person who brings educational know-how to bear on workplace issues, often issues of workplace change where people are looking together for new responses to new situations. We operate in the overlap between education and work so that learning and work are meaningfully connected.

Although our focus here is on literacies at work, we support a holistic approach to literacy that recognizes that literacies are more than just about work; they are equally about personal development, families and communities. We see a workplace educator as someone who plays a number of different roles that are connected to learning in the broadest sense. Our job is about learning in specific workplaces. We learn from workers about their views, interests and needs; from managers, supervisors and staff about their vision, values and strategies for success. We facilitate and problem-solve with workplace committees and partners. In addition, our roles can include teacher or instructor, researcher, needs assessor, program developer, instructor trainer, mentor, educational advocate and more.

We use the term "workplace education" to describe a range of workplace programs and activities that address the reading, writing, numeracy, second-language learning, basic computing and other identified educational needs of the work force (Folinsbee, 2000a). Educational programs that address these needs may be job specific, or a combination of job related and non-work related, and they may be for any member of the work force. They may take place on or off site in various formats. The union, jointly with management or in the community, may offer them. Adult educators or peer trainers may deliver them. Technologies may be part of the delivery method.

The list is extensive, even impressive. What do we do, exactly? What do companies, unions, educational institutions, governments or, most likely, joint steering committees from companies or sector groups pay us to do? Here are some examples from our own experiences as practitioners, and from the experiences of our colleagues.

Communication and collaboration are at the core of our work: We do it, investigate it, model it and always try to improve it. We start out by setting up an environment designed for collaborative practice: a joint endeavor between labor and management. We ask questions about work and learning for particular people in a particular workplace or industry. We ask about literacies, language, communication and skills. We do applied research to figure out which parts of a workplace problem might be understood through the lens of education, and which parts might not. We write reports documenting what people said, describing the findings of our research and possible courses of action. We make recommendations. We design customized courses and sometimes train others to facilitate those courses. We make recommendations for organizational change. And we always learn from the people brought together in a committee or in a workplace program.

We work with people to build knowledge about learning, about being a learner and knowing themselves as learners when they might be very disconnected from that idea. We teach people to read, to speak up, to be part of a meeting or to host a tour of their work area. We teach people how to use a computer for word processing, for databases, or for email. We tutor or work with small groups of people in worksite learning centers. We facilitate sessions for tutors who go on to tutor co-workers. We prepare workers to take the examinations for high school completion credentials. We connect workers with continuing education. We work with content experts to make technical content into learning that will work for everyone. We start reading circles and get people writing. We suggest company and union picnics include a family story time, and lunch rooms have a shelf for swapping pleasure reading material. We give people books and introduce them to libraries. We offer industry and labor the mind, the understandings, the attitudes and the heart of an educator.

Our practice is more than the sum of these examples. It is action, backed by thinking, planning, trying and reflecting. It is often part of a group effort. It is its own social practice, as we discuss later in the chapter. When we took on the job of researching and writing this book, we took on a new kind of practice, too. Our group of five became another frame of reference for practice. Our thinking about literacies became part of the weave of our work life.

ISSUES, INSIGHTS AND IMPLICATIONS

This part of the chapter is organized around issues in workplace education practice. They are listed in a rough order of the early issues in the relationship between educator and workplace, through those of a more ongoing or later nature. We did not want to write a how-to list that would simplify the very daunting tasks of applying a social practice lens to our work. We believe our work and our local meanings are as complex as anyone else's. We did not want to pretend that we have answers when, in fact, all we have are questions and a few insights.

In each case, the issue is linked with an example. It is now almost 2 years since we stopped collecting data from our worksites. In that time we have each tried to adapt what we do to reflect our new enthusiasm for literacies as social practice. We have each thought back to our previous work and tried to see it and ourselves through the lens of our insights. We invite you to ask yourself these questions and to reflect on your own practice, too.

How Can We See Literacies in the Weave of Work Life?

One of the most mundane things about cultural practices is that they are largely unquestioned by the people who live them. Paradoxically, it is difficult for workplace educators to focus on our own literacies, especially those that we apply in our long list of job tasks. But we agree that we are all in our field to learn.

We say that often, but we come into the situation less naive than we might like to imagine. To stay in the mind set of a learner, we may need to take a fresh look at ourselves even as we look at those around us in the workplace. For example, before we ever started this project, we knew that there are many kinds of reading and writing and uses of text, and many ways people use their abilities. Still, we did not use the specific notion of "literacies" as part of our way of thinking. Literacies as a plural was a new term for us, although we could all recite a list of kinds of literacy: prose literacy, document literacy, computer literacy and so on. Reflecting on literacies and competencies led Tracy to think about the discovery of what she called her "inner illiterate worker." It was an insight that has implications for how we think about ourselves and others.

Tracy found that at Metalco, as is common in manufacturing, products were described technically on engineering drawings. These large, complicated representations of the products were easy to find at almost every production workstation. Tracy was interested in these drawings, not just for what they revealed about the literacies in use at this workplace, but because she could not read them. Each drawing showed a product from three views: top, side, and a cutaway through the center. By convention, all the words written on the drawing to label or describe the product were in block capital letters. Reading these drawings meant interpreting the diagram from the angles presented to "see" the product in one's mind.

Tracy was fascinated with the discovery of this illiteracy within herself. She found she could pretend to read the drawings, and sometimes fooled people into thinking she was an insider with the same blueprint literacies everyone around her seemed to take for granted. After all, conventional thinking tells us that any form of literacy is generic and portable. It is easy to think of a person as being literate or having competencies as an absolute. But the blueprint reading reminded us of how dynamic, relative and relational literacies are in real life.

Workplace educators, all educators should remember that we cannot attain all the literacies possible, ever. Perhaps we don't read music, or French, or the cryptic comments on production bulletin boards. We are all on a learning curve. Tracy's example also reminds us that those we work with have highly developed understandings of literacies where we do not. Her example counters the commonplace ideas in the public arena (Castleton, 1999) that suggest workers lack basic skills and are responsible for the economic woes of companies and countries.

One of the simplest and most powerful insights from our study is that literacies are themselves work. Not separate, they are part of the substance and process of the work itself. In the language Barton and Hamilton (1998) used in their book *Local Literacies*, work is a textually mediated social practice, just like education, and leisure. Learning to use texts is part of almost every job. Acquiring new literacies is increasingly a part of what people get paid to do. As educators, we need to pay attention to those moments when literacies are work not only to support people learning at work, but to also attract the attention and support of workplace decision makers who decide whether these kinds of programs will go forward. At the same time, we might profit from paying closer attention to our own literacies, when and where we use them, and what they mean to us. How can we see literacies in work life? We have to look. We have to think twice about what literacies are, what we might be looking for, and we have to notice them.

How Can We Get Past the Surface to Understand Goals?

Sue is well known for her writing on needs assessments and collaboration in workplace education. Sue now sees the need for an educator to have a deeper and more complex understanding of company objectives and goals and the local meanings held by managers and workers in order to assist them in coming up with educational programs and strategies that both meet the interests of workers and are sustainable. In addition to understanding what a problem is, what it looks like, why it is happening from both managers' and workers' points of view, she now urges us all to look at the bigger picture of the situation across industries.

For instance, she wants to understand the importance of any single document or practice within the bigger picture of a system and how the systems fit into the company's business success. What stage, for example, are they at in implementing ISO? How do they describe their current practices with quality procedures in relation to ISO best practices? We know that these initial discussions usually help us see how things are supposed to work, but don't reveal how they really work in practice.

We see new questions that overlay our basic questions about what is going on with both managers and workers. These might include:

- What are the contradictions both in what they are telling us and in what we see?
- What aren't they telling us?
- What can't they tell us because they don't know?
- What is the difference, or the tension, between theory and practice? For example, between quality assurance theory and practice?

We want to work jointly with workers and managers to understand their different meanings for areas such as work practice, learning needs and possible strategies to address issues around documentation. Recommendations and action ideally come from what managers and workers can agree on in terms of realistic educational solutions and policy for implementing these strategies. We recognize that in many workplaces coming to an understanding or agreement may not be easy because of power differences between workers and managers, especially in nonunionized workplaces. However, through ongoing, developing understandings of what is going on, we have a better chance of helping to pose strategies and start conversations that may lead to meeting the needs of both. It could be that some employees want or need to improve their writing and would welcome opportunities at work to do so. However, we want to find out what this looks like from their point of view. Taking a social practice view of learning includes all the dimensions of how writing plays out in real life

For instance, we insist on using authentic print materials as learning tools, but we usually rely on our own interpretations or meanings of those documents. A social practice view means focusing on the meanings that people have for completing these documents or engaging in other kinds of literacy—their "meanings-in-use." In addition, we want to make the contradictions and issues that emerge around documentation visible to our worker and manager partners. Only when such issues are on the table will new learning be successful. Sue understands from the different local meanings of Non-Conformance Reports at her research site that using authentic materials in learning situations without considering these contradictions and issues will not necessarily result in improved use in practice.

Can Looking Back at Our Reports Help Us See Our Filters?

People have asked us why we bother to do ethnographic study, or even this kind of thinking about literacies and "essential skills" in the weave of work life. Why not just do job profiling to understand workers' literacies in use? The answer we have repeated most often is that skills profiling takes reading and writing and the other skills in that framework and removes them from the complexity and the reality of work life—it pulls out a thread and makes it easy to look at. And in pulling out that thread for any one individual or any job, we lose the "weave," the ways other jobs, other functions, and other people and systems act on and with the one we are studying. So in this study, we are trying to understand the picture without pulling it apart.

But there is another more powerful layer to this answer. Working and learning and literacies are all human constructs. These are human social practices. Although trying to look at any one part outside the influences of the other parts can be useful in some circumstances, it is also artificial.

Mary Ellen remembers her work as a consultant for Triple Z 4 years before the research. She worked with a joint committee to set up a workplace education program. They conducted an organizational needs assessment (ONA) (Folinsbee & Jurmo, 1994) for establishing workplace education programs and activities on site. The ONA document and the evaluation of the programs were part of the written materials that she reviewed in the beginning of the research to reacquaint herself with the recent history of the company and union in regard to educational needs and opportunities. When reflecting on her practice at the end of this new research process, she reread the ONA report and the evaluation again and came away with very different reactions.

This particular report had substantial data on language and literacy skills, communication practices and job training practices, with additional information on equipment, staffing and work procedures. For the workers, staff, managers and union officials who participated in the ONA, all these topics affected how they went about doing their jobs. As the consultant, Mary Ellen saw it all as rich context, but still background material for her focus on basic skills. The report was filled with the voices of people at all levels taking a hard look at their working conditions. They spoke openly about the contradictions and the power relationships that played out in communication practices and in getting work done. At that stage, she saw workplace education as affected by these issues, but still separate. The image she saw was composed of foreground (basic skills) and background (the context of the workplace), not a tapestry with threads woven into different patterns. At the time, she didn't have an understanding of language and literacies as embedded in daily practice, as being a part of the contradictions, affected by them and also shaping them.

In *Making Meaning, Making Change,* Auerbach (1992) lays out for teachers the role of context for education ("the context of the project shapes the possibilities," p. 24) and how people are "experts on their own reality" (p. 19). These ideas have much more potency for us now than when we first encountered them. Working within a social practice view of literacy, we find ourselves stepping into the complicated weave of workplace relations and practices and Auerbach's words make deeper sense. We see people as "experts on their own reality" because they know the meanings of actions, paperwork and communication patterns in their workplace. Understanding what the meanings are and how contradictory meanings exist at any one time leads us to see our role now not as fixing problems, but as revealing practices and understandings that make people use their literacies or not. If our role is to make these practices visible, then the role of the joint committee is to address those practices as they see fit.

In Triple Z's ONA report, participants painted a complicated picture of work in which many threads were woven together. People consistently pointed to social and power relationships when they addressed communication practices, motivation and incentives for education and training. "Recognition," "respect," "status," "listening to those who do the job"—all these comments appear repeatedly throughout the report. On the topic of communication, respondents mentioned eight "barriers to good communication" at their workplace, only one of which referred to skills. They talked about interpersonal relations characterized by arrogance, disrespect, back-stabbing, jealousy, an "us versus them" mentality, and work procedures that discouraged good communication practices. Language and literacy was just one of many barriers they named.

At the time, Mary Ellen was operating in a framework of assessing "skills in context." So the participants in the ONA had painted the context that she then tried to document accurately, one full of high emotions, contradictory meanings and rapid change. But then in her own practice, she pushed that context to the background and put skills as the centerpiece; she thought improved literacy and language skills would make certain workplace tasks doable despite the social picture. She did not consider that all the contradictions that people complained about would affect how or when people used their language and literacies. What she reported then as barriers to communication were really different aspects of social practice in the company —admittedly negative aspects, but powerful ones that affect literacy practices as well as any educational endeavors the committee might undertake.

For instance, if one of the aims of language classes is to help people speak up about issues at work, we have to consider whether anyone is listening to them. Is anyone willing to act on what they hear? If not, or if those opinions are not respected, then why would people try to speak up? If work practices remain the same and people don't see any change resulting from speaking up, then why use the language learned in the classroom out on the floor? Is this solely a skills issue? Of course not, yet Mary Ellen kept separating skills and treating them separately— skills for tasks, not skills in practice.

This approach is the dominant one in workplace education. Ultimately, effective change on the floor in language and literacy use depends on changes in social practices at work. At Triple Z, almost all of the joint committee's recommendations for communication were about practice, not about improving skills. They were aiming for structural changes that would affect all the tasks people performed, including literate ones.

This insight of Mary Ellen's about foregrounding skills and documentation, but not making sense of the nonskills concerns of people in a workplace, should give us all pause. We need to bring forward and consider all the contradictory meanings in making recommendations. We need to listen to people describing the weave of social and work policy patterns in their learning at work and not try to focus so closely on literacy or language or communication skills, when the most successful approaches might be ones that take a broader look at job training, meetings and other aspects of company culture.

How Can We "Read" a Workplace?

Trying to put our insights into practice led Tracy to "reading" a workplace to learn about needs in new ways. She discovered new ways of talking about learning by adopting the language of the high-performance manufacturing paradigm to describe educational practices consistent with good practice. For instance, Metalco was trying to move from a "push" system to a "pull" system for the flow of materials and processes. These terms refer to the goal of streamlining the manufacturing process so everything is done "just in time" and a minimum of resources are spent on waiting or wasted effort. People "pull" what they need only when they need it.

Off-the-shelf courses created for imaginary learners with no account of variation in starting places of prior experience and knowledge are an example of a "push" approach. The curriculum is static, and may or may not serve a specific need. In a "pull" approach, things vary to match the learner. Using this metaphor and explaining it to people in the workplace leads to new ways of approaching educational support. It suggests not classes that "push" content, but individual or even group learning plans and teaching support on the floor, by request and customized to the "pull" of the learners. Without an understanding of the overall changes taking place in that workplace, Tracy would not have made the link between her educator's preoccupation with needs, and the cultural change to a pull process. With this link made, understanding and support for a workplace education initiative were secured, and an evolution in practice was set into motion.

The capacity to recognize how groups of people interact and their struggles to learn and work together is an important kind of workplace literacy for us as educators. To do this work, we have to learn to read a workplace. We think there are many such links to be made. We encourage other educators already *reading work* as part of their practice to share their stories.

How Can We Bring Multiple Meanings Into the Picture?

If we try to approach our practice as educators with more emphasis on understanding the different meanings that activities and events hold for people in various parts of the company, we will have to find ways to make the social practices apparent to those people. Production workers, managers, engineers, office workers—all see things differently, and all experience contradictions between the ideal and the lived reality of work. We encourage them to articulate these different meanings and to set up meetings, training and other situations for more dialogue.

In order to understand the social practices around literacies in a workplace, we want to have access so we can spend time on the production floor, or beside people working. We found it very valuable at our research sites to sit in on meetings and training, and to just witness life outside training situations at work. This experience in observing work life on the production floor, in meetings and through job shadowing provides a rich understanding, and also gives us more opportunities to find the stories that help us explain multiple meanings and understandings to the joint advisory committee or others. People tell us stories, but we too seldom use those stories as illustrations. The ones we are a part of, especially where points of view collide, make good examples in building a case for paying attention to meanings.

We can use technology to provide another route to meanings besides words and observations. Tracy is using the digital camera extensively now, and putting it in the hands of production workers, often with an open-ended task like "Take pictures of quality," or "Show us what you think adds value here." The photographic images not only let us all see the photographer's point of view, but are a lasting reference for ongoing discussions. The images also aid memory and make it much easier to show and share what is going on in training. Through taking pictures, people can show what is meaningful to them, even if they cannot articulate exactly how the detail or person or place they have focused on is important.

Another way we have been trying to look for meanings is to give voice to the "hub" people, such as those in Metalco who worked in Quality Assurance. These kinds of people are often already translators between groups without a forum, to create cross-group understandings. Workplace education could enhance that opportunity. Along those lines, we are increasingly interested in co-teaching with content experts, and integrating literacy support or other learning with on-the-job training.

For some time in her practice, Tracy has been trying to support individuals and at the same time find and support groups of people who work together. This has been especially true in places where workplace education has been defined as a need due to rapid change. We see a great need to keep a place for individuals, but spend more time on groups of people and what they need to learn together. We need to make the most of what we already know and what we observe about how groups of people learn together. This includes everyone from the workers we are most familiar with, to managers, engineers and everyone else. It would be her goal, Tracy says now, to make everyone at the company smarter about learning, about themselves as learners, and about the simple idea that other people may not be just like them.

How Can We Explicitly Identify Contradictions and Local Meanings in Paperwork Practices?

Throughout our research-site chapters run stories about workers who do not complete forms and other documentation in the way that managers intend. At all of our sites, we have seen resistance to participation that goes beyond not having the required reading and writing or other literacy skill. Participation also had to do with social relations, power, risk and blame. Our stories showed that workers are not likely to want to participate in documentation practices that have no meaning for them or that are associated with blame for doing so.

We saw at Texco that workers had complex understandings of Non-Conformance Reports (NCRs) and might not complete them to protect themselves or co-workers from blame. At The Urban Hotel, floor managers rejected a system of documentation designed by a consultant that they thought would have resulted in more errors. Instead, they opted for a document designed by one of their own staff that satisfied their need for accuracy and reinforced social bonds. At Metalco, one group of workers didn't complete process charts partly because their production manager did not see the charts as important. At Triple Z, workers did not understand the importance of the documentation required by HAACP, the food safety certification program, and also saw a high degree of risk in participating in these practices.

What are we to make of all this? Paperwork is contested terrain in workplaces. We agree that an obvious implication for practice is that practitioners should never approach documentation as being a simple, neutral work task. If workers are in work groups and part of larger social units (and which are not?), then the workplace practitioner owes it to the worker-learner to set a frame of reference large enough to catch the group, the department and indeed the industry in the field of view. The implication we take away is that although we need to hold the individual in focus, we also need to have enough depth and breadth of focus to be able to see the relationships and the contested meanings that impinge upon the individual.

This is certainly the case where people write texts that they intend to keep outside the documentation system of their workplace. In all our sites we also saw that workers develop their own forms of documentation to assist them in doing their jobs well. Their own personally made charts, logbooks or manuals are concrete examples of their literacies-in-use. Workers might make them to help follow steps in a process accurately, to interpret and put in clear language complicated official documents, or to keep track of changes or their learning on the job—their own piece of worker research. Mary Hamilton (2000) refers to these personal forms of documentation as "vernacular literacy." At Triple Z and Texco, workers created their own bilingual books, which housed their knowledge about the job as well as new information that they could use in particular circumstances.

Workplace teachers rarely find out about these personal forms of job documentation. As unofficial documents, they could pose a risk in a controlled quality or safety system, so workers hide rather than display the fruits of their talents. Workers themselves may not see their documents as examples that are appropriate to share with us. Sometimes we find that workers who have been labeled as needing upgrading in reading and writing are producing these very documents. Their writing, unofficial and risky, gives evidence that literate practices are driven by the need to make work meaningful. These workers make sense of their jobs through their own personal forms of documentation as the managers do through their official documents. Workers exercise a certain amount of autonomy or personal power to gain control over work processes that they know are important.

As workplace educators, we can assume that workers are using literacies at work in ways that are unconventional, unofficial and personally motivated. These examples won't likely appear in a literacy audit. They are worth digging for because they not only reveal talents where some might see deficiencies, but also point to those meanings central to understanding how people, as individuals and groups, practice literacy at work.

Can We Learn About Social Practices by Paying Attention to Resistance?

Mary Ellen's example of her earlier work at Triple Z before the research study brings up the issue of how workplace educators can most effectively support people to find and explore the boundaries of their communication practices. In the final evaluation of that early project, its joint steering committee was criticized for not maintaining adequate communication with plant managers throughout the first phase of the programs. As facilitator for the committee, Mary Ellen had raised the issue of ongoing communication with managers, and the committee set dates for reporting. They agreed it was important, but they didn't follow through, despite much coaxing.

This type of "checking in" was certainly not part of practice in the plant generally; there were no previous examples, no forums to do so. Now Mary Ellen says she would explore their resistance and try to understand it within the social practices of the workplace. The plant manager had as much to learn as the committee did about maintaining contact and the supports in place to follow through. One staff person commented that there are no short cuts; everything has to be in place for programs to be successful. Once again, people who live the reality know it's complicated and that there is no easy fix in a workplace.

The implication for workplace educators, though, goes farther than this. To get to a place where meanings are visible or important to uncover, we may have to dare to explore the boundaries of practices in a workplace, and in particular, to pay attention to resistance. For some people, articulating the range of acceptable practice makes it easier to define what practices are taken for granted in their workplace. For a workplace educator, communication practices are a central issue. We might learn more about them and what they mean to people by exploring them from their edges rather than from the mainstream. And resistance can be a signal to pay attention. We hold this kind of insight as a watermark for our future practice.

Where Do Stakeholders Fit in the Weave of Meanings?

Acknowledging complexity might mean reconceptualizing some of our most central concepts like "stakeholder buy-in," repositioning the workplace needs assessment, or redefining the roles workplace educators take. If literacies are work, and can only be understood in the work tapestry, then holding an interest in the outcome is one way to talk about the weave. What do we mean by reconceptualizing stakeholder buy-in and the workplace needs assessment? We think of stakeholders as those people and those groups who have an interest in the literacies-in-use in a workplace. They are those people who have a concern, who have goals and who lend resources to a workplace education initiative. What if we think about their commitment, or buy-in, as stakeholders as an expression of the local meanings those literacies have for them? Attending to stakeholders' local meanings and making them explicit so they can be named and shared would become one of the reasons to do a workplace needs assessment, and, more importantly, the reason to remain open to new revelations or understandings of local meanings as they are revealed. We can talk about this process as changing understandings over time to be more honest, more real because they emerge through our growing interconnection with the weave of the workplace. If we anticipate these layered revelations and design our initiatives to be responsive and flexible, then as educators we will have the power to come up with ideas and educational answers that truly fit and serve the whole range of stakeholders in the workplace.

Workplace educators have the opportunity to offer insights into learning at a workplace. As outsiders with expertise in learning and teaching, we have a further opportunity to reflect back the local meanings we find. Making local meanings visible creates opportunities for dialogue and for new insights into multiple perspectives on complex issues such as choosing whether or not to participate in reporting your co-workers' non-conformance with procedures. Keeping more than one point of focus or holding multiple perspectives simultaneously sounds difficult, but it is part of best practices now for many workplace educators who try to satisfy multiple stakeholders and at the same time see that workers are recognized for their learning. We see value in practicing three-dimensional thinking, with multiple priorities, even when there may appear to be some contradictions. Complete resolution of these contradictions is unlikely, but acknowledging them is a step toward building a positive environment and a more effective educational program.

We have asked ourselves why many workplace literacy programs have a short life. Many last only as long as a startup grant, and fail to be sustained by those same stakeholders whose buy-in was documented at the outset. We wonder whether short-lived programs are often built on a superficial understanding of the lived meanings embedded in the work process, floating above the level of local meanings that would make them sustainable in a workplace.

Because our experience shows us that these meanings are revealed and recognized over time, rethinking workplace literacy initiatives and making changes over time as local meanings become clearer to the anticipating educator seems to be the way to go. When we think of projects we have been involved in that have lasted over time, we recognize some characteristics that stand out: attention to evolving priorities, change in response to workplace change, and delegating responsibility to the local people who really know the place. These efforts come through structured, collaborative, ongoing evaluation: a planning cycle that looks a bit like that prescribed by the international quality programs that guide our workplaces. Think, plan, do, check and set a new course. But this process needs to be respectful and responsive to the needs expressed by workplace learners themselves.

How Can We Explain Literacies as Social Practice to Other Educators?

During and after the research, Sue had opportunities to work with literacy workers. She facilitated a number of workshops on workplace literacy. She was anxious to apply her new learnings and insights from the research experience to these sessions. In fact her master's thesis (Folinsbee, 2002b), which she was working on at the time, focused on the critical analysis and self-reflection related to trying to make these connections. In one workshop on Organizational Needs Assessment, she tried to use a social practice framework. She used the tapestry metaphor developed by Mary Ellen to set this framework. She also told stories from her research and asked participants to both identify different interests in the stories and elaborate on how they would deal with these situations as educators.

But the concept of literacy as a social practice was not well received by workshop participants. Although they understood the concept, they resisted including social context in the definition of literacy. Many felt more comfortable limiting the role of the educator and defining literacy more closely within a skills framework as they knew it. Participants did not feel that the issues literacy was imbedded in were theirs to deal with. Their view was consistent with the dominant view of literacy that one would find in the literature in workplace literacy and was also consistent with the current government policy framework for literacy. One participant summed up this view: "'Responsible' means setting our limits as educators; what's the role of the ONA? The issues are greater than literacy. We need to limit the interests of what we can meet."

Sue learned that making the bridge from theory to practice was difficult and enormously more complicated than she had imagined. She relearned what we might have predicted, that any work on moving to this kind of thinking and working must start with small steps that begin from participants' own frameworks. She also had insight into the many barriers that would make it difficult, if not impossible, to move to a social practice framework. These barriers included a government policy that focused on individual skills, participants' lack of resources and time to develop the expertise to address these issues, and no existing framework for a more complex practice. Managers who decide on programs may also see literacy as an individual skill, and may not want an educator to examine and teach literacies as a social practice.

On a positive note, Sue saw that introducing stories and the tapestry metaphor in her workshops showed literacy educators how complex literacies at work are. This was often new thinking for some who thought it would not be difficult to transfer the kind of program they offered in their community-based settings to the workplace.

How Can We Focus on Content and Meanings?

Tracy has also been working with the ideas of literacies as social practice and struggling to apply them on a daily basis in her work with Mary, her colleague at Metalco. They have taken the idea of group learning to heart and have focused their work on learning groups that are work groups (often called "work teams"). The framework they are building allows for individual planning and attention that is concurrent with group learning. And always now, they ask the groups to talk about meanings. Not what does something mean officially at work, but what does this mean for you, for your group, what do you associate it with, how can you find an example of it? This kind of thinking takes their practice into regular work group meetings rather than only in special learning sessions for some individuals. They are comfortable with the inclusiveness of this arrangement, and especially appreciate the way it makes learning an equalizer rather than a solution for perceived deficits. This practice means that they are sometimes co-facilitating sessions with work group leaders. As production work groups reported positively on these new meeting topics, other groups of managers, office workers and engineers have been drawn in.

Both Tracy and her colleague Mary have found that attending to work ideas and processes as well as to people has helped make the workplace more real and more meaningful to them. It is possible, and perhaps common in workplace education, to see the actual work people do and the experiences they have through their workday as somehow separate from the people they are when they come to training or tutoring. Mary Ellen described this earlier in her thinking on how her earlier practice framework saw the workplace in terms of background and foreground rather than an integrated tapestry. But attending very closely to meaningful content in work life at Metalco has helped Tracy and Mary get into the very weave of work life. Much of what they do know starts with groups posing questions for discussion: "What does this mean to us?" And they don't reach for the manual to find the official definition; they sift through their understandings to find stories and examples that express what it means in lived experiences. They share the ways they read their workplace. These are lessons that have taught us a lot about the workplace, their work, themselves and us, too.

The Social Practice of Workplace Educators

Through this research, we have come to see that power, risk and blame are also part and parcel of a workplace educator's social practice. As illustrated by Sue's experience, the kind of practice that an educator is able to engage in might reflect the government policy of the day, institutional support and support from a workplace. For example, Schultz (1997) found that the majority of programs she studied used a competency-based, functional context approach. In fact, this framework was a condition of funding for most of the programs. Such conditions impose their own power structure on the work of individual educators, who then must decide how much risk they are willing to take to bend the rules to reflect their own educational philosophies. Other researchers (Kalman & Losey, 1997) conclude that for teachers to deliver a more participatory approach to workplace literacy, they need to believe that change is educationally sound, they need adequate support and preparation time, and students too need to be convinced of the merits of a nontraditional approach.

In our own experience, we find that there is often resistance among educators to an approach that embraces the complex and contradictory issues introduced by a social practice or sociocultural framework. There are many good reasons for this resistance. Educators may not feel equipped to deal with a more complex picture that they feel is outside their comfort level, expertise and experience. They may receive no support or rewards for doing so from the organizations they work for. They may see such an approach as dabbling where they shouldn't, and one that might have risky consequences for their reputation or business. All these are legitimate and compelling concerns, but we hope not completely paralyzing.

Although we acknowledge these issues of risk for the educator, we also want to present another way to think about these dilemmas. We believe that by reducing literacy issues to their simplest terms and avoiding the workplace complexities that literacies are intertwined with, we are focusing only on single threads without considering the tapestry into which they are woven. In missing this bigger picture, we can actually make our educational initiatives less effective, and less likely to succeed.

For ourselves, we are interested in stretching our notions of literacies in the workplace and what this might mean in terms of new ways to improve our practice, starting with small steps and making changes in places that seem most possible. We recognize that this means building on our knowledge and experience incrementally rather than waking up one morning and trying to do everything differently. We see the process as first gaining awareness, then reflecting on new understandings, then beginning to act on them, and continuing to reflect.

One of the important discoveries that has been sharpened by our research is that there are no neutral places. Either by going along with the status quo (staying in places that are safe for us as educators) or by going out on a limb, we are taking a political stance. Staying in our safe places may have consequences for the very people we believe we are trying to assist. We know of a situation where educators took at face value a manager's request for a literacy test score for all workers so a company could offer training selectively to those employees who needed it. They failed to delve deeply enough into the context to discover an unstated agenda to use those tests to lay off workers with the lowest scores, which had far-reaching and unanticipated consequences. Such outcomes are part of the risks faced by educators who want their work to serve the best interests of workers as well as managers.

One of the important insights we carry away from this research experience is the power and value of approaching workplace education from a perspective that anticipates complexities and sees past individuals and their personal skills through to the weave of relationships, systems and cultures they work in. We have tried to think from that perspective and what it will mean in the various phases of our working relationship with a place or a group.

We want to explore how seeing the workplace and the people in it as an interconnected system or tapestry influences what we do as workplace educators as we move forward from *Reading Work*. We want to continue to examine the threads of power, risk and participation for both educators as we do this work and all those who participate in our educational initiatives. We hope that our reflections have sparked thinking about practice for other educators in a positive way that enhances what they already know and do.

BUILDING THE BRIDGE THROUGH COMMUNICATING IN PRINT

As workplace educators, we need to write more about what we do, why we do it and how we think about it: our best innovations and our biggest disasters, our ordinary days, our exhilarating triumphs. We are all puzzling hard over paradoxes and problems in our work. We are thinking and trying to see our work in new ways, and through the eyes of our partners. We need to share our insights and our reflections. Keeping them to ourselves prevents a cycle of practice evolution and theory development. It implies that we do not have knowledge to share with the wider community. It makes it harder to build the bridge. There needs to be more opportunities for both workplace educators and academics to write in the same journals.

Much of what we write is kept internal to the company or the group: applied research, facilitator's guides, teaching and learning materials. We don't have a tradition of dissemination. We don't have incentives to share; we don't have forums for publishing. Many workplace educators present their work at conferences, but conferences for educators and for learners do not require papers. Nor should they. Writing a paper is a whole layer of work that we do not get paid to do. Educators turned graduate students have written most of the published accounts of workplace literacy practice. Conferences should encourage diverse types of publications to be submitted from the many different kinds of presenters and participants. We need journals or space in journals for educators' accounts of their work, and for workers, managers, unions or government representatives to offer their ideas on the understanding and practice of workplace literacies and workplace education. The Internet is another forum for discussion; it is one easy way to disseminate an idea or send out a serious reflection and get a serious response. Because the number of workplace educators is relatively small, we often find like-minded or interested colleagues far from home. Virtual community is a real possibility for workplace educators; perhaps the bridge will be built through the Internet.

As educators, we believe in the power of workplace education to meet real learning needs. We believe learning and learning at work can be transformative. We see workplace learning as one of the front lines of adult education where real-life problems and learning needs are defined and addressed. We want our reflections on practice responding to workplace complexity to add to understandings of literacies, learning and workplace education. We want to welcome the complexity of workplaces. And especially, we want to respect our colleagues and their work. We hope to enrich people's practice through insights into working life. Our project gave us an unusual opportunity to investigate issues that are important to workers, and to influence how they read, write, communicate, how they learn what employers want them to learn, and even how they learn what really excites and motivates them at work.

As members of a growing profession, we think these issues need to be on the agenda for dialogue. We know that individual educators are sometimes very well aware of these issues, and sometimes not. Sometimes we fail to see how important these complex factors are in terms of participation and practice, and sometimes we see but may not know how to act. No one person will have all the solutions to these dilemmas, and one solution will never work for all. Like the workers in our stories, we exist in a community, and believe that the best solutions to our challenges will come from dialogue with each other. This book is our contribution to that dialogue, and we hope it will stimulate others to tell their stories.

7
Implications for Theory

Judy Hunter

WHAT DO WE MEAN BY "THEORY"?

Although most people tend to see theories as the domain of "experts" and academic researchers, in fact everyone has theories. Frank Smith (1978) says theories help us generalize our experiences, make sense of new things and learn more about the world. Teachers have theories, for example, about how students learn that they've developed through their own learning, their training and experience with students' successes and failures. Teachers' theories are modified through professional development, discussions with colleagues, reading about their subject areas and ongoing experience. The kinds of theories that make sense to teachers depend a lot on their personal values and attitudes, the sociocultural values of the times, their colleagues and workplace and their access to professional development and reading. Academic theories and research have similar influences.

Whether academic or practical, all theories are there to be reflected on, tested and modified. This chapter invites you to learn about the social theories of workplace literacy that we have drawn on in our In-Sites research. It invites you to test these theories against our findings in the four research sites, and to reflect on them in light of your own understandings.

One way to look at research-based theories is as answers to questions researchers ask about their subject area. Researchers ask questions about particular subjects, how things work, how they are related to each other. The answers to their questions are theories. These answers can be described in various ways. For example, they can "narrate a story" (Brodkey, 1992, p. 316), or be "the best summary of ... [the] data" that's been collected (Smith, 1978, p. 70), or a "set of generalizations ... [that] ground beliefs and claim to know things" (Gee, 1990, p. 15). Moreover, research-based theories are derived from research data that is systematically gathered and examined in light of the research questions. In that sense they differ from the informally developed theories we may have about many aspects of the world. Associated with theoretical questions and answers are also sets of assumptions, values, beliefs and principles that drive the questions, help interpret the "data" and then shape the answers and their implications. These "starting points" of theory may reinforce or challenge particular sociocultural and political trends in society.[1]

WHAT ARE LITERACY THEORIES ABOUT?

Theories of literacy tend to answer questions about how people read and write, how they make sense of written texts, and how they learn to do so. Most traditional academic theories of literacy parallel popular theories. They start by assuming that literacy is an activity that entails composing and comprehending written words. They see that activity as an individual thinking skill. Their research questions focus on the "cognitive strategies" used by readers and writers. They associate thinking and meaning and texts with the ways that different types of texts reflect and demand different complexities of thinking. They see a hierarchy of thinking and meaning and text, in which "higher level thinking skills" are required for texts where the meaning is all in the text—for example, in their view, academic essays. At the other end of the spectrum are texts where "lower level thinking" is required, where readers simply decode words, like exit signs, and derive much of the meaning from the surrounding context, like a doorway just below an exit sign.

It isn't surprising that the assumptions and starting points associated with cognitive theories of literacy are traditionally popular. The views of these theorists are similar to many popular ideas that "academic" literacy and thinking are deeper and more abstract than everyday literacy and thinking. Academic thinking is learned through years of education. And most people, even those who do not engage in academic literacy, learn to read and write via school instruction. What's

---

[1] I owe much in this opening discussion to conversation with Chris Holland.

more, it seems intuitively "right" to assume that reading and writing involve thinking. When a person reads or writes, we commonly think of the activity as involving one person and a text. So, following this line of thinking, when we look at workplace literacy, often seen as simply filling out forms correctly, we may think of simple skill-based reading and writing tasks. But when we begin to involve new technologies, or forms that require more information, we might see higher level demands on thinking and skills.

Cognitive theorizing about literacy was at a height in the 1970s and 1980s. Many literacy theorists asked how literacy affected societies, how it affected thinking. They espoused the notions that literacy changed one's mind, allowing people to think in more abstract, complex ways. For Jack Goody (1986), research findings were drawn from history. For instance, he theorized that high levels of social organization enabled by literacy facilitated British imperial expansion through colonization. Olson (1977), who linked the development of literate societies in the West with schooling and literacy, maintained that literacy was an agent of higher thinking. And Walter Ong (1982) interpreted historical data to assert that only literate societies could develop disciplines like science and philosophy. Writers like these three well-known theorists were concerned with showing how literacy related to thinking. They drew on contrasts between the knowledge and technologies developed in nonliterate, "oral" societies and those of literate societies, and contrasts between the mental abilities of preschool and school children.

Other cognitive theorists wanted to know what thinking strategies expert, experienced, educated writers used when they went about writing an essay or article, as opposed to the strategies of novice writers. Their research answers revolutionized older educational theories about literacy that drove school curriculums and teaching methods. They found that "good" writers didn't think and compose in a straightforward, direct manner as previously assumed. Their thinking and writing were messy, cyclic, and involved setting and solving problems and juggling numerous goals and constraints. These theorists had a major impact on Western school writing instruction. They provoked a move away from formulaic, prescriptive "how to" teaching toward "process" writing, where students brainstormed, gave peer feedback and wrote many drafts.

Despite their different angles, these two aspects of cognitive theories share the premises that reading, writing and particular thinking skills go hand in hand, for individual readers and writers, and for societies. This direct link between text, thinking and meaning, and readers and writers continues to work as a driving force in the widely popular "functional" theories of literacy. In this view, literacy has been seen as "the ability to understand and employ printed information," "a broad set of information processing competencies" and a "multiplicity of skills" (OECD & Statistics Canada, 1997, p. 14). In the past decade, educational and literacy assessments, practice and "common sense" notions of reading and writing have been shaped from this perspective. For example, the IALS test of literacy is based on this premise. It draws on Kirsch and Mosenthal's (1990) cognitive theories of reading processes that relate "difficulty" to levels of complexity in texts and the kinds of things readers must do with texts. Results of the IALS assessments have been influential in national literacy policies throughout the West. In fact they have taken on greater emphasis than just measurements of literacy, and are widely seen as linked to national prosperity and economic success.

WHERE DO SOCIAL PRACTICE THEORIES COME FROM?

In the 1980s, several developments in theorizing and ways of seeing the world challenged cognitive theories. One was the literacy research of Sylvia Scribner and Michael Cole (1981), and of Shirley Brice Heath (1983). Another was the proliferation of Paulo Freire's popular "emancipatory" literacy of the 1970s, together with theories of critical pedagogy. And the third was the rise of postmodernism, a change in worldviews that affected many subject areas. Scribner and Cole's and Heath's work spoke directly to those involved in theorizing about literacy, whereas postmodernism was a historical movement in thinking that affected many subject areas. Freire's work (1970, 1985) and that of critical pedagogy theorists turned the focus in education to marginalized groups and issues of power. They were attempting to liberate and empower communities and individuals through a focused definition of literacy alongside a critical view of society.

Scribner and Cole (1981), linking anthropology and psychology, explicitly countered the historical analyses of earlier work to look at individual literacy practices. They investigated the literacy of a Liberian people called the Vai, some of whom learned to read and write in the community, without formal schooling. Others did attend school and learned school literacy. They found that literacy competencies and related skills were linked to their contexts of learning, and not necessarily related to schooling in itself. Heath spent a decade in the American Appalachians studying language and literacy among three communities: rural Whites, African Americans, and White middle-class town residents. She found that the family and community literacy practices of the middle class most closely matched those of the school, and predisposed them to school success. Further, she found that children were not "illiterate" in the other communities, but that their literacy practices were different from those valued by the school. Heath concluded that the two groups were not prepared for the kinds of teaching and assessment activities common in schools. The findings of both of these studies led a major shift in thinking about the nature of literacy and thinking.

Friere's work (1970, 1985) and critical pedagogy shaped a growing ideological approach to literacy in the 1980s. This school of thought explores identity politics and the oppression of marginalized groups, gives moral edge to concepts of power in postmodernism, and draws attention to issues of power and dominance in literacy and society. It was enormously influential in literacy teaching, with an emphasis on seeing reading not as a technology, but as an interpretation of the world and of experience, of seeing teachers as teacher/learners and education as political and artistic.

Postmodernism is a way of making sense of the world in current times. Rather than a single, tightly focused and well-defined theory, it presents a challenge on several fronts to modern ways of seeing the world. Postmodern concepts include the perspective that there is no single truth; that all knowledge is a social construction; and that power can no longer be seen as held by just the state, but is local, dynamic and distributed unevenly in society through different structures or agents. Accordingly, it is important to explore issues of diversity. Postmodernism considers that individuals have many different identities (like mother, student, writer, cook), and that there are many forms of marginalization (Hemphill, 2000). As we will see in further discussions of context and discourse in literacy, Gee's and others' views reflect many of these notions in postmodernism, in the ways they relate to literacies, to identities, discourses, and power relationships.

SOCIAL PRACTICE THEORY VERSUS COGNITIVE SKILLS THEORY

In the academic world, it is generally taken for granted that disciplinary knowledge progresses by building on existing theories (see Kuhn, 1962, for a well-known source), partly by identifying their limitations. What this means is that new theoretical ideas are often presented by critiquing older, accepted theories and by showing how the new ideas overcome the flaws of the older theories.

Accordingly, much of the social practice theorizing on literacies has established itself by critiquing cognitive theories and showing how these new views contrast favorably to the older ones. Some of the early social practice research on workplace literacy was Sheryl Gowen's (1992) American hospital study. Gowen showed that managers wrongly interpreted reasons why workers did not follow written directions. Their assumptions about people's low literacy skills led them to program workplace literacy classes for workers. In fact, the reasons for workers' non-compliance were that they resisted the message of the text and what it represented in the context of the workplace, as well as its meaning in the broader sociohistorical context of race relations in the American South. The workers felt insulted that managers, who knew little about the nature of the workers' jobs, felt compelled to instruct them in literacy skills, based on how they completed workplace instructional documents. The managers misinterpreted documentation practices through the lens of cognitive skills.

Hull, Jury, Ziv, and Katz (1996) studied literacy practices in California's Silicon Valley and saw workplaces where workers had considerable responsibility in terms of literacy activities. They described an incident when workers failed to follow labeling instructions that served as records for traceability and accountability in circuit board production. One explanation for the problem was that the workers didn't read the instructions. But Hull and her colleagues found two more that illustrated how literacy skills alone offer an inadequate, misleading explanation of the incident. First, workers had organized themselves so that one was designated to communicate special instructions to the rest; on the day of the error that worker was absent. Second, the workers were unaware of the significance of labeling for the company. Hull's group identified the need for access to more complete knowledge about the literacy demands of the workplace, so that the purposes of work would be recognized.

In another report on the Silicon Valley research, Hull (1995) tells of a lead hand who was an effective, creative problem solver, who used literacy as a tool to deal with problems in the manufacturing process. Although this worker solved production problems, he was not allowed to employ his solutions without higher authorities' approval, which he spent a great deal of time obtaining. As Hull pointed out, the texts he created "were not sanctioned by the company and ... had no authority" (p. 20). Hull's findings belie the official claims of the "new" workplace, claims of high performance, more complex literacy skills requirements, and flattened hierarchies. In this workplace, the worker used complex literacy competencies to surpass the limitations of his job description and his status. But because this work was not officially sanctioned, it was also not recognized.

Studies like these, and other research findings cited in the introduction to this book, have established an alternative understanding of workplace literacies. They have challenged the bases of cognitive skills theories, which make close links between words on the page, "correct" readings and adequate skills. These studies show us that if we assume readers and writers make sense of texts simply by dealing with words on a page or screen, we can easily misinterpret the link between literacy and meaning. They show that meanings, or "readings," and use of text don't just depend on understanding words on the page, but are closely intertwined with the social environment. In Gowen's 1992 study, managers assumed that workers couldn't read if they didn't carry out written instructions; they did not see resistance. Hull, Jury, Ziv, and Katz's 1996 research found that not following written instructions was due to workers not understanding the significance of the instructions for the company. And for Hull (1995), one worker's complex literacy skills related to his work simply were not recognized in the organizational hierarchy. We see several examples of this kind of misinterpretation in the In-Sites research findings discussed in the rest of this chapter. We also gain a richer understanding of social practice theories of literacy and of how literacy at the In-Sites workplaces illustrates the theories.

HOW LITERACY RELATES TO SOCIAL PRACTICE

What Do the Theorists Say?

Most current theorists see social practices as cultural ways of doing things. The "things" literacy is involved with are, in Barton and Hamilton's terms, "utilizing written language" (1998). Others broaden definitions of literacy: Gee (1990) refers to literacy as reading, writing and talking. To Kress (2000), literacy is "socially made forms of representing and communicating" (p. 157), and to Hull (1997), "cultural symbol systems" (p. 19). In other words, for those like Kress, literacy includes dealing with images and formats as well as words, because meaning in texts is carried through all these means. Along with the expansion from printed words to cultural symbol systems as the concrete objects of literacy, is a move to include multiple modes of communication. Books, reports, the Internet, computer databases, and symbol systems used to operate technologies are all now considered modes of literate communication. Many popular views of workplace literacy share this perspective; they agree that reading and writing involve many different modes and symbol systems. But to all the theorists just cited, literacy as a social practice focuses on how people create meaning: meanings of the information in texts,[2] meanings of the texts themselves, and meanings of the ways texts are used. They all consider that meanings are embedded in the contexts of how people use texts.

Some theorists emphasize the practice, the "doing" aspect of literacy, that is not just the text meanings. They look extensively at how texts are used and the meanings of those uses. They focus on the activities around texts that also involve "values, attitudes, feelings and social relationships ... existing in the relations between people, within groups and communities" (Barton & Hamilton, 1998, p. 7).

To illustrate, David Barton (1994b) tells a story of his visit to a hotel to book a conference. As Barton and his colleague met with the conference manager, the manager consulted a book. At the meeting, Barton

---

[2]"Text" is generally a catch-all term for complete units of written language or even graphic and spoken language. For example, an ISO form, a menu, an employee handbook, a novel, and a television commercial can all be considered texts.

reports that the manager held the planning book and as decisions were made about the conference arrangements, he noted them in the book. Barton points out that simply these actions shaped power relationships among those present. Because the manager carried the book and recorded information in it, he held the power in the interaction. At the same time, Barton, focusing on the manager's power, wasn't equally aware of his own power to accept or reject the arrangements. Barton also describes the social roles around the use of the book and the interweaving of oral and written language in the meeting. He further notes that there were specialized ways of writing understandable only to the hotel personnel and not to the academics.

Although Barton's definition emphasizes relationships between individuals and within groups, his example also shows literacy dynamics across groups: the academics holding a scholarly conference and the hotel's organizational world. Analyzing these aspects of that event —the interweaving of activities and modes of communication with reading and writing; the specialized knowledge and skills required for understanding the text; and the interpersonal roles and power relationships—is key to social practice theories of literacy.

The words and form of texts are also a focus of study for social practice theorists. Gee (1990), for example, points out that language forms are not "definable neatly and directly in terms of a set of meanings" (p. 75). Gee (1990, 1996) claims that different types of reading require different background knowledge and different skills. He argues that safety labels on medicine containers are carefully written to protect drug companies, and that if readers understand only the words and sentences on the labels, the dosage message to consumers isn't always explicit.

Another example: Consider the image brought to mind by the sentence, "Superman raised his hand and stopped the truck." The ability to decode the words of the sentence does not ensure a clear interpretation. Judging whether Superman raises his hand as a signal or uses it as a physical force depends on prior cultural knowledge. People who don't know of Superman would picture the scene much differently from those who do. For social practice theorists, the meanings carried by the texts are always embedded in the social context together with the words and form of the text.

What Does the In-Sites Research Show Us?

Like Gee, Hull, and Kress's views, and like many "basic skills" notions of literacy, literacies at our research sites involved many kinds of systems. Many employees across departments in the hotel used highly technical databases to keep records, but they also used scraps of paper placed beside the computer and hotel pens and planning books. like the manager in Barton's story. They also used credit card swipe machines, telephone codes, radio pagers and paper reporting forms.

They added information to computer hard copy with colored markers, special ways of folding papers and individualized marks and symbols. They posted paper documents and notes on bulletin boards and doors, taped them to desk tops and computer monitors, carried them in their pockets, filed them in notebooks, and boxed them away in storage areas. Similarly, in the manufacturing sites, workers handled the production lines, simultaneously measured and read machine outputs and fine-tuned their machinery. They kept paper and computer records of their work. They consulted and created work manuals. They filled out continuous reports on work quality and progress to feed the overall production data. All these ways of dealing with, storing and modifying text were significant in each of our workplaces to those who used the texts.

As in Barton's meeting with the hotel conference manager, social and power relationships played an important part in the literacy practices at all our research sites. That is, what people did in relation to texts was important to the ways they were used and interpreted at our workplaces. Employees' interactions with documentation showed ways that they helped each other interpret and learned ways to work well. The Texco workers who wrote books as personal manuals got feedback from more experienced workers. They collected information for their books from their own experience with the machines they worked on and from co-workers with whom they shared their books. The front desk Guest Service Agents at The Urban Hotel took it for granted that they shared information about the workings of the ever-changing database system in the hotel. They frequently commented to newer employees that they too were once new and needed information from others, for the in-house training prepared them only for the basic operation of the system. The creation of the uncontrolled, homemade chart was interpreted with little distress at Metalco, illustrating decisions based on co-workers' respect for and knowledge of each other's expertise and experience.

Relationships of power also stood out in the literacy practices at our sites. Tensions around privilege, status, workload, autonomy, blame and risk were reflected in the ways people used and interpreted texts, although the issues were not readily apparent just by looking at documentation. Yet we found them to be more complex than Barton noted in his discussion of the hotel meeting. Barton saw the power difference there between the banquet manager who held the book and the customers who didn't have the same information. Gee (1990) has also written about power and literacy, mostly in terms of groups with different status and power in society, like teachers and students, for example. Although we saw power and literacies related to managers with power over workers, we also found power and literacy issues among workers, and workers challenging the power of managers through literacy practices.

Power conflicts were an important issue behind the problems with HACCP documentation on the production line at Triple Z. In-Sites' research shows us that managers tended to impose HACCP on employees without their clear knowledge of its purposes. Its meanings were clear to managers, but not to workers. And workers felt the imposition of standardization and discipline around the paperwork was superfluous and illogical. They didn't see it as contributing to better production. It would be easy to think that all the managers needed to do was explain its purposes clearly to the workers, and they would be happy to comply. In fact, that's a response we've received from a number of practitioners about the research. But that solution would ignore another crucial aspect of the issues around power at Triple Z: The workers knew that they risked their managers' blame for filling out their forms if there was a production error; that was a strong disincentive to doing the paperwork. They also experienced errors in production that they felt were intensified by the increased workload of the documentation. In the end, managers and supervisors used their power to place workers in a situation of potential blame whether they completed the forms accurately or not, for they would be disciplined if they chose not to comply.

At Texco, In-Sites research found that employees used ISO Non-Conformance Reports to assert power with co-workers. Although the official meanings of these reports was that they fed into the quality control program by documenting errors or things that needed to be fixed, they weren't always used for these purposes. Managers thought that workers weren't thorough enough in completing the reports, perhaps because of low skills, low confidence or poor English. But we found that workers used the reports to blame each other for unsatisfactory work. Some workers "with a sense of power and security" wrote Non-Conformance Reports to blame others for work they judged as problematic, to call it to their and others' attention. Others wrote reports on co-workers to protect themselves from blame for production errors.

At The Urban Hotel, Room Attendants sometimes failed to keep track of their room checklists, and Floor Managers had to search for them on the supply carts and then ask for the information. Although the Floor Managers officially had power over the Room Attendants, this small bit of forgetfulness or resistance slowed down the Floor Managers' work and, however briefly, reversed the hierarchy. On a larger scale, the Floor Managers together resisted a consultant's imposition of new documentation practices, also challenging the workplace hierarchy.

In other words, we saw power issues as a part of literacy issues in several ways at our work sites. And although the three examples just reviewed show power as a negative force or as resistance, it's important to remember that power and literacy practices are not just negative. The power of HAACP and ISO literacy practices contributed to Triple Z's and Texco's legitimacy with suppliers and to the companies' income and profit. The complex documentation systems at The Urban

Hotel helped ensure that guests received the services they wanted. The culture of documentation at Metalco contributed to uniform quality control. In all of our sites, literacies were designed to work as powerful tools for company success. What our research shows are the dynamic, complex, and often unforeseen ways that power is interwoven with literacies in actual practice.

As with other aspects of literacy as social practice, the In-Sites research shows not just how people use texts socially, but how the meanings they give to texts and take from texts are socially shaped. Throughout our research, it was frequently clear that interpreting and producing information in texts were importantly related to a close working knowledge of the purposes of people's work, of the ways things were organized, or of the physical settings people worked in, for example. Even as supposedly highly literate researchers, we could not always make sense of documents until we understood the work processes and the tasks they referred to. From the onset of our work, we realized how much of the documentation required of employees at our sites was often incomprehensible to us or even to others outside the immediate work area. In describing a display board at one work station in Metalco, Tracy Defoe equates understanding the display to reading "the work of a production cell in a few key numbers and words ... where relationships and layers of significance reveal themselves only to the most knowledgeable readers, and ... [where] readers may draw meanings not apparent to writers."

There was a memorable incident in my own research site where I misread a formatting convention of skipping lines between items in a list as being inconsequential. It actually had important practical significance for Room Attendants, and in "helping out," I slowed down their work. Coordinators typically skipped lines between each set of rooms on a floor when they wrote up checklists for the afternoon shift Room Attendants. That way, in reading the checklist as the shift began, attendants could quickly scan the number of floors they were working on. That was important information in judging their workload and assessing the need to organize their time. Each floor had its own supply cart, and room attendants had to make sure each one they needed was sufficiently stocked up. Formatting the checklist helped them to plan their shift efficiently.

At Triple Z, Rosa, a woman with what's often called "limited" English, created her own system for recording cleaning tasks on her job checklist. Its meaning was not readily apparent to auditors, but because she had created a meaningful, consistent marking system for herself and was able to explain it, it was considered acceptable. In other words, she defined what she considered significant distinctions in the tasks she was responsible for, and she devised a system for recording them. What's more, she was able to "translate" them in ways that outsiders recognized as meaningful, too.

So far we've talked about how theorists now define "literacy" as creating and making sense of many ways of presenting information, with a variety of symbol systems and modes. They see social practice in terms of doing things with texts and of interpreting the meanings of texts that are both tied up with social context in the workplace. We've also seen how the findings of the In-Sites research illustrate this concept of literacy as a social practice. Next, we look more closely at the theoretical concepts of "discourse" and "context," which are not quite the same as the everyday notions of the words.

WHAT ARE THE CONCEPTS OF "CONTEXT" AND "DISCOURSE"?

What Do the Theorists Say?

"Context" is an important idea in social practice theories of literacy. As is common in theoretical jargon, it's an everyday term used with a special meaning, to represent an important part of the new ways of looking at literacies. For language teachers (and for many others in everyday use), the "context" of a word traditionally refers to the surrounding words or text, and students learn to "guess meanings from context." For example, they learn that "rare" has a different meaning in the context of a restaurant menu than in the context of a book about coins or stamps. But when social practice theorists talk about literacies and meanings as embedded in context, they mean something much more than the words on the page.

Researchers such as Lave and Wenger (1991), who write about learning rather than specifically about literacy, have had a strong influence on the way of thinking about context in literacy theories. They believe that "learning, thinking and knowing are relations among people in activity in, with and arising from the socially and culturally structured world" (p. 51). That is, they see meanings of words and texts as part of people's ways of doing things together, as part of the cultural nature of the environment. They might consider the word "rare" on a menu and see its meaning not just as how well done a serving of meat is, but as a meaning shared by a class of people who like eating expensive cuts of meat in restaurants. Lave and Wenger also see meanings as "produced, reproduced and changed in the course of activity" (p. 51). So, for instance, when people are dining out, they speak and read the word "rare" in reference to the meat they're eating, but when they're engaged in stamp collecting they use "rare" in another way. This way of looking at meanings isn't really difficult to understand, and many people would acknowledge that social context is intuitively related to meaning. But the difference is that in popular terms there are two sets of meanings: a "core" meaning sometimes changing according to the text or the setting, and then maybe an extra "connotation" that has to do with social use. Lave, Wenger and the new literacy theorists don't see separate sets of meaning. They see meanings as always "embedded" in social relationships and activities, in the ways diners or stamp collectors talk, read, write and share meanings.

The idea of contexts of shared meanings and ways of doing things among groups is emphasized in Lave and Wenger's (1991) widely used term "communities of practice." They stress that communities of practice such as midwifery or tailoring share much more than a set of mechanical skills. They also share "understandings about what they are doing and what that means in their lives and for their communities" (p. 98). To be full "participants" in the midwifery community of practice, women learn the shared ways of talking, reading, writing and problem-solving that other midwives engage in and that mark them as all being midwives.

James Gee refers to a "Discourse"[3] rather than a community of practice and describes it at length in his writing (e.g., 1990; Gee et al., 1996).[4] Discourses are similar to communities of practice; Gee emphasizes that they are created by shared objects, arrangements of space, appearance, language, knowledge, attitudes, values, sense of shared history and behavior. Displaying and adopting these attributes allows people to be members of discourses, and to show they have that particular identity. Gee et al. (1996) give the example of law school as a discourse, through which teachers and students act, think, read and write "in certain characteristic, historically recognized ways, in combination with their own individual style and creativity" (p. 10), and thus present themselves as members of the law school discourse. That is their identity as lawyers.

Gee (1990, 1992) extends the concept of shared beliefs and practices beyond Lave and Wenger's (1991), though. He claims that we all belong to many discourses. We may be mothers, daughters, students, teachers, investors and gardeners simultaneously. We may have many identities. Two things are important about this concept of multiple discourses for literacy theories. One is that discourses are hierarchically valued, and the other is that they often conflict with each other. For instance, in schools, although students all participate in a shared discourse of schooling, those who also belong to nonmainstream discourses outside of school may find that some of their behavior, ways of talking, reading, and writing conflict with those of the school. Mainstream home discourses may be more in tune with the dominant school discourse, and more highly valued. Issues of power come to the fore as members of more highly valued discourses exercise power over members of less valued ones.

---

[3]Gee distinguishes "Discourse: with a capital D" from "discourse," the linguistic term used to describe a stretch of text. I use the small d to roughly cover the "community of practice"/"Discourse" notion.

[4]Discourse is similar to the notion of discourse in postmodern writing, particularly Foucault (see, e.g., Foucault, 1980).

The terms "discourse" and "community of practice" aren't quite the same thing as "context" in terms of literacy theories, but they are widely referred to in discussions of social theories of literacies. And these theoretical concepts have been widely used as a framework to cover all of the aspects of the environment that are relevant to literacy events and practices. Context is seen to include social groups, relationships, the objects, arrangements of space, appearance, language, knowledge, attitudes, values, history and behavior that may relate to particular uses of literacy. These related concepts have dramatically expanded the view of what's relevant to meanings in literacy practices. At the same time, when we consider context, we need to remember that it may include several overlapping, merging, complementary or conflicting discourses, so it can't be correspondingly equated with discourse.[5]

Janet Maybin (2000) defines context more explicitly. She outlines the scope of social practice analysis of literacy activities and their contexts as threefold: "a) individual activities, understandings and identities, b) social events and the interactions they involve, and c) broader social and institutional structures" (p. 198). Maybin goes on to identify the importance of looking at the relationships among various levels of contexts that figure in the meanings of literacy events. She cites, for example, physical setting, local background knowledge, and insider knowledge about institutional practices as important to the ways people take up meanings from texts.

In summary, the concept of "context" in social practice theory has dramatically extended what's important to consider in understanding the meanings of texts and literacy practices. It includes social relationships, roles, power, solidarity and conflict, time and space, technologies of communication, attitudes, values, beliefs, experience and knowledge. All these aspects of context change over time, they are valued differently in society, and they may often conflict with each other. And because context involves individuals and groups of people rather than objects, it is not easily defined as a fixed formula. Let's return to some of the In-Sites work situations to see how these concepts apply in real life.

What Does the In-Sites Research Show Us?

We've already seen several examples of how context is relevant to literacies in the In-Sites research we've been discussing here. Interactions around documentation mentioned earlier are one aspect of context. Experienced workers helping new employees understand document practices, individuals' unauthorized notes and manuals

---

[5]In fact, several theorists are beginning to question the concept of community of practice as having unrealistic boundaries and as unable to explain how power or attitudes, for example, move across communities. They see them as much more fluid and "permeable." See Hamilton (2001) and Prior (2002) for a further critical discussion.

on work procedures, along with supervisor support or lack of support for such initiatives, the worksites themselves, and the worldwide corporate trends to document quality control were all part of the literacy contexts. Those contexts were integral to workers' sense of the documents they worked with, and for us, looking at their literacy practices, to understand how they took up and "made" meanings from them. The issues of power and conflict and the difficulties in understanding paperwork conventions from outside one's work area also illustrate the important nature of context in the literacy practices we observed.

We can also look at examples of context more in relation to discourses and identities at our worksites. In The Urban Hotel, the literacy practices of each job marked employees as having certain work identities, with a clear status in the hotel hierarchy. Employees who carried and wrote in notebooks, and who could give and take paperwork to and from others, were also employees who wore uniforms that looked more like everyday business dress than those who wore cleaning uniforms. We could say that they belonged to a particular discourse: middle-level hotel supervisors, called Floor Managers. Floor Managers could ask Room Attendants to show their checklists, but Room Attendants could "mislay" the forms, or not hear the requests. The status of Floor Managers' jobs gave them certain powers with documents. But at the same time, when they interacted with Room Attendants, the context was sometimes one of conflict arising from status differences and resistance to control.

At Triple Z the research focused on a large segment of the line workers who were older Italian immigrants with little formal education. Many of these workers had been working at the plant for decades. They had "a collective memory of working together, living together, growing up in Canada ... at this plant, speaking Italian and singing Italian songs while they worked." At the same time, the group identity they shared also marked them as having inadequate language and literacy for the new document-driven workplace. Although they saw themselves as having built up the company, the perception that they lacked language and literacy skills made them a liability rather than an asset in the new workplace. With that image (as well as the company's view that enough had been invested in upgrading language and literacy skills, especially when it was government funded), it was easier for managers to see them as not up to meeting the new documentation demands. I don't believe their collective identity as unskilled was the only reason for not looking deeper into the reasons for their non-compliance with record keeping, but it must have helped managers to place the blame on them. With a social practice approach we were able to look beyond skills alone or others' perceptions of their identity to understand their lack of participation in the HACCP documentation.

HOW ARE LITERACIES LEARNED IN SOCIAL PRACTICE?

What Do the Theorists Say?

Social practice theories of literacy look to sociocognitive or sociocultural theories to understand literacy learning. The best-known theorists in this area are Lave and Wenger (1999). In 1991 they published a monograph, *Situated Learning: Legitimate Peripheral Participation.*[6] According to Lave and Wenger, learning is a process through which learners become fully participating members of a community of practice. They define "community of practice" as "participation in an activity system about which participants share understandings … [of] what they are doing and what that means in their lives and for their communities" (p. 98). By "legitimate peripheral participation" they refer to the ways that people participate in a social practice where learning is an integral part. To illustrate the theoretical concepts they introduce, they present several apprenticeship case studies. They describe how Mayan girls learn to become midwives, for example, by gradually increasing their participation in midwifery over several years. They are not formally taught, but learn by accompanying a midwife, often a female relative, absorbing both cultural and skills knowledge over time, until ready to practice on their own.

It's easy to see how Lave and Wenger's (1991) approach dovetails with notions of discourse and literacy as social practice. Although this theory has some ambiguities (for example, it is not always clear about issues of power), it has been widely accepted as part of social literacy theory. Indeed, much of their terminology is used by literacy theorists.

Situated learning theory calls into question the cognitive-based notion of de-contextualized, generic skills that can be learned in a formal setting and then transferred to other situations. Lave and Wenger (1991) argue that "abstract representations are meaningless unless they can be made specific to the situation at hand" (p. 33). Likewise, Billet (2000) criticizes the notion of basic generic workplace skills. He draws largely on research by Stasz (1997), who found that across several workplaces, competencies defined as generic were actually not common competencies. That is, they were not the same competency in each workplace. For example, problem solving in one workplace might involve identifying and fixing problems. At another it might mean collecting information and interpreting it. Out of context, the generic skill could not be easily defined. Moreover, Billet points out that workers need to apply "context-specific knowledge" in order to complete what was termed "higher order" work procedures.

Other recent research on the nature of workplace knowledge also supports this view of literacy learning in the social context of the work-

---

[6]Lave had earlier published with Sylvia Scribner and also researched the Vai in Liberia, so there was a common base with Scribner and Cole's 1981 approach to some extent.

place. Hopkins and Maglen (2000) report on research into the ways people learned their jobs. Across four manufacturing and service sector sites they studied, personnel tended to learn their current positions while on the job, through co-workers. They reported much less learning through courses (inside or outside the company), computer packages or seminars. Although this area of research focuses on knowledge rather than literacy, literacy is widely seen as closely linked to acquisition, forms and display of knowledge.[7]

What Does the In-Sites Research Show Us?

Although we had opportunities to observe much more daily work practice than formal learning over time, we did see instances of learning among new employees, which illustrated Lave and Wenger's (1991) situated learning theories. We're not attempting to refute formal learning here, but to show observed evidence of situated literacy learning.

First, at Metalco, Tracy describes a conversation between Frank, a worker on the job for only 2 weeks, and George, a more experienced Machine Operator. In this exchange, George shows Frank how to check the gauge adjustment. But he also reminds Frank that they will be sending the chart to Quality Assurance, how it will be interpreted and responded to, and what they should make of the response. He also reminds Frank of crucial responsibilities they have to measure accurately and assures him of their knowledge and confidence in the job they do. In explaining the machinists' role, he uses "we," including Frank as part of the team. He also explains to Frank the reason Quality Assurance needs to see the forms, and why the forms are important for warranty purposes in the company. As Tracy tells us, in this way, "the workers' knowledge is passed along; their meanings are shared. The new worker is brought into the group of machine operators."

At The Urban Hotel, much of the time I spent shadowing workers was also a job literacy experience for me, learning that I couldn't have accomplished outside the work context. However, beyond just learning that it was important to skip lines between rooms on different floors, I learned ways to deal with problems of keeping track of data that the computer program could not handle. For example, I sat in the action center for two mornings while operator Jan managed what seemed like hundreds of incoming calls and redirected them to the proper departments. There were problems of blocked toilets, questions about where to buy cheap socks, rooms that needed immediate cleaning, guests who wanted special supplies like humidifiers. She had to follow up each call to make sure "action had been completed." At the same

---

[7]For further reading on workplace knowledge, look at Garrick and Rhodes (2000), or Gerber and Lankshear (2000).

time, she had to log each call and action on the computer, and had to keep track of its completion.

As Jan logged the information, she demonstrated and explained what she was doing. But at the same time, she taught me how to manage the computer, for the limitation of the computer screen was its size. Once the screen was full, earlier entries began to scroll off and they were no longer visible. That meant she could easily forget the calls and their status. For that reason she used a pencil and paper to keep track of the records. She had created a special scheme to mark each call's status and whether she'd entered it on the computer as well. I'm sure I could not have learned the job, or even kept up with it, if I hadn't had the opportunity to learn about it in place, to observe an expert worker, to see how she used her skills and knowledge and to benefit from her critical adaptation of text and technology. Certainly I wasn't with her long enough to really learn the job, but what I saw gave me an important window on the kinds of expertise I would have needed.

SOCIAL LITERACIES AND COGNITIVE SKILLS IN THE IN-SITES RESEARCH

Early in this chapter cognitive skills perspectives on literacy were compared to social practice views. We return to that discussion now in closing, with a fuller sense of social practice, and apply it to the In-Sites findings.

Rosa, the cleaner at Triple Z who created her own job checklists, is particularly remarkable. Her limited English and assumed limited literacy practices would suggest low-level cognitive skills if we didn't consider the context of her work. Rosa's literacy practice was meaningful in terms of her work, and meaningful to auditors whose intentions and interpretation she did not know. ("What's the paper for? For me it mean nothing. For them and the government, it mean something.") It's also notable, though, because it shows her creative thinking, initiative and problem solving concerning a simple document. These skills are often considered "higher order" thinking, which supposedly goes hand-in-hand only with "higher" literacy levels, that is, use of more complex, linguistically dense texts.

Skills-based and cognitively oriented theories would also see the thinking behind Rosa's checklist system as something that resides in Rosa's head, as an individual. Certainly Rosa may have had these kinds of skills more or less than other individuals, but if we think in terms of social practice, we can see additional sources for her abilities. She was confident and experienced at her job. Mary Ellen Belfiore notes that "cleaning Triple Z [was] like cleaning her own home." Rosa worked with autonomy, making her own decisions and disciplining herself. It appears from this account that she got little interference, possibly because her work wasn't seen as essential as production or because her supervisors didn't know much about her work. As Mary Ellen points out regarding other workers who take literacy initiatives, Rosa had an investment in her work, experience and knowledge of the job, opportunity and autonomy. All that supports creativity and initiative.

Indeed, many employees at our research sites personalized ways of keeping track of their work and creating memory aids that didn't necessarily conform with standards. But because they harmonized closely with the best ways they had learned to perform their jobs, they were often more significant for effective work than standard forms. Sue Folinsbee discussed the use of three workers' notebooks at Texco. She found that they developed their own books, first because the official manuals were not always accessible and closely suited to their immediate work needs. She notes that the workplace response to such a situation might be to "'teach' participants document literacy skills so they can read the manual." Yet at Texco, the manuals were inadequate, not the workers. As Sue says of one of the manual writers who might have scored low on conventional writing assessments, "She was able to make literacy do what she wanted, have control over her work and do her work well."

Just as in Gowen's hospital and Hull's Silicon Valley worksites, In-Sites researchers found contradictions between official claims about the ways literacy fit the workplace organization and the workers' own experiences. These contradictions would not have been so apparent without a social practice understanding of literacy events. The most salient were the issues of blame at Texco and Triple Z. At both worksites, paperwork considered important by managers regularly did not get completed. At Texco, managers suggested "fear of being blamed for a mistake, not having the big picture, and conflicting expectations" as reasons why workers did not adequately fill out R&D forms. Signing off on incorrectly labeled production runs was one example of problems with record-keeping at Triple Z. One manager's response was to call a meeting to go over the procedures; another's was to force compliance through progressive discipline. Yet at both sites, the issue for workers was blame and contradictory messages from employers about the meanings of proper documentation.

At Texco, workers were ostensibly told that paperwork was important, but when production was rushed, they were pushed by middle managers to prioritize production over paperwork. In the end, line workers were blamed if the work was slow *and* if the paperwork was incomplete. At Triple Z, line workers were asked for input about labeling failures, but their reasons of work overload were ignored, and they risked blame both if they signed off errors and if they avoided signing off. As in the Silicon Valley site, workers never really understood the full reasons for HACCP documentation.

We've seen how looking through the social practice lens at workplace literacies helps us understand workers' abilities and knowledge better than drawing on assumptions about their reading/writing skills. We've also seen how we can gain a much richer understanding of how deeply literacies are interwoven in the relationships and activities of workplaces.

WHAT CAN PRACTITIONERS MAKE OF SOCIAL PRACTICE THEORIES ABOUT LITERACY?

By including this chapter in our book, we have intended to include practitioners and others in the discussion about literacy and social practice in the workplace. We hope that this chapter opens the door to the discussion for those less familiar with research and theorizing. We do not see academic theory as the final word on literacy, to be received and digested by practitioners. Nor do we see theory as something to be dismissed by practitioners as incomprehensible prattle. Now that we've looked at literacy through the lens of social practice theories, we can see how skills alone cannot explain how literacy practices are followed at workplaces.[8]

What we hope is that practitioners may bring their knowledge to the field, to take an active part in critical analysis and development of these theories, to take on the idea of theory to inform themselves and enrich their practice. We believe, in Robert Scholes's (1985) words, that "theory can help us solve curricular and pedagogical problems ... teaching can help theory pose and elaborate those problems ... teaching and theory are always implicated in one another" (p. ix).

---

[8]For those interested in reading further about social practice theories of literacy, Sue Folinsbee and Judy Hunter have prepared an *Annotated Bibliography of Workplace Literacies*. The bibliography is available online at www.nald.ca/insites

8

Conversation on Collaborative Research

Joys and dilemmas! Taking on academic research rather than the applied type of research I had become used to doing left me with contradictory feelings: stunning highs, awful lows; but more often, a puzzled sense with bright moments and some dungeons of confusion.—I tried to hold on to what I thought I understood and then was thankful that there were five of us and that someone would rescue me. Certainly, we have to be ready to be confused and to dwell there for awhile. —(*Mary Ellen*)

This conversation on collaborative research among the five researchers spans a number of topics: our initial excitement about this project and its importance to each of us, our different understandings of theory and practice, and our thoughts on the inevitable tensions in a long-term and long-distance working relationship. In the final section, the three educators converse about the joys and dilemmas of switching roles from workplace educators to researchers.

We designed the research as a collaboration between workplace educators (Sue, Tracy and Mary Ellen) and academics (Judy and Nancy). We felt the research could then draw on the insights and strengths of both practice and theory, with benefits for both. We all expected an eye-opening experience, but we didn't realize on how many levels this would take place.

For this chapter, we each wrote about our own understandings of the collaborative research process, then responded to one other. This conversation took place over several months at different times during the project. We used a conferencing Web site that we had access to throughout the research to post all of our correspondence.

SIGNING ON

Tracy: It was several years ago when we first started saying that "someone" should propose research aimed at understanding workplace learning and literacy as being more complex than anything that could be measured through charting individual workers' skills. At that time, I was not thinking that we (Sue, Mary Ellen and I) would be the researchers, and I didn't know Nancy or Judy. I was thinking that we would advocate for attention and for money, and someone else would do the long, hard lonely work in the field and at the computer. But when it came back to us to do, I didn't hesitate to sign on. I felt I knew more or less what I was getting into and I would be able to do it well—and I was excited to work on something innovative with this group of women.

Nancy: I joined in this conversation very keen to work with people who spend their time in workplaces. I guess that's because I've been focusing my academic research and writing on workplace social issues for a long time, but don't get to spend much time actually hanging around in workplaces. In fact, I didn't get to do that in this project either, but I got to share in the benefits of all the time spent by others. I considered this a pretty lucky opportunity.

Judy: After my thesis I thought I might never get a chance to do an observation ethnography again. It had been one of the most exciting, challenging experiences in my professional life. This one would give me a chance to do it again, and to try to do better. When I first met the other women researchers on the project, I was really impressed by their competence, confidence and strength. They were all experienced, accomplished consultants and teachers in the workplace. They were labeled the "practitioners" and Nancy and I the "academics" on the team. It was a term I hadn't ever really applied to myself. I've spent 25 years teaching ESL and writing, experience that I thought made me a practitioner, too, albeit not a workplace one, but I know well what teaching is like. This project would be an opportunity to do something really exciting, to meet and work with interesting, intellectually curious women, and to have a clearer sense of how school and workplace literacy teaching and practices related.

Sue: My interest in a collaboration began with reading critical perspectives and research by writers such as Glynda Hull, Sheryl Gowan and Charles Darrah. I thought that this work had much to offer me and other workplace educators in terms of how we might view the complexities of the workplace and improve our practice. I felt that their stories rang true to my experience in workplaces. However, these writers made very few links to how their research and analysis might actually shape and influence practice. In fact, I found that they sometimes seemed critical of educators without understanding their lived reality. I was hopeful that our In-Sites group might be able to make these links between theory and practice that I hadn't seen in the literature.

Mary Ellen: Like Sue, I was immediately engaged when I first read Gowan, Darrah and Hull. Rather than feeling that their observations rang true for me, I remember saying to myself that I had a lot to learn about workplaces and workers. This was a layer of literacy life that I had not observed or examined. But I knew it was a dimension I wanted to investigate first-hand. Unlike Sue, I didn't start out with a desire to link theory and practice, or even to improve my own practice. I just wanted to know more about literacy practices at work, not sure of where that would take me. My first reason to do the research was to have an excuse to be on the floor, in the meetings and at the training sessions for months, not just for a few hours or a day. Theory wasn't part of the attraction; seeing, experiencing, understanding as an educator (not a researcher) were the lures. For me, it was a one-time opportunity to engage in cultural exploration.

DISCOVERING ETHNOGRAPHY AND A SOCIAL THEORY OF LITERACY

Sue: Personally, I was thrilled to have the opportunity to learn to do ethnographic research and through this research understand the realities of workers' lives on the plant floor. I have always been interested in the larger picture of the workplace as a culture and how people, language and literacy, and education activities fit into this culture. I thought that the rich, complex descriptions and understandings that came from ethnographic research could provide some answers for practice.

Theory (the more critical perspectives) and practice could be tied together to offer more satisfying strategies to consider issues of print and oral communication at the workplace. I was frustrated in my own work when time after time managers seemed uninterested or unable to deal with systemic issues around print and oral communication that came up in every organizational needs assessment. I began to realize later that perhaps I could position these issues in a way that would be more useful to them.

Mary Ellen: I have always been drawn to the discoveries of ethnography, to questioning assumptions and to discovering the details of lived experiences that change the way I understand behaviors, attitudes and values. I saw this collaboration as an opportunity to get into the complexities of workplace education. For ethnographic studies in the workplace, messiness and tangles would be the norm rather than the exception. My own work as a teacher, consultant and facilitator in workplace settings told me that the tangle was indeed the norm. Yet when I wrote teacher reference books, I was always trying to get beyond those messy complexities (or was it really just pushing them aside?) to write about generic knowledge and concrete steps that instructors could use in workplace education. Finally, I decided that manuals were not my style of writing. I wanted to revel in the details, the contradictions and the way it really is. I wanted to do an ethnographic study.

Nancy: For me, theory is most exciting when it is put to the test in the real world. So this chance to do sustained workplace observation through the lens of social practice theory was really attractive. I felt that this project would give us enough time to reflect on what we were looking at, and to really learn something worthwhile.

Judy: I returned to graduate school after a decade of teaching ESL in the occupational training division of a local community college. I had reached a point in my teaching where I needed to know more, more about how language worked, how written texts came to be valued or not, how learners learned. I ended up on a project observing children learning how to write in a multicultural, working-class, inner-city classroom. Everything changed when I stepped into their classroom and sat down beside them. Only a few of them lived in the school's world. Their interests, intentions, concerns, conflicts and desires played out both in their writing activities and in the stories they produced. They were most engaged with writing to align themselves with friends, to provoke others, or to play out desirable media identities. They wrote only superficially to meet the teacher's requirements; as a result, their texts did not match school standards. Most of all, I learned through this ethnographic study that their texts could never be meaningfully assessed or interpreted without understanding the social dynamics of the classroom. I could never again look at literacy and literacy learning solely as text or as a set of mental processes.

Mary Ellen: In discussing my experience with a social theory of literacy, I need to go back a few steps and position myself in my community of practice as a workplace educator. Despite years of experience, reading and investigating, I never had a grounding in either language or literacy theories. Teaching, applied research, program development and even writing for teachers didn't demand an obvious theoretical grounding. Even after my own brief foray into ethnographic research a decade before this project, I didn't have a real understanding of what it would mean to take a theoretical position and use it to direct data collection and to analyze the data we got. I went through the steps before, but didn't dig deep enough to reach the ground I stand on now. This project is the first time I have tried to understand a theory and use it; or perhaps to understand a theory through use and in use. It's the first time I have struggled with thought in this way: the grasping after an idea, the fleeting moments of insight, the confusion in the dark. This experience of struggling to understand a theory at the same time as we use it to analyze our data is what the social practice of research for newcomers is all about, I suppose. This dynamic relationship between theory and data, changing and shaping as we proceed, has been enlightening, confusing, exciting, exasperating, tiring, isolating and communal: the full load of contradictions.

Sue: Like Mary Ellen, I found it was the first time that I was guided by a formal theory—that of literacy as a social practice. It was working in a new culture because everything that we analyzed and wrote had to be in tandem with this theory. I found myself straddling two worlds, the world of practice where I had my own theories and the world of research where I was trying to apply and use the theory of literacy as a social practice in understanding what I was observing at my research site. The one thing that really disappointed me was that I felt my experience as a practitioner was undervalued in this research work. The only use I felt my practitioner experience had to offer was to make me feel very comfortable in the manufacturing environment I was in because I had worked in similar environments many times before. In fact, at times I felt my knowledge and experience as a practitioner hindered my ability to understand and apply the theory. In all of these ways I didn't feel that the research work built on my strengths or knowledge.

Judy: When the chance came to study workplace literacy, I didn't hesitate. I knew the dominant line from the voices of business and industry, the popular press, and many education circles: that the new workplace required a highly skilled, highly literate workforce, and the current educational system was inadequate because a substantial percentage of the workforce could not handle the skill demands of the changing times. I saw several parallels between the classroom study and the workplace: social and commercial institutions labeling a group of readers and writers as deficient and guilty of not meeting others' expectations. In both settings, I saw the interpretation of the problem based on psychological models of text comprehension and production. In neither case did I see an official recognition of the kinds of social forces involved in literacy practices that I saw in the school classroom. I thought it would be very enlightening to look at literacy practices in terms of social practice in the workplace to understand what other important dynamics figured in workplace reading and writing.

Mary Ellen: Once I got into the readings and the research, I started noticing that researchers and writers in other disciplines such as history and medicine were operating with a similar view—not only academics, but also artists and media people. For instance, here is Felipe Fernandez Armesto (2000), a Spanish historian, in *Civilizations:* "People are part of the awesome continuum of nature and you cannot encounter them except in the tangle of their environments and the mesh of the ecosystems of which they form a part" (p. viii). Or Dr. Patricia Baird, a geneticist at the University of British Columbia: "The evidence is overwhelming that the determinants of common chronic diseases of modern life are complex, interrelated, act over time and are embedded in a social context" (Valpy, 2001, p. A13). I now feel part of a much larger community, one that has the diversity I prize and yet a common view of the world that creates a sense of unity. Because our workplace literacy community is small, this discovery gives me more hands to join, more smiles and more comfort.

COLLABORATING ACROSS DIFFERENT WORLDS

Nancy: I had not collaborated with four researchers before, and I have to admit that I was a bit worried about such a large group, particularly of people who had not worked together before. And I was nervous about such a long time commitment: A lot can change in two or three years (in fact, three of us have changed jobs and two have moved to different locations). I was also aware of how much trouble academic researchers have working together, even when their backgrounds are more similar than our group's. But I figured we would take one step at a time and deal with whatever unfolded. I'm forever the optimist.

Tracy: "Collaboration" is a word that I embrace. I have thought, talked and written a lot about what it means to me to work in diverse groups—how it is so challenging and so slow, yet the only real way to get things done in a workplace. This is certainly not the most difficult group I have ever worked with, not by a long shot. In fact, looking back, I am not sure we have been very collaborative—not yet.

Sue: As a group, I think we came to this project with a sense of anticipation and goodwill. But we all had different interests and concerns about the project. I felt that there was always a sense of generosity and good spirit in how we helped each other and worked together. But sometimes we spoke different languages because we were operating in different worlds. This created tensions and underlying currents that were difficult to name.

Nancy: I agree about the underlying tensions. But I think these too have been a source of valuable learning, and might even be interesting to other groups who are trying to collaborate.

Judy: I see now that the ways I approach knowledge are quite academic: that is, the way I think, talk and debate about ideas; the language conventions I follow in presenting ideas; and the values I have incorporated about these ways of thinking and acting. That didn't figure strongly in my impressions of how I fit into the group in the beginning. But our different discourses were to figure in tensions through the project. Sue, Tracy and Mary Ellen all shared a different discourse with a different knowledge base than I had. They knew what they wanted to do. The question was focusing and coordinating it. At first, we talked about our different strengths and what they could bring to the group. Things might be tricky, but we were all full of energy and anticipation.

Sue: I do think the collaboration between our group as academics and educators provided an opportunity to learn how to do ethnographic research and gain a deeper understanding of literacy practices and workplaces. But little did I know or understand how difficult or painful it would be to make the links between theory and practice. The worlds of academia and practice seem so separate and far apart. This is my observation from struggles in our group and my firsthand experience as a graduate student. I feel that I am in both these worlds and neither of them. It is hard to know where my many years of experience fit anymore.

Nancy: I was also surprised how hard it was to manage our differences in personal style. But seeing how things unfolded, I now think that our personal styles might be partly an extension of our differences in background knowledge and experience. For instance, in our research group, we seem to have different kinds of comfort and confidence with various kinds of talk and writing. Maybe these are not just personal, but professional traits as well. I mean, academics do a lot of our work through writing. Perhaps workplace educators do more work through talk. Also, academics spend a lot of time turning concrete details into abstractions. We call that analysis. Then we swap these abstractions and call it debate. It is like a common currency among academics to talk and write like that. That's probably not true for everyone.

Judy: I too assumed that we would debate theory and ideas, that we would all disagree and argue back and forth. That's what we were going to do together. The silences didn't mean disagreement to me, at first.

Sue: What Nancy and Judy say are interesting examples of different ways of communicating based on our background knowledge and experience. I sometimes found it difficult to find a space for my ideas because I was not used to the kind of talk we were engaging in. I find that I have to mull things around for a while before I contribute. Unfortunately, by that time, people are on to something else!

Tracy: I think I imagined when we started that we would each interpret things we found in the research sites from what we knew or from what we read. Not that we would all try to get up to date on the various thoughts and strands in those academic discourses. Or that Judy and Nancy would try to learn how to be workplace educators, for example. I imagined that we would be okay as who we were. We would help each other equally.

Mary Ellen: I knew I wanted to do some reading, but I can see now that I hadn't envisioned being fully immersed and up on it. I already feel that I will only go so far with pushing my intellect to grapple with different aspects of theory. I know there are still many leaps I could take in understanding social practice, not to mention all the other theories that overlap but are different. I think I've come to a plateau and I'll probably work for awhile with what I now know. I feel very much like I did after my graduate work. I had to stop—I had to get out there and do, teach, get grounded.

Judy: I know that academics often over-ponder, over-talk, lack action and may not have a clear sense of real-world applications of theory. But I also know that the simple, flashy, clever and quick fix can be seductive and often effective in the corporate world, but not in research.

Nancy: I also noticed that we have different habits around tacit knowledge. Academics, maybe ethnographic researchers in particular, are often interested in drawing out the tacit knowledge they have about a setting so it can be shared and examined more closely. So that means we may want to talk about things that seem boringly obvious to others, because we think that's where the new insights will come from: looking at familiar events through a new lens. This is a kind of specialized way of thinking and working. Workplace educators are accustomed to working with a lot of background knowledge too, but perhaps you don't need to make all those understandings explicit—it would take too much time. You are not getting paid to describe problems in detail, but to fix them. That is almost the opposite of research. You go straight from understanding to action. So, you always need to know a lot more than you take the time to write down.

Sue: Yes, one of the things that I did learn through this research and my graduate work was the beauty and power of making tacit knowledge explicit. One thing I never liked to do was journal. I would rather talk about an issue with someone. Doing ethnographic research is an ongoing journaling process where you are constantly testing and retesting your thoughts, ideas and analyses around something you have observed by writing things down. Sometimes it feels tedious and tiring to never be finished. The intensity of this process can be very painful, but I think that's where true, long-lasting learning occurs.

Mary Ellen: I did not anticipate the tensions that we have experienced as an educator/academic collaboration. In hindsight, it seems predictable that we would play out those same tensions that any systemically unequal work group does. Our own messiness and tangles are a story too, and one that other such work groups have experienced and referred to. I always thought of the group as five contributors. My focus on the different contributions people could make to this collective effort perhaps blinded me to the equality and power issues that were always at play. I named them "communication problems" or "personal styles," just as they have been named in the workplace. It was a revelation to see how we experienced these power issues in the same way as others have in the many workplaces where we have been consultants.

Judy: I don't think our tensions are just personal, just political, or just system oriented. To me, they are a combination of the ways each of us manages (or tries to manage) our everyday personal, work and social lives. How each of us presents and sees ourself in the world, our fears of failure and exclusion, our (in)security about what we don't know well and our projection of that baggage onto each other. Each of us has a different mixture of styles, personal strengths and insecurities. So we've both meshed together supportively and collided on this project. When I think about the equality and power issue, most of all I think of its dynamism. Power shifts and coalesces in different ways. It's multifaceted. And power imbalances are felt most keenly by those with less in the power balance, an experience that's been felt variously across our group over these three years.

In future group work I'll try to apply what we've learned here. I think it's important to watch for and bring out the sources of potential tensions before they become impediments to the work. It's hard to do when you're not quite consciously aware of them, but each person in the group needs to take responsibility for that.

Nancy: And I think we all found it helpful when we were eventually able to name some of these issues. Like how being silenced felt when trying to be the observer/researcher and not the facilitator/educator in those workplaces; or some of the writing blocks that came from a sense of power imbalances in our group.

Mary Ellen: Although I have tried to understand these tensions, I don't think I have experienced them with the same rawness as others have. Perhaps because my stake in this project is more personal than professional. And also perhaps because I have taken on the responsibility of managing the daily life of the project, which has given me a certain amount of power others have not shared. In this role, I get to use some of my facilitation skills, which means I'm not powerless. Another reason might be that I have bought into the hierarchy of the academy and see myself as the student with no ambitions to become an academic researcher. Both the collaborative process and the content of this research have been an awakening to me with all the emotional upset that goes with any startling endeavor.

Tracy: I don't think we three are so typical of workplace educators, or maybe it is just that workplace educators are such a diverse group, so that generalizing about how they deal with knowledge or might prefer to work in a group will just not make sense. One thing we do share is that we are used to working for inclusion. For example, making space for everyone on a joint committee to bring their best ideas forward in whatever ways they can. I know some of my frustrations came from the way we used our time together in our research meetings. I kept looking for more variety in the day. Five people at a table or in a circle just didn't work for me over long days. I needed a chance to take on something with one other person, to change the physical setting, to plug into modes other than oral/aural. All of us in a room listening, speaking and taking notes took the creativity and fun out of it for me. I like playing with new ideas and I am a multimodal learner. Sometimes that was really discouraging for me.

WORKPLACE EDUCATORS AS RESEARCHERS:
JOYS AND DILEMMAS

Mary Ellen: My joyful moments were certainly about new understandings of work, people doing work, and about literacies and language. I had the greatest luxury—time—to see complexities revealed and to get used to looking at the world of work with new lenses.

Tracy: One of my joys was just having the time to really do this. The field work and what understandings I gained there, not just about literacies but about the ways people think about work, manufacturing and all the goals they have—those understandings have really helped me make my work more relevant than it has been in the past. I feel really grounded with a wide view. Many of the things I now "know" most people there have never thought about, or they haven't moved around enough to see patterns. So time was a joy.

Sue: I really felt that through this project I was about as close I would ever get to standing in someone else's shoes. It was an exhilarating experience to be able to put 100% of my concentration on my conversations with people around me and what they were doing. I could see things that I couldn't see before. It was like doing a puzzle with millions of little pieces that finally came together in one big picture. The big picture allowed me to see systemic trends, issues, contradictions and patterns of inequality that exist in every workplace. In my everyday life, I find that there is lots to distract me from seeing what is going on around me as closely as I could when I was at the research site. In addition, it was humbling to work on the line with the workers at my site. The work was difficult for me to do, but they were always respectful, never made fun of me as I struggled with tasks they were trying to teach me. I had such a healthy respect for the work that they did, which came more from my heart and spirit than from my head.

Mary Ellen: I also gained an immense appreciation of how working people live with contradictions and manage to keep their selves intact despite believing one thing and having to do another. These contradictions are part of how people use print, too, of course, and will always be present in some form. As an educator, I would jump to solutions for eradicating those contradictions around print; but now I am driven more by curiosity than by a desire to fix it first.

Tracy: I love field work, and I also really do enjoy the writing. Those are joys, too. I guess the dilemma that goes with that is that the time I was researching and meeting and writing took me away from some of my usual circles. I lost touch with other colleagues and got pretty isolated from my local peers. You can't really talk about this work while you are doing it. That is isolating, too.

Sue: I found that doing this research created separations between me and other practitioners and people I used to work with. I also found that it did not help me get work or enhance my career as an educator. In fact, I would suggest just the opposite. Initially, I often felt discouraged because I seemed so out of sync with other people in workplace education. However, I now feel that I have met a lot of new allies who are more in tune with the ideas we have been working with. I also find that other people are interested in these ideas, which makes me more hopeful. Although I gained a new perspective, these ideas go against the grain in terms of mainstream literacy policy. The reality is that I often have to work in old ways without acknowledging what we have learned, living with the contradictions of new knowledge and old ways of doing our jobs. But I'm always looking for the spaces that will hold the new perspectives.

Tracy:　I am used to working with a "joint committee," a labor–management advisory group to check with during all phases of a project. I missed those other interested people who really know the place as insiders. We were sounding boards for each other, and there were people at Metalco who had an appreciation of what I was doing, but it just wasn't the same. I think it was another way of being isolated. And as a researcher I had no defined job role in the workplace. You really need to be self-motivating to do this and then to write it up.

Mary Ellen:　For me, the motivator for being an educator/consultant in the workplace is that desire to fix, to be useful, to facilitate processes for improvements. We work collaboratively, setting agendas, starting up educational opportunities, getting things done with tight timelines, then moving on to the next project. So dilemmas began to surface early on for me when I experienced the slow and careful pace of ethnographic research. I was now in the workplace with a different purpose, not to offer assistance in the short term, but to understand at a much deeper level. To get that far, I found I had to be open to whatever came along. My own agendas and targets for accomplishing things were detrimental. Better to hang out with no fixed agenda and make sure there was lots of time with "nothing" to do but observe, listen, talk and think. I found myself leaving the house not knowing what to expect that day or what I would be doing. At first, I felt the fear of going into the workplace with no particular task in mind; then, the knowledge and quiet smile of certainty that there would always be something happening that would be important for me. And I was never disappointed.

Getting to that point required a higher tolerance for ambiguity than I was used to, not only as a consultant, but also in my personal life. I had little control over what happened, but I realized that didn't matter. More importantly, whatever happened would be one more knot in the tapestry to explore. I came away with a lot more trust in how people, issues and patterns of behavior reveal themselves over time.

Tracy: So maybe, Mary Ellen, this is part of what we take from this as practitioners, a little more appreciation for the time it takes to know and understand the knots and layers. It is easy to say that we all know trust takes time. And that we get to know a place and the people there over time, but we also get asked to make recommendations based on a quick look-see and our own best judgment. It is a dance. We will need courage to talk about ambiguity and exploration.

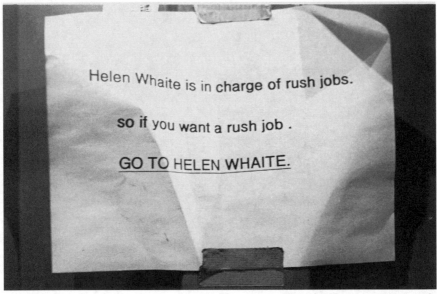

Photo by Vincenzo Pietropaolo

Appendix:
Notes on Ethnography
as Research Method

Nancy Jackson

This book is the product of a collaborative research project that spanned nearly 5 years from conception to publication. That is a long journey, with lots of learning along the way. In the other chapters, we have reported quite a lot about what we learned, but not very much about how we learned it. Many kinds of activity go on behind the term "research." So we would like to demystify the process a bit by making visible some of the daily dilemmas and decisions that moved us forward, step by step. By doing so, we hope to illustrate how this kind of research actually gets done, and perhaps encourage others who might want to get involved in research themselves. This appendix is not meant as a handbook on how to do research, but rather a glimpse behind the scenes. It provides a brief overview of the stages of our research, along with some tales from the field to try to illustrate what these stages look like in real life.

But in research as in other matters, there is no one right way to do or to think about issues of method. One size never fits all, and there are many and competing versions of the theory and practice of ethnography. We have focused here more on practical procedures than the theories underlying them. But we have included a few footnotes suggesting a further readings that are relatively consistent with the way the research in this book has been conducted.[1]

GETTING FOCUSED

We have described this research as "ethnography," or a series of ethnographic case studies. Briefly, ethnography is a way to investigate a chosen topic by spending a period of time in a suitable setting and asking "What is happening here?" and "How do things work?"

For example, in our research, the topic we were investigating was workplace literacies, and we chose four workplace settings where we knew there was activity relating to literacies. Right away, some people might think, "Isn't that biased?" The answer is, not at all. As ethnographic researchers, we are not trying to prove whether literacy is an issue in workplaces. We are trying to understand how and why literacy is an issue in some workplaces, and what is going on when people think there are literacy problems. To answer such questions, we must first go where we know we can find some activity that fits this description. Then we pose a whole range of questions and leave our minds open to the answers we will discover. There are always more and different things to learn than we anticipate.

Usually, ethnographic researchers start with a few general puzzles they want to investigate. For instance, What is happening in this workplace? What are the different jobs here? What kind of literacy practices are involved in this work? Who thinks there is a literacy problem here, and why? Does anyone think there is not a literacy problem, and why? Gradually the questions get more focused as the researchers understand more about the setting. Sometimes this is called an "emergent research design." For example, after a while we might start to ask, How do you use this checklist? How do they want you to fill it out? Does it help you do your work? How or how not? Where does this form go once you have filled it out? Do you know who reads it? Each answer generates new information, leading to new questions. It's a bit like a treasure hunt.

There are many approaches to ethnography and many debates about the theory, power and politics underlying this and other kinds of research methods. But broadly speaking, ethnographic methods share some general features that distinguish them from other approaches, such as statistical studies or clinical experiments. For example, they mostly don't use statistics or numeric measurements, or pre- and posttests. Instead, ethnographers investigate their topic by talking, listening and systematically observing the ordinary ways that people make sense of things in everyday life. As we look and listen, we use

---

[1] For a broad, general introduction to qualitative methodology, try Bogdan and Biklen (1998).

our own methods of "making sense" to understand what we see and hear, which means we are part of the same process we are investigating. This is called "reflexivity," and a lot has been written about this tricky issue in textbooks about research methods. Sometimes this kind of research is also called "interpretive" and the sense-making work of the researchers is called "human-as-instrument."[2] The key point here is that every single method of discovery that researchers use leaves its mark and sets limits in some way on what they discover. This is no different in ethnography than in science. In ethnography, we try to be aware of and make these influences visible or "transparent," so others can judge for themselves about the trustworthiness of the information we collect and the conclusions that we draw.[3]

READING OTHER WRITERS

Although we mostly think of research as taking place in the field or the research "setting," in practice it starts long before that (and continues long after). Most researchers begin the research journey by reading other research reports and theory related to their topic so they are familiar with other influential ideas. Some of these will be ideas they expect to agree with, and others they hope to challenge. But in either case, researchers need to know what others are writing, so they have an informed perspective and don't reinvent the wheel with every new study.

For example, for this research we read recent theoretical debates and previous studies about the changing nature of both workplaces and literacies. We have described some of this literature in other chapters of this book. Reading and reflecting on this research literature was essential to thinking broadly about what we were seeing, and allowed us to compare our "findings" or interpretations of events with what others have been saying about similar situations. That way, each new piece of research can make a contribution to the "discourse" or ongoing conversations taking place (largely through publications) in every field.

GATHERING DATA

Data can refer to anything that helps to answer the research questions. Sometimes we don't treat certain information or events as data when we first encounter them. But later we realize how much they help us understand about our topic, so then they become data. Data could be found or acquired in many ways: by observing, listening, asking casual questions, conducting formal interviews, or by reading texts in the re-

---

[2]For a discussion of basic philosophical issues in interpretive research see Maykut and Morehouse (1994).

[3]For a very accessible introduction to trustworthiness and related issues see Eisenhart and Borko (1993).

search setting. But perhaps ethnography is best known for the informal data gathering technique of "hanging out." That is, ethnographers go into a setting and try to learn primarily by just being there, using all their powers of comprehension to understand what is going on. This sounds a lot simpler than it turns out to be, as those who try it soon learn. But in general, it involves using very focused attention to try to learn things that others already know because they are "insiders" to the research setting.

Our research settings were workplaces, and we wanted to know how literacies work there. So we chose to focus our attention on what certain employees did every day that involved various kinds of literacy practices. Notice that this already required us to decide what counts as being a type of literacy. What do literacies or literacy practices look like? Sound like? What counts and what does not? These are important but taken-for-granted theoretical decisions that are also part of the data-gathering process. This is where some of that advance reading came in handy, in preparing our minds to see through fresh eyes, or to "make the familiar strange."

We wanted to learn how literate activities and events came about and what meanings they had for different individuals. We learned by watching people, talking to them informally and sometimes interviewing them, if possible with a tape recorder so we could keep a close record of what they said. Doing this over a period of days, weeks or months, an ethnographic researcher begins to understand events from the complex and often multiple perspectives of insiders. This issue of perspective is important because how insiders see things is often quite different from the ideas and understandings with which the researcher began the study. So in this case, the members of the setting are the experts and the researchers are the learners. The learning curve is often high, and this can be very challenging.

Fitting In

Right off the top, we learned to make various adjustments to our personal styles of dress and speech to participate comfortably in the research setting. As Judy says in Chapter 3, she learned to smile a lot, wear suits, and say "Excellent" in order to fit into the hotel culture. Tracy found a way to fit into the mostly male working environment by wearing "nondescript" clothes, casual trousers and a gray zippered jacket with a Ryerson University pin, in contrast to the more brightly colored professional clothes she wore as an educational consultant in the same workplace. Mary Ellen was required to wear a hairnet and lab coat to enter the food-processing floor, and had to learn to read lips in order to have conversations next to roaring machinery and hissing steam. Sue had to exchange her trademark large, colorful jewelry for steel-toed work boots in order to conform to safety standards in the textile plant. On the one hand, these small adjustments to personal identity could be seen as trivial at best, or manipulative at worst. But in the world of ethnography, they are all part of learning to walk in the shoes of other people and to apply all our senses and creative capacities to the task of understanding someone else's reality.

Figuring Things Out Along the Way

Data gathering is a constant process of making small decisions. What is important to write down and what is not? Who shall I talk to next? How can I get this person to talk to me? How could I get an invitation to that meeting? So it goes, a relentless stream of tiny choices that seem insignificant, but in research turn out to be quite important. This requires a lot of concentration to do well, and adds up to a tired mind at the end of the day. We cannot begin to recount all the decisions we had to make along the way, of course. But we hope telling a few bits will indicate what is meant by terms like "emergent design." It mostly means using a lot of common sense and making educated guesses about what is best.

In each of our four research sites, one of us "hung out" as an ethnographer for a period of 6 to 8 months, 2 or 3 days a week. During that time, we used a variety of standard data-gathering techniques, including different kinds of observations, interviewing, tape-recording and note taking, depending on what seemed possible and appropriate at the time. All of us had some kind of previous research experience, and we had spent several months together reading and talking about fieldwork strategies (as well as theory) before we began. Nevertheless, for the most part, we didn't know when we started out what would be possible in any of our sites. So when we arrived on site, we each had to figure out our actual data collection procedures as situations presented themselves. The following sections illustrate with a few practical examples from our sites.

Observation Strategies

As things unfolded, we found ourselves using quite different strategies and styles of observation in our four sites. At Texco, Sue got permission from the company to become a full "participant observer." This meant she got on-the-job training for a number of the job functions and she actually worked full shifts alongside the other workers in the textile plant. By doing this, she was trying to discover not only what they did with their hands, but also what it felt like to be inside their jobs, their understandings of events, and their working relationships.

In contrast, both Tracy and Mary Ellen were more conventional, "nonparticipant observers," by following people around, standing beside their workstations watching and taking notes, asking questions, trying not to be in the way. But they too had some level of insider status in their sites, because in both cases they were known to quite a number of both workers and managers from serving previously as education consultants and/or teachers in the same companies. So they too had the benefit as ethnographers of some prior knowledge and relationships with insiders to help gain "access" to the site and its employees, to break the ice once they were there, and to promote open communications about issues of interest.

At the other end of the spectrum was Judy's experience in The Urban Hotel. Not only was she previously unknown to the hotel managers or workers, but she also had no previous insider knowledge of a hotel setting from an employee's perspective. So she had to start from scratch in negotiating research access with the hotel managers and in understanding the events, vocabulary and relationships of the setting. When it came to observing, Judy was not allowed to record or take notes in the "front of the house" where she was in public view. She had to sneak off for little breaks in the coffee shop and the washroom to write field notes on her observations. This is a common problem, and individual researchers get very inventive about finding their own solutions. Fortunately, in the "back of the house," Judy was permitted, like Mary Ellen and Tracy, to follow people around, ask questions and take notes as they worked.

In fact, at Metalco, Tracy realized that she was finding it a lot easier to observe and ask questions of managers and engineers than of machine operators, in part because they work in quiet places instead of with noisy machines. Of course, this too had an impact on what kind of data she actually managed to get. These are all common variations in opportunities and strategies for observation and understanding. All are recognized in the research literature as legitimate means of gathering data, and any of them must be adapted in the moment to fit the particular circumstances of the setting. It is never possible to see and hear "everything," so every researcher must make choices.

Interviewing Strategies[4]

The same kind of improvising was needed when it came to interviewing people. We found that we did whatever worked in the situation, and usually that could not be planned until the individual researcher was immersed in the setting. Mary Ellen found she had good success sitting in the cafeteria in Triple Z and talking with people on their lunch breaks or other spaces in the day. The cafeteria turned out to be a good "research office" for her because it was away from the noise of machines and she could have reasonably private conversations. Out on

---

[4]Here we have focused on practical logistics of interviewing in a field site. For a good discussion of techniques for understanding and managing the interview process see Seidman (1991).

the floor, she could only talk to workers when the production lines were down. Sometimes she was able to ask planned interview questions and use a tape recorder in private rooms that staff arranged for her to use. But sometimes she found that in order to understand what was going on for people, she just needed to listen to what was on their minds rather than ask prepared questions.

At Texco, Sue did a lot of her talking to people while actually working beside them on the job. This did not lend itself to private conversations or tape recorders. Like Mary Ellen, she started out with lists of proper interview questions, but soon learned that if she used simple and familiar openers instead, like "What's up today?," she would often get an earful of useful information. As Judy did, Sue found it impossible to take field notes while actually working on the line. So she scribbled little reminders to herself on a notepad whenever she could during the day (the washroom comes in handy again). Then she realized she could capture lots of her own observations by talking into a tape recorder in her car on the way home from her shifts. This didn't provide 100% recall. But she grew to realize that no technique is perfect, and anyway, ethnography is more of an art than a science.[5] Sometimes she was able to interview co-workers on tape at another time, like over coffee or dinner after their shifts, and recapture some of the same discussions they had on the floor.

At Metalco, Tracy found that many of her engineering informants didn't mind at all being tape-recorded in both formal and informal interviews and, in fact, loved chatting with her about their jobs. In contrast, she did not speak the first language of many machine operators, so found that she did many fewer interviews with these workers. These are the kinds of variations in access and opportunity that inevitably shape the data. Sometimes translation is used to overcome such barriers, but that too shapes the data in ways that are often hard to judge, because a third party is mediating the sense-making. There is no pristine solution.

In Judy's case at the hotel, language was not so much a barrier as culturally defined behaviors. For instance, in order to understand the work of the employees in the housekeeping office, she had to learn how to fit in with the fast and easy humor of the Caribbean women. She also learned to make field notes after the fact, or in ways that drew the least attention to her presence, such as using a clipboard just like the housekeeping staff and floor managers did.

Text as Data

Along with watching, listening and asking questions, ethnographic researchers usually read or examine a variety of technical source materi-

---

[5]See Fine (1993).

als. Some of these are background documents that explain the principles or the logic of activities going on in the research setting. But writing of this kind is usually found only on a bookshelf or a desk in the manager's office. In our case, this included literature about the HACCP food safety system, ISO systems in manufacturing, and systems of quality assurance and competitive ranking in the hotel industry. We read standard texts on high-performance management to increase our understanding of terms like "Non-Conformance Reports" and "push versus pull" models of manufacturing. In these and other ways we learned many things that employees took for granted about their working environments and may not have explained to us. Like them, we needed this background knowledge in order to make sense of things around us.

Other kinds of texts we read as data included those that people in the research setting used every day to do their jobs. For example, we read charts and diagrams or photos on the wall, instruction manuals, checklists, and other routine forms, regulations and guidelines that were sometimes in print form, sometimes on computer screens in email or "intranet" systems. These texts were absolutely central to our attention because they are our topic: workplace literacies. But they are included in this discussion of methods for a different reason. That is, regardless of the topic, researchers can learn a lot of crucial information about the research setting by examining workplace-related texts to help them understand what is going, and what meanings may be shared and taken for granted by insiders to the setting.

Leaving the Field

After many weeks or months in the field, it is sometimes hard to know when to stop. Methods texts sometimes say that ethnographic fieldwork should stop when questions keep turning up the same answers over and over. This is sometimes called the "saturation point." In real life, such cues are not always obvious, and most often the recurring views we encounter are not the same, but rather a recurring pattern of differing opinions. But at some point we have to stop anyway, sometimes when the time or money runs out. We stop with the realization that our knowledge of the setting will never be complete, and that we still face the challenge of trying to make sense of what we have seen and heard.

Usually after a long period of fieldwork, researchers' own thinking about the original topic has changed quite a lot, and they often feel more confused than when they began. Some of these new understandings will reflect what (some) insiders had to say, and this means the researchers have been good learners in the research setting. But this merely underscores the challenge of bringing together a chorus of differing possible views about the same workplace, and drawing some conclusions as a researcher that will have some legitimacy. This is the job of analysis.

ANALYZING DATA

In practice, analysis does not occur only at the end of this kind of research. The process of analysis or making sense of gathered data begins the moment the ethnographer enters the research site, even before.[6] If the setting is completely unknown to the researcher, everything is new and must be figured out—even simple things like which parking lot and which entrance to the building are okay to use, or which lunchroom to use and why. This too involves analysis of meanings.

But even if the setting is a familiar one, the research role may be new, and that means orienting to different questions and answers than while wearing another hat in the same setting. This transition can be very demanding, and may take a while to achieve. As literacy researchers, as opposed to teachers for instance, what should we be paying attention to? What do we have time to think about in this role, and how broadly should we look? When we were teachers, we may have been working for the Human Resources Manager; now who are we "working for"? How many different perspectives on daily events do we want to hear, and why? What do we do about the disagreements that surface? What do we do with any confidential or sensitive information we may get?

As a group of five researchers, we gave a lot of discussion time to this issue of what we were actually looking for and why. We spent a lot of energy early in our fieldwork reporting our experiences to each other, whether in pairs, in the whole group, on the phone, or in person, including several 3-day workshops where we tried to "immerse ourselves in our data." We talked extensively about what we were trying to understand and why, comparing notes about our sites, our observations and how they fit with what we had read about in the research literature. We pushed ourselves to examine events more closely, to question our own assumptions, to start noticing common issues as well as differences, dynamics and tensions across all our sites. It took a couple of months of this kind of dialogue before we began to see, with some relief, that there really were similarities as well as differences across our sites. What we were seeing about literacies did begin to make sense to us in light of some, and in contrast to other, research literature. Slowly, we began to feel that we were all in the same conversation and that we might really have something to say as researchers at the end of all this. At the end of our most energizing days of searching for our story lines, we would say to each other, "Now we just have to go home and write it." Famous last words.

---

[6]For an excellent discussion of problem solving throughout the research process see Weis and Fine (2000).

Despite this growing sense of direction and confidence, we still faced a painful transition when the time came to actually stop visiting our sites, stop talking to each other, and just write, write, write. One member of our group summed up the writing phase of our work as "pain, pain, pain!" We each spent weeks and weeks surrounded by a sea of paper, poring over field notes and transcripts, pacing the floor, fretting. We couldn't tell which was more painful: the isolation of trying to write alone at each of our desks, or trying to write collaboratively with each other. Both were fraught with tensions: fear of the blank page, anxiety about our different writing styles, different ways of seeing the same material, our perfectionism, procrastination, distractions, false starts, fear of the unknown.

We tried to begin gently by writing basic site descriptions first, to familiarize each other more deeply with all four sites. But even that was a challenge: What is important to describe about these sites and why? Why is the color of the walls important, or the location of the parking? Eventually, after a lot of talk, we agreed to start writing stories to illustrate dynamics involving the uses of literacies in each of our sites. This too was a challenge, as we constantly revisited the question, What's the point of this story? Slowly, draft by draft, after hours of feedback and soul searching, months of writing and rewriting, pacing the floor and sleepless nights, the stories began to emerge along with our sense of what they were all about. Eventually we started going to conferences and making panel presentations about our findings. "Talking" our stories seemed a bit less scary than writing them, but we still had terrible nerves before every presentation. When people at conferences seemed to recognize what we were talking about, we felt encouraged. A couple of times, nobody at all came to our sessions. We tried to reassure ourselves that we weren't that boring; we must just have been at the wrong conference!

Conclusions Are Made, Not Found

Little by little our conclusions or "findings" began to emerge from the sea of details in front of us. We read, reread, pored over photographs from our sites, smiled again at the jokes and the stories that people had told us, thought things over while standing in the shower, got up in the middle of the night to write when we couldn't sleep. Sometimes we figured things out in order to write; sometimes we wrote in order to figure things out. Sometimes we talked and then wrote; sometimes we wrote and then talked. In this meandering way, the stories gradually took shape, along with our growing sense of what they were about. Sometimes we turned stories upside down, told them another way around and then they seemed more clear. All the time we struggled to see through a fresh lens the familiar events and activities of literacies-in-use and workplace teaching and learning. Slowly we began to see not only our research sites, but also our own roles and identities as educators through a new lens as well. This was not always comforting, but there seemed to be no retreat from what we had learned: The experience had changed us, too.

In this organic way, it is the job of ethnographic researchers to systematically and painstakingly carve conclusions from the data, and reveal them through some form of narrative that will both tell and show others what they have learned. To be sure, the aim of this kind of research is not to make grand claims about truth for all time, or all places or all people. But the point is certainly to make an argument that is of interest and relevance beyond itself. In the case of our research, our writing had two aims. The first was to present coherently and convincingly a particular way of understanding literacies-in-use in our four workplaces. The second was to illustrate our views and arguments in such a lively and transparent way that our readers would be able to see how we came to our conclusions, and how our conclusions might be relevant for other workplace settings as well. This is a common qualitative approach to the quest for "generalizability." More simply put, it is the "Aha!" factor, or "Oh yes, I recognize that ... it's the same where I work." It is one sign of the trustworthiness necessary for good ethnographic research.

By putting forward research findings in this way, ethnographic researchers become part of an ongoing conversation across time and space. Academics call this "making a contribution to knowledge in the field." But we hope this conversation will extend beyond academic circles. It may include people who are insiders to the actual setting where the research was conducted, and/or insiders to settings where the analysis strikes an "Aha!" response. It may also involve people with widely different roles and reasons to be interested in the research topic. For our project, we had in mind the following range of readers: educators or trainers in a variety of settings, workplace supervisors or team leaders, human resource officers or managers, workers or union officials interested in literacy programs, students or others preparing to work in any of these roles, and policy-makers in literacy and workplace training. Writing conclusions with such diverse audiences in mind takes some care, strategy, courage and sometimes restraint. But it can increase the potential impact of the study.

Indeed, the most hopeful scenario may be that different parties will find something new, useful, even challenging in our research process and reports. Some findings may fit comfortably into established ways of thinking and acting. Some others may be controversial, both inside and outside the original setting, and serve to stimulate debate long after the project itself is finished. Those studies that offer challenging results often come to be seen as key points of reference for future work. In fact, even studies that elicit the "Aha!" response will hopefully stimulate new thinking and contribute something beyond the everyday understandings of insiders. This is a goal in some but not all forms of ethnography. But in our view, it is an area where ethnographic researchers can make a uniquely valuable to contribute, by reconceptualizing or "reframing" familiar issues.

For example, in our worksites, the everyday views of front-line workers often included blaming the attitudes or personalities of their supervisors for the job rules they found unreasonable. However, by following our own trail of questions and answers, we were able to discover that the actions of both "nice" and "mean" supervisors were often driven by stiff rules, regulations, manuals and audits (ISO, HACCP) over which they too had little control. Thus, the everyday tensions around literacy practices were often part of a broader picture of systemic change in the nature and organization of work that placed heavy demands on workers and supervisors alike. As we have argued throughout this book, understanding this weave of broader connections is essential knowledge for workplace educators seeking constructive and collaborative solutions to "literacy problems." But making such discoveries depends in large measure upon the methods we use to look for them.[7]

Invisible Labor

In addition to the recognized categories of research methods we have used in the preceding discussion (like data gathering and analysis), there is a whole layer of less glamorous work that rarely gets mentioned in methods texts, but is equally consequential. It goes on before, during and after all the activities just outlined. That is the often-thankless work of planning and administration. We perpetuate this invisibility unless we include here at least a brief version of the nature of this essential work in our own research process.

First, we spent weeks and weeks of proposal writing and rewriting, all on the off chance that we would actually get funded. We didn't know each other well at that time, and in fact (like now, as we finish) we were living on different continents. So doing this work was the beginning of figuring out who we were and what we might do together. Even so, as Tracy says in Chapter 8, "Conversation on Collaborative Research," we may not have been making all the same assumptions about the meanings behind our words. Eventually we did get funded, but it doesn't always turn out that way. So the work of proposal writing is speculative, unpaid labor, and may come to nothing.

We also spent many hours learning how to read and understand the budgets and financial reports for our multiyear project, as well as learning the ropes in the research administration department of a large university. Fortunately for us once again, the research adminis-

---

[7]For a suggestive discussion of nuances involved in "looking" and "listening" to discover the broader picture, see Devault (1999).

tration office turned out to be efficient, helpful and pleasant to deal with. But we didn't know that in advance. So here too we were taking a leap into the dark.

In addition to satisfying the requirements of the university that administered the funds, we spent time communicating directly with our funding agency. This involved monthly activity reports, intermittent phone calls to get questions answered, and occasional meetings with the whole group. In this process we negotiated budget changes as our needs and plans evolved, and kept the agency informed of our progress. Fortunately, most of us had some prior working relationship with this funding agency, and knew it to be reliable and flexible, which gave us confidence. In particular, our project officer was known by us to be enormously knowledgeable, helpful and patient. If it weren't for her faith and skill in steering this project through the system, there never would have been a study or a book. But all this too is part of the invisible work of initiating and sustaining research.

The End Is a New Beginning

There are endless details that we could report about the research process, and possibly something to be learned from most of them. But perhaps we have said enough to encourage others to think that ethnographic research may be messy and even organic, but not a complete mystery. In our experience, the process has not always been easy; perhaps it has never been easy. With hindsight, we could say that above all it has been a continuous learning process. We started out to learn about the meanings of literacies in our worksites. Along the way we learned a lot about changing work and workplaces, and the complex pressures facing learners as well as workplace educators.

We also learned to see ourselves differently. As researchers, we learned about working together and collaborating across multiple dimensions of space, time and our own identities. We also learned to think differently about our role as workplace educators. We learned and we are still learning. We are learning as we write and revise this book. We learn as we begin to see this book through the eyes of others who have not lived through the process of discovery with us in the field. We learn as we emerge from an intensive focus on this work, and try to rejoin the circles of our peers in both workplace education and academia. We learn as we go "back to work," in workplace education, as we said in Chapter 6, and try to figure out how our learnings can make a difference.

We do hope others will take the plunge into research. At the same time, it is probably not a good idea to try to do so without any preparatory research training. Even with training, it is probably wise to work with some people who have previous research experience, to help get through the bumpy parts. Research does not need to be a 5-year project like this one. In fact, something smaller would be a better place to start. No project is too small if it helps to answer our own questions about how to improve the teaching and learning of literacies, in the workplace as elsewhere. In fact, the title of a recent review of international experience with literacy research-in-practice sums it up well. As Quigley and Norton (2002) say about practitioner-based research: "It simply makes us better."

About the Authors

Mary Ellen Belfiore is an independent adult educator, workplace consultant and researcher. She has written teacher reference books and learning materials for language and literacy in the workplace. She has taught language and literacy in workplaces, in the community and in the university, and has delivered practitioner training. As a consultant, Mary Ellen has worked with joint business and labor committees for both nationwide projects and local organizations. Her academic research includes investigations of language and literacy use, and her applied research includes briefing papers and numerous reports to labor, business, government and education.

Tracy Defoe is an adult education consultant and researcher specializing in workplace education. She has been a part of many first-time projects including curricula for peer-led courses, authored reports and articles and presented at many conferences. She has taught language, literacy, writing and cross-cultural communication as well as teaching methods to adults in colleges, universities and the workplace. A regular consultant to business, labor and government on learning and literacy, Tracy is an advocate for plain language. She is currently puzzling over the challenges of worker participation in continuous improvement manufacturing.

Sue Folinsbee is a long-time workplace educator who has worked across Canada and the United States to set up collaborative workplace

291

education programs in diverse sectors. She is also an experienced practitioner trainer and writer of practical handbooks, articles, and research related to workplace literacy. She operated a national consultancy for 5 years. Presently, Sue is acting Co-Executive Director of the Ontario Literary Coalition in Toronto.

During the In-Sites project, **Judy Hunter** was an Assistant Professor in the Department of English at Ryerson University in Toronto, where she taught courses in English as a Second Language, writing and literacy in society. Her teaching experience includes academic and community ESL programs, ESL for occupational training and professional development for teachers. She has conducted ethnographic research on language and literacy in school, university, and workplace settings. She continues to focus on the above interests in New Zealand, where she is affiliated with Auckland University of Technology. Judy was the Principal Investigator for the In-Sites project.

Nancy **Jackson** is Associate Professor in Adult Education at the Ontario Institute for Studies in Education, University of Toronto. She teaches in a graduate program in Workplace Learning and Change, including courses on workplace literacy and workplace research. Her past research and writing are focused on critical analyses of workplace skills development and skills training policy. She has worked as a consultant in the labor movement on large-scale training design and development, and taught in education, women's studies and labor studies in Canada and Australia.

References

Armesto, F. F. (2000). *Civilizations*. Toronto: Key Porter Books.

Auerbach, E. (1992). *Making meaning, making change*. Washington, DC: Center for Applied Linguistics.

Barton, D. (1994a). *Literacy: An introduction to the ecology of written language*. Oxford: Blackwell.

Barton, D., & Hamilton, M. (1994b). Literacy practices and literacy events. In M. Hamilton, D. Barton, & R. Ivanic (Eds.), *World of literary* (pp. vii–x). Clevedon, Avon: Multilingual Matters, Ltd.

Barton, D., & Hamilton, M. (1998). *Local literacies: Reading and writing in one community*. London: Routledge.

Belfiore, M. E., & Folinsbee, S. (2002). Close up: Job training, language, and literacies. *Contact: Special symposium research issue, 28*(2), 103–115.

Billet, S. (2000). Performance at work: Identifying smart work practices. In R. Gerber & C. Lankshear (Eds.), *Training for a smart workforce* (pp. 123–150). London, Routledge.

Bogdan, R., & Biklen, S. (1998). *Qualitative research for education*. Boston: Allyn & Bacon.

Boyett, J. H., & Conn, H. P. (1992). *Workplace 2000: The revolution reshaping American business*. New York: Plume Penguin.

Brodkey, L. (1992). Articulating poststructural theory in research on literacy. In R. Beach, J. Green, M. Kamil, & T. Shanahan (Eds.), *Multidisciplinary perspectives on literacy research* (pp. 293–318). Urbana, IL: NCTE.

Cappelli, P., Bassi, L., Katz, H., Knopke, D., Osterman, P., & Useem, M. (1997). *Change at work*. New York: Oxford University Press.

Castleton, G. (1999). Inspecting the consequences of virtual and virtuous realities of workplace literacy. *Research and Practice in Adult Literacy, 39*(3), 13–17.

Castleton, G. (2000). Workplace literacy: Examining the virtual and virtuous realities in (e)merging discourses on work. *Discourse: Studies in the Cultural Politics of Education, 21*(1), 91–104.

Cook-Gumperz, J. (Ed.). (1986). *The social construction of literacy*. Cambridge, UK: Cambridge University Press.

Cope, B., & Kalantzis, M. (Eds.). (1999). *Multiliteracies: Literacy learning and the design of social futures*. London: Routledge.

Darrah, C. N. (1990). *Skills in context: An exploration in industrial ethnography*. Unpublished doctoral thesis, Stanford University.

Darrah, C. (1997). Complicating the concept of skill requirements: Scenes from a workplace. In G. Hull (Ed.), *Changing work, changing workers: Critical perspectives on language, literacy and skills* (pp. 249–272). Albany: State University of New York Press.

Devault, M. (1999). Talking and listening from women's standpoint: Feminist strategies for interviewing and analysis. In *Liberating method* (pp. 59–83). Philadelphia: Temple University Press.

du Gay, P. (1996). *Consumption and identity at work*. London: Sage.

Eisenhart, M., & Borko, H. (1993). Standards of validity for classroom research. *Designing classroom research*. Boston: Allyn & Bacon.

Fairclough, N. (1989). *Language and power*. London: Longman.

Fairclough, N. (1995). *Critical discourse analysis: The critical study of language*. London: Longman.

Fine, G. A. (1993). Ten lies of ethnography. *Journal of Contemporary Ethnography, 22*(3), 267–294.

Folinsbee S. (2000a). *Looking back, looking forward: A conversation with workplace educators*. Hull, QC: National Literacy Secretariat.

Folinsbee, S. (2002b) *Linking critical perspectives on literacy and work to the program Planning Process*. Unpublished master's thesis. Antigonish, NS: St. Frances Xavier University.

Folinsbee, S., & Jurmo, P. (1994). *Collaborative needs assessment: A handbook for workplace development planners*. Toronto: ABC Canada.

Foucault, M. (1980). *Power/knowledge: Selected interviews and other writings, 1972–1977* (Trans. C. Gordon). New York: Pantheon Books.

Freire, P. (1970). *Pedagogy of the oppressed*. New York: Herder & Herder.

Freire, P. (1985). Reading the world and reading the word: An interview with Paolo Freire. *Language Arts, 62*(1), 15–21.

Garrick, J., & Rhodes, C. (Eds.). (2000). *Research and knowledge at work: Perspectives, case-studies and innovative strategies*. New York: Routledge.

Garrick, J., & Usher, R. (1999). Flexible learning, contemporary work and enterprising selves. In *Conference proceedings & researching work and learning* (pp. 61–69). University of Leeds.

Gee, J. P. (1990). *Social linguistics and literacies: Ideology in discourses*. London: Falmer Press.

Gee, J. P. (1992). *The social mind*. New York: Bergin and Garvey.

Gee, J. P. (1996). *Social linguistics and literacies: Ideology in discourses* (2nd ed.). London: Falmer Press.

Gee, J. P. (2000). The new literacy studies: From 'socially situated' to the work of the social. In D. Barton, M. Hamilton, & R. Ivanic (Eds.), *Situated literacies* (pp. 180–196). London: Routledge.

Gee, J. P., Hull, G., & Lankshear, C. (1996). *The new work order: Behind the language of the new capitalism*. Boulder, CO: Westview Press.

Gerber, R., & Lankshear, C. (2000). *Training for a smart workforce*. London: Routledge.

Goldstein, T. (1994). We are all sisters, so we don't have to be polite: Language choice and English language training in the multilingual workplace. *TESL Canada Journal, 2*(2), 30–43.

Goldstein, T. (1997). *Two languages at work: Bilingual life on the production floor.* Berlin: Mouton de Gruyter.

Goody, J. (1986). *The logic of writing and the organization of society.* Cambridge: Cambridge University Press.

Gowen, S. G. (1992). *The politics of workplace literacy.* New York: Teachers College Press.

Graff, H. J. (1979). *The literacy myth: Literacy and social structure in the nineteenth-century city.* New York: Academic Press.

Graff, H. J. (1997). The persisting power and costs of the literacy myth. *Working Papers on Literacy.* Working Paper No. 1, pp. 3–5. Montreal: Centre for Literacy, Dawson College.

Graham, L. (1995). *On the line at Subaru-Isuzu.* Ithaca, NY: Cornell University Press.

Hamilton, M. (2000). *Sustainable literacies and the ecology of lifelong learning: A Global Colloquium Supporting Lifelong Learning Presented by The Open University.* http://www.open.ac.uk/lifelong-learning/ index.html

Hamilton, M. (2001). Privileged literacies: Policy, institutional process and the life of the IALS. *Language and Education, 15*(2&3), 178–196.

Heath, S. B. (1983). *Ways with words: Language, life and work in communities and classrooms.* Cambridge, UK: Cambridge University Press.

Hemphill, D. F. (2000). Incorporating postmodernist perspectives into adult education. In V. Sheared & P. Sissel (Eds.), *Making space: Merging theory and practice in adult education* (pp. 16–28). London: Bergin and Garvey.

Hodgetts, R. M. (1998). *Measures of quality and high performance: Simple tools and lessons learned from America's most successful corporations.* New York: AMACOM Books.

Hogg, D. (1999). *Achieving global competitiveness: Success through world class performance.* Ontario: High Performance Solutions and the High Performance Manufacturing Consortium of Ontario.

Holland, C., Frank, F., & Cooke, T. (1998). *Literacy and the new work order: An international literature review.* Leicester, UK: National Institute of Adult and Continuing Education.

Hopkins, S., & Maglen, L. (2000). Learning through working: Views of managers and personnel. In C. Symes (Ed.), *Working knowledge, productive learning at work—Conference proceedings* (pp. 243–250). Sydney, Australia: Research into Adult & Vocational Learning, University of Technology Sydney.

Hull, G. (1993). Hearing other voices: A critical assessment of popular views of literacy and work. *Harvard Educational Review, 63*(1), 20–49.

Hull, G. (1995). Controlling literacy: The place of skills in 'high performance' work. *Critical Forum, 3*(2/3), 3–26.

Hull, G. (Ed.). (1997). *Changing work, changing workers: Critical perspectives on language, literacy and skills.* Albany: State University of New York Press.

Hull, G., & Grubb, W. N. (1999). Literacy, Skills and Work. In D. Wagner, R. Venetsky, & B. Street (Eds.), *Literacy: An international handbook* (pp. 311–317). Boulder CO: Westview Press.

Hull, G., Jury, M., Ziv, O., & Katz, M. (1996). *Changing work, changing literacy? A study of skill requirements and development in a traditional and restructured workplace. Final report.* Berkeley: University of California.

Hunter, J., Belfiore, M., & Folinsbee, S. (2001). In-Sites research: Literacy and language threads in workplace tapestry. *Contact: Special research symposium issue, 27*(2), 20–31.

Imai, M. (1997). *Gemba Kaizen: A commonsense, low-cost approach to management.* New York: McGraw-Hill.

Jackson, N. (2000). Writing-up people at work: Investigations of workplace literacy. *Literacy and Numeracy Studies, 10*(1/2), 5–22.

Kalman, J., & Losey, K. (1997). Pedagogical innovation in a workplace literacy program. In G. Hull (Ed.), *Changing work, changing workers: Critical perspectives on language, literacy and skills* (pp. 84–116). Albany: State University of New York Press.

Katz, M.-L. (2000). Workplace language teaching and the intercultural construction of ideologies of competence. *Canadian Modern Language Review, 57*(1), 143–172.

Kirsch, I. S., & Mosenthal, P. B. (1990). Exploring document literacy: Variables underlying the performance of young adults. *Reading Research Quarterly, 25,* 5–30.

Kress, G. (2000). Design and transformation: New theories of meaning. In B. Cope & M. Kalantzis (Ed.), *Multiliteracies: Literacy learning and the design of social futures* (pp. 153–161). London: Routledge.

Kuhn, T. (1962). *The structure of scientific revolutions.* Chicago: University of Chicago Press.

Lankshear, C. (1997). Language and the new capitalism. *The International Journal of Inclusive Education, 1*(4), 309–321.

Lave, J. (1996). Teaching, as learning, in practice. *Mind, Culture, and Activity, 3*(3), 149–164.

Lave, J., & Wenger, E. (1991). *Situated learning: Legitimate peripheral participation.* Cambridge: Cambridge University Press.

Legge, K. (1995). *Human resource management: The rhetorics, the realities.* Basingstoke: Macmillan.

Mawer, G. (1999). *Language and learning in workplace education: Learning at work.* New York: Addison Wesley Longman.

Maybin, J. (2000). The new literacy studies: Context, intertextuality and discourse. In D. Barton, M. Hamilton, & R. Ivanic (Eds.), *Situated literacies* (pp. 197–209). London: Routledge.

Maykut, P., & Morehouse, E. (1994) *Beginning qualitative research: A philosophical and practical guide.* London: The Falmer Press.

Monden, Y. (1998). *Toyota production system: An integrated approach to just-in-time* (3rd ed.). Norcross, GA: Engineering and Management Press.

O'Connor, P. (1994). *Thinking work I: Theoretical perspectives on workers literacies.*

OECD & Statistics Canada. (1997). *Literacy skills for the knowledge society.* Ottawa: Author.

Olson, D. (1977). From utterance to text: The bias of language in speech and writing. *Harvard Educational Review, 47*(3), 257–281.

Ong, W. (1982). *Orality and literacy: The technologizing of the word.* London: Methuen.

Pollert, A. (Ed.). (1991). *Farewell to flexibility*. Cambridge, MA: Blackwell.

Prinsloo, M., & Breier, M. (Eds.). (1996). *The social uses of literacy*. Capetown and Amsterdam: Sached Books and John Benjamins.

Prior, P. (2002, June). *Disciplinarity: From discourse community to dispersed, laminated activity*. Paper presented at the 2nd Knowledge and Discourse Conference, Hong Kong.

Quigley, B. A., & Norton, M. (2002). *It simply makes us better: Learning from literacy research in practice networks*. Edmonton: The Learning Centre.

Scholes, R. (1985). *Textual power*. New Haven, CT: Yale University Press.

Schultz, K. (1997). Discourses of workplace education: A challenge to the new orthodoxy. In G. Hull (Ed.), *Changing work, changing workers* (pp. 43–83). Albany: SUNY Press.

Scribner, S., & Cole, M. (1981). *The psychology of literacy*. Cambridge MA: Harvard University Press.

Seidman, I. E. (1991). *Interviewing as qualitative research*. New York: Teachers College Press.

Smith, F. (1978). *Reading*. New York: Cambridge University Press.

Stasz, C. (1997). Do employers need the skills they want? Evidence from technical work. *Journal of Education and Work, 10*(3), 205–233.

Story, J. (1994). *New wave manufacturing strategies*. London: Paul Chapman.

Street, B. (1984). *Literacy in theory and practice*. Cambridge, UK: Cambridge University Press.

Street, B. (Ed.). (1993). *Cross-cultural approaches to literacy*. Cambridge: Cambridge University Press.

Taylor, M. (1997). *Transfer of learning: Planning effective workplace education programs*. Ottawa: NLS.

Turk, J., & Unda, J. (1991). So we can make our voices heard: The Ontario Federation of Labour's BEST project on worker literacy. In M. Taylor, G. Lewe, & J. Draper (Eds.), *Basic skills for the workplace* (pp. 287–280). Toronto: Culture Concepts.

Valpy, M. (2001, January 27). Perfection, but at what price? *Globe and Mail* [Toronto], pp. A12–A13.

Weis, L., & Fine, M. (2000). *Speed bumps: A student-friendly guide to qualitative research*. New York: Teachers College Press.

Womack, J. P., Jones, D. T., & Roos, D. (1990). *The machine that changed the world*. New York: Rawson Macmillan.

Index